Sexual Fantasies

Mariah Larsson/Sara Johnsdotter (eds.)

Sexual Fantasies

At the Convergence of the Cultural and the Individual

PL ACADEMIC RESEARCH

Bibliographic Information published by the Deutsche Nationalbibliothek
The Deutsche Nationalbibliothek lists this publication in the Deutsche Nationalbibliografie; detailed bibliographic data is available in the internet at http://dnb.d-nb.de.

ISBN 978-3-631-64940-4 (Print)
E-ISBN 978-3-653-04032-6 (E-Book)
DOI 10.3726/ 978-3-653-04032-6

PL Academic Research is an Imprint of Peter Lang GmbH.

Peter Lang – Frankfurt am Main · Bern · Bruxelles · New York · Oxford · Warszawa · Wien

This publication has been peer reviewed.

www.peterlang.com

Contents

Acknowledgements

There are a number of foundations, institutions, and individuals that have been helpful in the work with this volume. First of all, we would like to thank our contributors, who throughout the process have dedicated themselves not only to researching and writing their respective chapters to the volume, but also to offering insightful response to the other contributions and to the volume as a whole. Sven-Axel Månsson kindly read and commented on the introduction in its final stages. In addition, we would like to thank those contributors who travelled far to participate in the workshops that were arranged during the project, and Ylva Hernlund who worked efficiently with language revision of all our texts. Any remaining mistakes are not due to her reading. Our colleagues at our respective home departments at Malmö University and Stockholm University have provided stimulating scholarly environments.

This volume is produced in association with the newly started Center for Sexology and Sexuality Studies at Malmö University. The two workshops – one in Skanör, the other in Vitemölla – were generously supported by the Department of Social Work at Health and Society, Malmö University, and the Crafoord Foundation. We are deeply grateful for this support.

Finally, and as always, our warmest thanks go to our families.

Mariah Larsson & Sara Johnsdotter

Introduction: At the Convergence of the Cultural and the Individual

Fantasy and imagination are vital parts of what makes us human beings. Our capacity to form mental images or concepts of things that are not actually present, together with our ability to let our minds and imaginations wander, aid us in our everyday lives. Although we can fantasise about many different things – from positive daydreaming about more or less attainable goals to nightmare visions about accidents or illnesses – one significant aspect of fantasy has to do with our sexual worlds. Sexual fantasies might be shameful or embarrassing, they might create awkwardness in real-life situations, or a questioning of one's own sexual identity, but they might also be rich and rewarding, a path that leads to exploration, self-discovery, and pleasure. Moreover, they contain a weird paradox: on the one hand, they are the most private and secretive in people's lives (some never admit their sexual fantasies even to a partner who is very close); on the other hand, they are both shared by many and, in some way, dependent on a world that supplies structures, images, symbols, narratives, and so on, that can be deployed in various ways within those fantasies. On the one hand, fantasies emanate from the individual; on the other, they are produced in interaction with the world around us.

Using the terminology from sexual script theory by Simon and Gagnon (e.g., 2005[1973]; 1986), one could say that sexual fantasies are the place where the cultural scenario and the intrapsychic script converge and/or conflict. Sociologists Simon and Gagnon presented the sexual script theory in the early 1970s, and developed it through the years to come. 'Script' is a metaphor for how sexuality is not biologically determined but shaped in and by a social context. From an early age, individuals form their perception of sexuality through various bits and pieces of information; through taboos and misapprehensions; through sex education and other informational materials; through glimpses snatched from films, literature, and real life; through experiences and feelings aroused by erotica or pornography. Simon and Gagnon describe scripting as occurring on three different levels. The first one is that of the intrapsychic, or individual, scripts. At first glance, this is where sexual fantasies are located – they are a 'symbolic reorganization of reality in ways that make it complicit in realizing more fully the actor's many-layered and sometimes multivoiced wishes' (Simon & Gagnon 1986: 99). As personal, private, and (often) secret parts of the self, sexual fantasies quite definitely belong within the intrapsychic scripts. The second level is that of the interpersonal scripts – here, two or more people interact in accordance with both expected codes of conduct within sexual activity and with their own intrapsychic scripts. As Simon and Gagnon explain it, the scripts in this case are rather a kind of template or a set of instructions for improvisation. For instance, that sex is 'supposed to' begin with kissing and petting in order to continue on to penetration and intercourse, is such a template within which two or more people can improvise. Included in the interpersonal script is everything from flirting to post-coital behaviour.

The cultural scenario is the third level. This is at once quite abstract and quite concrete: the cultural scenario provides the information from which individuals piece together their knowledge about sex, the inspiration for the personal, intrapsychic scripts, as well as a backdrop – or even a stage – for our interpersonal scripts. It is both a contemporary social context and a historical legacy of cultural tradition.

In this volume, we mainly approach sexual fantasies as they are expressed, conveyed, and disseminated on a cultural level, for instance through various media. This is not because we find that the research done on individuals' sexual fantasies is faulty, or even looking in the wrong places, but rather because we want to expand the notion of sexual fantasies from the field of psychology and into the realm of cultural studies, anthropology, philosophy, sociology, and analyses of cultural phenomena. Our conviction is that individuals' sexual fantasies cannot be understood without the backdrop of social culture, or, in Simon and Gagnon's terminology, the cultural scenario. Accordingly, the contributors ask questions about how such fantasies may be navigated in the convergence with the personal on an individual level but also how such fantasies are understood or interpreted in society, what they might mean in a given social culture, and what effects they may have. In a review of research on sexual fantasies, Leitenberg and Henning observe: 'Certainly it is by now a truism that one's brain is at least as important a sexual organ as one's genitals. [...] Understanding sexual fantasies therefore seems central to an understanding of an important aspect of human sexuality' (1995: 469). We might, however, add that understanding sexual fantasies is an important aspect of understanding our culture, and that our culture is one way to understand sexual fantasies. Fantasy, as Cultural Studies scholar Martin Barker observes, belongs 'in the zone of the relations between bodies, selfhood, and social and cultural permissions and forbiddings' (Barker 2014: 157).

Thus, the emphasis in this volume is not on mapping the prevalence of particular fantasies in certain people, but on how sexual fantasies can be multifaceted and ubiquitous; how they may be individualised but seldom unique; and how they interconnect with a multitude of other psychological, social, and cultural phenomena. This volume also examines how sexual fantasies and their various expressions may be used for liberating ends, such as exploring one's sexuality in therapy, and for finding alternatives to stereotypical depictions of sexuality.

Secret gardens

Since people are secretive about them, sexual fantasies are hard to research. Previous studies have attempted to investigate people's sexual fantasies by surveys, open-ended questionnaires, or by asking subjects to record their fantasies in journals over an extended period of time (Leitenberg & Henning 1995). These methods are problematic, since they – like much sexological research – rely on honesty in a subject that is fraught with taboos, social norms, conventions, expectations, and even legal regulations. Nonetheless, researchers have reached some tentative results regarding sexual fantasies in individuals as relates to gender, age, and correlation to for instance sex crimes (Leitenberg & Henning 1995).

There are collections of sexual fantasies, where people have submitted their fantasies in writing or in taped interviews. Nancy Friday's classic, bestselling *My Secret Garden: Women's Sexual Fantasies* (1973) is one such collection. Born out of the sexual revolution, second wave feminism, and the curiosity about sexuality which permeated much of the late 1960s and early 1970s, *My Secret Garden* is not a scholarly book – Friday made requests for sexual fantasies through ads and articles, thus creating a selection of fantasies which came from those who would offer them – but it does not really make that claim, either. Instead, it is written as a call for liberation (from shame, guilt, and oppression by the ideal of the 'good girl') and openness. Friday would go on to write about (among other things) men's sexual fantasies (1980) and returned to women's sexual fantasies in later publications (1991; 2009).

Another form of sexual fantasy research is the psychologist or therapist who relates a number of cases and discusses what the fantasies might mean to the individual who has them and how he or she can be able to negotiate, for instance, a tension between everyday sexual life and fantasy (see e.g., Bader 2002; Kahr 2009). Here, the sexual fantasy might cause problems that need to be resolved in order to establish a functioning intimate relation. One such example, where the fantasy fetish had led to a cessation of sexual activity between husband and wife, is, together with the therapy treatment, described in McCarthy and Breetz 'Confronting Male Hypoactive Sexual Desire Disorder: Secrets, Variant Arousal, and Good-Enough Sex' (2010).

Through its on the one hand graphic explicitness and its on the other hand role as fantasy, pornography holds a paradoxical position in relation to fantasy and reality (Barker 2014). The legalisation of pornography in the Western world during the 1970s, as well as the severe debates around pornography, gender, and sexuality from the late 1970s and into the 1990s, brought a new kind of discussion about what sexual representations are and how they relate to actual sexual practices, as well as to dominant ideology and hegemonic conceptions.

For instance, are women's rape fantasies an expression of an inherent wish in women to be dominated by men – is femininity masochist by nature? Or are they a way for women to allow themselves to enjoy sex, to not have to bear the responsibility of sexual activity because someone else made them do it, the so-called blame avoidance theory? Or is it just an example of how women have internalised patriarchal oppression and come to embrace sexuality as male domination and, even, violence? Might it be that women dream of being so desirable that men cannot resist them? All of these – and other – explanations have been proposed through the years and none is really sufficient (Bivona, Critelli & Clark 2012). When men fantasise about being dominated, is it because they need relief from the role of always being powerful, in control, active, and aggressive?

Although more women than men seem to fantasise about being dominated in one way or the other (being tied up, raped, beaten/whipped etc.), studies show very varied results on how many women actually have such fantasies. Between 31% and 57% of women have had fantasies of being forced into sex, but for only between 9% and 17% such fantasies are frequent or favored (Critelli & Bivona 2008). Thus, to say that it is a common female fantasy is actually very likely something of an exaggeration. It can be said that it is not uncommon for women to have such fantasies, but the only way it could be described as common is by ascribing fantasies of submission a negative character (like colds or Chlamydia are common). Nonetheless, since these fantasies are highly controversial, they become highlighted in reports of research. Explanations become politicised, because such fantasies could seem to endorse rape myths, such as the idea that women want to be overpowered, or they could cement gender roles such as that women are passive and men active.

Nonetheless, in research, it seems that sexual fantasies have little bearing on life outside the bedroom – sometimes even outside the mind and body of the fantasiser (Leitenberg & Henning 1995). Only a very small number of individuals act out fantasies that could be harmful to others or to themselves (about rape, sex with minors, asphyxiation, violence). Although some fantasies may have a correlation to attitudes, this applies to men who fantasise about dominating a woman and who have stronger rape myth acceptance, and not to women who have rape fantasies (Zurbriggen & Yost 2004). Some people have fantasies that do not have an equivalent in their sex lives – for instance heterosexuals who fantasise about sex with someone of the same sex.

Thus, from a socio-political perspective it might seem that it is of little importance what people fantasise about. However, Michael Kimmel and Rebecca F Plante argue that sexual fantasies reflect the social construction of gender in society in general (Kimmel & Plante 2005). In sharp contrast with biologically oriented explanatory models, Kimmel and Plante claim that gender differences in sexual fantasising come out of 'deep social structures. Differential sexual scripting, with the goal of reinforcing socially constructed gender role identities, is the primary axis of disparity. With socialization into a binary gender system that also assumes heterosexuality, gender is enormously powerful in the construction of the sexual self' (Kimmel & Plante 2005: 62). For Kimmel and Plante, the 'grey areas between fantasies and realities' are rather the result of reality's (in the form of social structures) influence on fantasy, and a palpable gender disparity in sexual fantasies is likely to cause problems in intimate, heterosexual relations (2005: 63). With script theory terminology, gender differences in the cultural scenario influence the intrapsychic scripts, which in their turn translate into a possibly problematic (heterosexual) interpersonal interaction.

This might be a more convincing explanation for gender differences in sexual fantasies than, for instance, claiming that fantasies involving multiple partners are typically male fantasies because of a biologically male imperative to reproduce with many women whereas women more often fantasise about famous men because they need a strong provider (Wilson 1997). One reason is that the pervasiveness of such fantasies is not significant enough to substantiate such claims. Although the group sex fantasy seems quite common among men (42%), the famous person fantasy for women was only slightly more frequent than for men (17% versus 16%) (Wilson 1997). In the study by Kimmel and Plante (2005), the famous person fantasy was actually more common among men (6.59% as compared to 1.61%).

Two neuroscientists, Ogas and Gaddam (2011) have used Internet searches for sexual content in order to describe and explain the human sexual mind. Arguing for their method, they refer to an experiment on anonymity conducted in the 1970s in which a psychologist let people enter a completely darkened room (Gergen 1973). Some of the subjects took the opportunity to touch and kiss, and almost 80% reported sexual excitement (Ogas & Gaddam 2011: 6). The Internet, Ogas and Gaddam claim, is like 'put[ting] a billion anonymous people in a virtually darkened room' (ibid.: 6).

Of course, the perceived anonymity of the Internet provides an occasion for people to do things they otherwise would be too embarrassed or ashamed to do.

However, the motivation for the searches that Ogas and Gaddam have compiled and investigated may rather be fantasy than reality. Simply finding out what people do when they believe they are completely and safely anonymous, does not readily allow itself to be interpreted as having found out the truth about what people want. An important reason to question both Ogas and Gaddam and Wilson is that, as mentioned before, fantasies do not necessarily guide our actions in real life. And if and when they do, they might not do so in predictable and universal ways. The potential impact of fantasies on everyday life has to do with whether they provoke a sense of shame or of joy, how the individual organises his or her sex life in practice, how much space the actual fantasies may be given (or demand), whether they facilitate or complicate interactions with others, and so on.

As we see it, our fantasies are informed and shaped by the world and others, and the cultural and the individual live in a constant dialogue with one another. Since human beings are social, our private fantasies are not sanctuaries free of civilisation's dos and don'ts but neither are our social situations completely out of our control, because we shape them by our interactions in them. One of the recurring themes in this volume has to do with the relation between fantasy and reality. Issues that come up are whether fantasies can have an effect on us and our dispositions even though they are not acted out; what happens when a potentially dangerous fantasy is acted upon and put into practice in reality; how we understand and experience fantasy although we know it is not for real; the consequences when reality does not meet our fantasised expectations; or what happens when our fear of actual abuse in reality guides our regulation of the mind; and so on.

The comparatively small correlation between what people fantasise about and what they actually do in real life may be hard to accept. Partly, perhaps, because we want to believe that people's inner lives are more true and authentic than the selves they present to the world. Accordingly, by looking into what people 'really' think, we tend to think – like Ogas and Gaddam – that we can achieve a greater knowledge of what people are 'really' like. The notion of a 'true', hidden self comes out of a vulgarised Freudian conception of the world within which civilisation is regarded as forcing us into controlling our true natures. On the other hand, radical feminist theories that claim that women internalise patriarchal dominance and male violence – thus explaining feminine masochism by such a complete socialisation as to overpower even individual agency and free will (e.g., Brownmiller 1975) – bring that conception to its logical end point. At the other end of the spectrum, however, explanations that come out of sociobiological theories, neurology, or evolutionary psychology are no more open to the agency of the human mind.

We avoid placing any value judgements on the fantasies presented in this volume. Sexual fantasies cannot be expected to be politically correct, no more than they can be regarded as revealing of a true self or explained by theories of internalisation. In addition, for all of the contributors to this volume, the aim has mainly been to understand rather than to prescribe. For example, although we do discuss, as in Daniel D. Hutto's chapter, women's rape fantasies, these are used as an example to test the credibility of pretend theory – which denies that we have true emotions in response to something that we know is fiction.

Another recurring theme in the contributions is the distinction between sexual fantasies – arousing, erotic fantasies – and fantasies about sex, that may be arousing and feed into our sexual fantasies but may also have other functions. One example would be pornography, which contains several fantasies about sex, such as a plenitude of sexual pleasure; large, erect penises, insatiable participants, and so on. At the same time, it is quite obvious that pornography functions not only as a fantastic space for sex (as 'pornotopia') but also has strong connections to what people actually fantasise about. Another example would be the fantasies we create about the Other – be it a political Other or the religious and cultural Other as Western conceptions about the Oriental Harem.

Chapters and contributors

The chapters of *Sexual Fantasies: At the Convergence of the Cultural and the Individual* are located within different scholarly practices. The contributors come from not only philosophy and psychology, but social anthropology, sociology, social work, film, media and cultural studies, science and technology studies, and gender studies. They use a variety of theoretical approaches and methods. Some chapters are more argumentative, others more descriptive. Several of the contributors are sexuality scholars teaching at the masters' program in Sexology at Malmö University in Sweden, and moreover, their research is associated with the newly started Center for Sexology and Sexuality Studies also at Malmö University. In addition, the editors have striven towards coherence and scholarly exchange through two workshops, one arranged early on in the work on the volume and the second held only a few months before the final deadline. Almost all contributors have participated in at least one of these workshops.

Comics and sexuality scholar Emma Vossen opens this volume with a defense of the bestselling erotic *Fifty Shades*-trilogy. The enormous success of these novels by E.L. James which began as fan fiction to the Twilight novels has prompted questions of what women actually want and a quite massive critique of the trilogy as lousy literature, both for its ostensibly low literary quality but also because it is regarded as antifeminist for encouraging abusive, misogynistic relationships. In her chapter, Vossen argues that both criticisms stem from the problem of viewing the book as a work of 'literature' as opposed to one of pornography. What women desire in pornography (and fiction) does not directly translate into what they want in a real life relationship.

Continuing on the theme of written erotica, anthropologist Sara Johnsdotter explores the way sexual fantasies are encoded in language through written narratives. Focusing on the use of the word 'cum' in written erotica, Johnsdotter describes a transformation in the meaning of the word since it began to refer to female cum as well as traditionally, male ejaculate. What is often called 'dirty talk' is a significant element in sexual excitement, used within pornography, fantasy, written erotica, and between sexual partners. In written erotica, words are what is available in order to induce sexual feelings and arousal in the reader. While erotic narration offers free reign for fantasy, depicting all kinds of activities that could be socially, culturally, and possibly criminally taboo in real, non-fictitious, social interaction, it is still regulated by standardised genre-specific scripts and subcultural standards: some fantasised scenarios seem to work better than others to elicit sexual arousal.

Deborah Blizzard takes on a very different projection of sexual fantasy. In 'Making the Fantasy: Consumption, Relationships, and the RealDoll', Blizzard turns the attention to sex dolls, more particularly the RealDoll. Technological advancement has made it possible to make quite life-like dolls, and the RealDoll began to be marketed in 1996. Blizzard discusses what the representation of the human body in the form of a doll that promises to be perfect might mean, both to the purchaser of such a doll and on a larger, societal scale.

The West has been accused of constructing an eroticised Other, especially with regard to the veil. Hence the *unveiling* of the oriental woman can be regarded as a classical Western sexual fantasy. In 'The Politics of Sexual Fantasies: The Inversion of Sexual Fantasies in Orientalism and Occidentalism', ethnic relations scholar Pernilla Ouis deconstructs Western fantasies about the Oriental, sexual Other, as well as Oriental conceptions about the sexualised West. These types of sexual fantasies and ethnopornography have had and still have political implications for the conquest and submission of the Other.

The role of sex as a religious motif and religious views on sexual fantasies is explored by anthropologist Aje Carlbom in 'Blocking out Sexual Fantasies for a Fantasy of Eternal Sex: Islamist views'. Carlbom, whose anthropological research has concerned Islam and Islamism, discusses both how a paradise of sexual abundance is promised for the afterlife of the devout Muslim and how imams relate to sexual fantasies that are disclosed in online sexual advice-seeking.

Focusing on what happens when sexual fantasies – even potentially dangerous sexual fantasies – are put into practice, Charlotta Carlström has contributed with a chapter on BDSM (an acronym for Bondage, Dominance, Submission, Sadomasochism). Carlström received her Masters degree in sexology at Malmö University and is currently working on a PhD project on BDSM. Her contribution focuses on the ritualistic aspects of BDSM and how fantasy is transposed into real life sexual practices in interpersonal, intimate relationships.

Carlström uses interviews with BDSM practitioners as empirical material in her research. Although also focusing on BDSM as fantasy and practice, Ingrid Ryberg, on the other hand, is a film scholar and consequently uses a different material to discuss political fantasies and expanded realities. Her chapter examines how two films, Morty Diamond's *Trans Entities: The Nasty Love of Papi and Wil* (2007), and Emilie Jouvet's *Much More Pussy* (2010), treat 'reconciliation' between fantasy and reality in queer, feminist, and lesbian sexual representations. Ryberg considers how in the two films fantasy, rather than being reconciled with reality, unsettles it and therefore potentially expands reality and everyday lives.

The relation between reality and fantasy, as visualised in images, is the topic of the next chapter, as well. In 'Fantasies Made Illegal', film and sexuality scholar Mariah Larsson discusses the criminalisation of child pornographic drawings, using a Swedish court case as example. Larsson considers the laws regulating child porn, especially images that do not have a 'real' object. Swedish law makes a distinction between graphic images of any kind and written narratives about sex. The latter are protected by the Swedish constitution under freedom of expression and freedom of the press. Whether an image of a child in a sexual situation is degrading to all children, regardless of whether it is an actual photograph or a computer generated image, is at issue.

Sven-Axel Månsson's research on sex work and prostitution spans five decades. He has been involved as an expert in official inquiries on sex work and on violence against women. In this chapter, he takes a closer look at the sexual fantasies of men who seek sex from female sex workers. By way of the numerous studies that have been made on sex work and prostitution, Månsson pieces together various themes that seem to be prevalent among men who pay for sexual services. Some of these themes are continuous, whereas others seem to be changing. Some are overtly sexual and have to do with for instance an idea of the skillful, 'bad' woman, whereas others have more to do with how the client perceives himself.

Philosopher Daniel D. Hutto contributes with an inquiry into the well-known puzzle concerning the rationality of our responses to fiction. 'Just Faking It? Pretend Theory Meets Sexual Fantasising' discusses, as mentioned above, the paradox of fiction. Using women's rape fantasies as a case study, Hutto compares two competing, fundamentally different, frameworks for understanding the mind. On the one hand, classic cognitivism sees the computational manipulation of subpersonal representations as the essence of mental life. Opposing this is radical enactivism, which characterises cognition in terms of non-representational embodied interactions. Radical enactivism assumes that contentful and discursive forms of cognition exist, but that they only emerge when individuals successfully master socially grounded practices, such as the creation of narratives.

Concluding this volume is Gunnel Brander's chapter, which deals with how sexual fantasies can be used in therapy, and what they might mean for an individual, both sexually and in everyday life. In some cases, the disclosure of sexual fantasies to a partner can evoke feelings of disgust or estrangement. In others, even a completely secret fantasy can diminish a person's sense of self and bring on self-doubt and anxiety. Conversely, the lack of sexual fantasies can lead to loss of self-confidence and ability to claim a necessary space for oneself. Brander draws from rich experience and knowledge after having worked for many years in therapy, couples therapy, and sex therapy. In addition, she has taught sexology and sexuality studies at Malmö University.

In one way, these last two chapters encompass the approaches of the contributions to this volume. The philosophical perspective questions easy assumptions about how the mind works. Elaborate cognitive processes that we still know little about cannot be explained by simple cause-and-effect logic. As we are interested in what happens between the individual and the surrounding world, the discussion of how the brain understands fiction is significant. The abstract reasoning of the philosopher, however, does not preclude very empirical and hands-on accounts of the possible uses of sexual fantasies. Rather, Brander's contribution points to how, with a humble, respectful, and non-normative approach, therapists can find a helpful tool in their clients' sexual fantasies.

References

Bader, M.J. (2002) *Arousal: The Secret Logic of Sexual Fantasies*. New York: Thomas Dunne Books.

Barker, M. (2014) 'The "problem" of sexual fantasies'. *Porn Studies* 1(1–2): 143–160.

Bivona, J.M., Critelli, J.W. & Clark, M.J. (2012) 'Women's rape fantasies: an empirical evaluation of the major explanations'. *Archives of Sexual Behavior* 41(5): 1107–1119.

Brownmiller, S. (1975) *Against Our Will: Men, Women and Rape*. New York: Simon & Schuster.

Critelli, J.W. & Bivona, J.M. (2008) 'Women's erotic rape fantasies: an evaluation of theory and research'. *The Journal of Sex Research* 45(1): 57–70.

Friday, N. (1973) *My Secret Garden: Women's Sexual Fantasies*. New York: Trident Press.

Friday, N. (1980) *Men in Love: Men's Sexual Fantasies: The Triumph of Love Over Rage*. New York: Delacorte Press.

Friday, N. (1991) *Women on Top: How Real Life Has Changed Women's Sexual Fantasies*. New York: Simon & Chuster.

Friday, N. (2009) *Beyond My Control: Forbidden Fantasies in an Uncensored Age*. Naperville, Il.: Sourcebooks.

Gagnon, J.H. & Simon, W. (1973) *Sexual Conduct: The Social Sources of Human Sexuality*. Chicago, Ill.: Aldine Pub. Co. (2. ed. 2005. New Brunswick: Aldine Transaction).

Gergen, K. (1973) 'Deviance in the dark'. *Psychology Today* 7(5): 129–130.

Kahr, B. (2009) *Who's Been Sleeping in Your Head? The Secret World of Sexual Fantasies*. New York: Basic Books.

Kimmel, M. & Plante, R.F. (2005) 'Gender of desire: the sexual fantasies of women and men'. In M. Kimmel (ed) *Gender of Desire: Essays on Male Sexuality*. New York: State University of New York Press.

Leitenberg, H. & Henning, K. (1995) 'Sexual fantasy'. *Psychological Bulletin*. 117(3): 469–496.

McCarthy, B. & Breetz, A. (2010) 'Confronting male hypoactive sexual desire disorder: secrets, variant arousal, and good-enough wex'. In S.R. Leiblum (ed) *Treating Sexual Desire Disorders: A Clinical Casebook*. New York: The Guilford Press.

Ogas, O. & Gaddam, S. (2011) *A Billion Wicked Thoughts: What the World's Largest Experiment Reveals About Human Desire*. New York: Dutton.

Simon, W. & Gagnon, J.H. (1986) 'Sexual scripts: permanence and change'. *Archives of Sexual Behavior* (15)2: 97–120.

Wilson, G.D. (1997) 'Gender differences in sexual fantasy: an evolutionary analysis'. *Personality and Individual Differences*. 22(1): 27–31.

Zurbriggen, E.L. & Yost, M.R. (2004) 'Power, desire, and pleasure in sexual fantasies'. *The Journal of Sex Research* 41(3): 288–300.

Emma Vossen

Feminism and Sexual Fantasy: Reading and Defending *Fifty Shades of Grey* as Pornography

History and context

E.L. James' erotic romance novel *Fifty Shades of Grey* (2011) has sold over 100 million copies worldwide. Reports indicate that the first novel in the series is one of the fastest selling books of all time (Bosman 2014) and it has been followed up by two additional best-selling novels, *Fifty Shades Darker* (2012a), and *Fifty Shades Freed* (2012b). Beyond this commercial success, the *Fifty Shades* series is now unquestionably one of the most famous erotic artefacts of our time. Despite this notoriety, many critics and detractors seem to know almost nothing of the tone, characters, or story itself other than its inclusion of BDSM sex, and its roots as fan fiction of Stephenie Meyer's *Twilight* saga. Because of both its prominent status in the public eye and its overwhelmingly female audience it has become 'hot' to hate *Fifty shades*.

Like many books that appear to be an overnight sensation, the popularity of the *Fifty Shades* series was actually a slow build towards success; the series was accruing fans and readers for years online before it became a runaway bestseller as an ebook in 2011. *Fifty Shades* was first 'published' online in 2009 as fan fiction of the *Twilight* series with the title *Master of the Universe*. The series was a part of what is known as the 'alternate universe' genre of fan fiction, which involves a story that is uprooted from its original context and given new meaning in another time and/or place (Tan 2012: 293). *Master of The Universe* is still focused on the relationship between Bella and Edward (the protagonists from *Twilight)* but takes place in the real world in which vampires do not exist: Edward is an obscenely rich business man, and Bella is an intelligent but innocent college student. When publishing her work, James changed the names of her main characters from Bella Swan and Edward Cullen to Anastasia Steele and Christian Grey, and created new names for the peripheral characters in order to avoid direct association with *Twilight (*Boog 2012).

Master of The Universe makes use of the characters and the already established dynamic between them in order to tell an entirely new story that is more sexually explicit than its predecessor. One area where the two series diverge drastically is through their discussions of power. The power relationship between Bella and Edward was mostly implied by Meyer and heavily speculated on by fans. For example, Bella would agree to or refuse Edward's various demands, but the power relationship between the two was rarely discussed or analysed within the text. We know that Bella clearly thinks Edward is too demanding and controlling, but we receive very little of her own thoughts about how his demanding nature would affect their ability to be together. Furthermore Bella rarely questions the validity of her entanglement with Edward; she is constantly convinced that they will be together forever, no matter the circumstance.

Fifty Shades, on the other hand, is fraught with discussions of power relations and the validity of the relationship. Sometimes the conflicts take place in Ana's head, and often they take place in arguments or discussions between the two main characters. Ana frequently questions if she should be in a relationship with a man who is so demanding and she is more than willing to end the relationship when she feels his demands are becoming too high. In the first book of the series, *Fifty Shades of Grey*, this discussion of power takes place through the construction of a 'submissive' contract which Christian draws up for Ana to examine and sign. Ana knows that despite the fact that she is falling for Christian she cannot, and will not, sign the contract because she does not want a purely physical relationship. Throughout the series, the discussions of power relations move away from sex, and instead revolve around their ongoing, monogamous, and increasingly committed romantic relationship. I highlight the difference between the two relationships because it is important to note that Christian and Ana's relationship is not one-sided, nor is it simply a replication of the relationship between Bella and Edward. I am sure some of the appeal of the series comes from the desire to see a woman like Ana work through a smorgasbord of sexual activities and state, firmly and honestly, how she feels about each one.

The series does not appeal to everyone and has endured vast and heavy criticism. The reactions from the general public, feminist critics, and the fanfiction and erotica communities have ranged from celebratory to damning. The perception of the series overall leans much more towards the heavily pejorative than the positive, not unlike the larger cultural attitude towards the *Twilight* saga. Some critics claim that the characters portray anti-feminist stereotypes, while others argue that the books will turn men into abusers and women into willing participants who tolerate physical abuse (Flood 2012). Some have even gone so far as to argue that *Fifty Shades* and *Twilight* both reflect the downfall or end of feminism (Cox 2010; Gold 2012). I argue that many of these criticisms are vastly underselling the complexity of the series and, more importantly, the intelligence of its readers. These critics often oversimplify the narrative, the characters, the relationship, and the sex so that they reflect stereotypical negative depictions of female sexuality, BDSM, gender roles, and female readers. Many of these critiques lack any medium- or genre-specific analysis, and examine the texts as social commentary while also holding them to the standard of literary novels, instead of acknowledging that the texts are functioning within the specific conventions of pornography.

Within this chapter I will discuss the generally negative perceptions of these books as well as more specific criticisms. I will demonstrate how many of these negative perceptions have very little to do with the actual content of the books and much more to do with sexual negativity, suppression, and most importantly: a fear of women consuming pornography. Contrary to many critiques, what women want within their pornography and their fiction (as with what they experience in their sexual fantasies) does not translate directly into what they want in their sex lives, or their relationships. There seems to be a double standard at play in which male consumption of pornography created and marketed towards men may be considered immoral by some, but is at the very least considered a perfectly ordinary occurrence by most; yet women who desire to consume and enjoy pornography that was intended for a female audience (as opposed to consuming male-oriented porn), are considered both laughable, and of a lower intelligence (Hamer 2012). Not only have *Fifty Shades* and other erotic ebook titles encouraged millions of women to embrace some form of sexual fantasy and pornography, it has also brought female sexuality to the forefront of the popular consciousness. The popularity and ubiquity of the *Fifty Shades* series is allowing countless women the type of exploration of sexual fantasy and role playing that fan fiction provides for its small subculture of women, and that mainstream pornography has long provided men.

But what is pornography, really?

In the *Feminist Porn Reader* the editors give a lengthy definition of what constitutes 'feminist pornography'. For all that I will not assert that *Fifty Shades* meets all the points of their definition (mostly because I do not think James' exigence for writing was political), I will say that these books are, at their core, pornography created by a woman, for women. The texts do meet a portion of the editors' definition, as they 'unsettle conventional definitions of sex, and expand the language of sex as an erotic activity'; the texts also function as 'an expression of identity, a power exchange, [and] a cultural commodity' (Taormino, et al. 2013: 10). Many pieces of feminist pornography have existed in the past, but none have reached the level of publicity or consumption that *Fifty Shades* has achieved.

Therefore this text has worked to 'unsettle the definitions of sex, and expand the language of sex as an erotic activity' for millions of women, many of whom may have never consumed pornography or thought about sex conceptually before reading *Fifty Shades*.

For some, the use of the word 'pornography' may be unwelcome or seem misplaced when discussing *Fifty Shades*, but I choose to use the word as an umbrella term for a variety of distinct works and sub-genres. My definition of pornography is one that includes no implications of quality or artistic merit. Pornography is: a genre containing explicit or implicit depictions of sexuality or sexual activity, in which the chief intention of that text and its creator is to sexually arouse the reader, using a variety of strategies and/or tactics in order to stimulate erotic feelings that may or may not be accompanied by aesthetic or emotional feelings which may or may not be expected by the audience. This definition puts weight on the rhetorical positioning and mechanics of pornography as a text instead of its cultural baggage as a genre. Many definitions of pornography emphasise that the text is in fact enforcing a stimulation of erotic rather than aesthetic or emotional feelings. Conversely, I hold that, more likely than not, there will be erotic stimulation adjoined by both aesthetic and emotional feelings when pornography is consumed. Moreover, there is a cultural idea that pornography is something that is used exclusively for the purposes of masturbation, which I also believe to be too restrictive a definition, as some (women especially) might consume porn and experience sexual gratification without having an orgasm or masturbating. Many aspects of the definition that we now know of as 'pornography' are concerning a phallocentric view of the medium/genre, and exclude many of the female oriented offshoots that may or may not be as sexually explicit, and may or may not be used for sexual gratification. This is a result of a continued failure in the history of sexuality to 'imagine [woman's] pleasures outside a dominant male economy' (Williams 1989: 4).

The double standard around pornography is furthered when women attempt to speak about it. This problem is articulated perfectly by pornography scholar Linda Williams who explains that it is important for her 'not to perpetuate the pervasive attitude among feminists that pornography is both the cause and the symptom of all women's problems' (1989: xi). She admits that when studying pornography, not admitting 'some enjoyment is to perpetuate an equally insidious double standard that still insists that the nonsexual woman is the credible "good" woman' (1989: xi). In line with Williams, I will admit that I do not feel that pornography itself is *inherently* a problem for women, but I do feel that women's marginalised status within pornography and, most importantly, their continued exclusion from the industry as producers and consumers is a *massive* problem. Furthermore, I will admit to not just reading but enjoying the *Fifty Shades* books as pornography. I think it is important to understand these texts *as* pornography in order to grasp their true cultural significance. If we cease to examine these texts as simply 'bad', 'harmful' or 'offensive' (as pornography *or* as literature) and begin instead to acknowledge the complexity and instability of the text at hand, we will be able to come to more productive conclusions about why the series is so popular, and why it has struck such a chord with women at this particular point in time. Instead of focusing on the simple question of 'should women be reading this?' discussion needs to advance towards 'the power and pleasure' that these texts 'hold for us' (Williams 1989: xi). Since consuming pornography is a voluntary act that many people enjoy, we, as feminists, should be placing the agency with the reader, and examining what pornography does for readers and consumers, not to them.

Ana's/reader agency

Globe and Mail reporter John Barber has gone as far as to say that the *Fifty Shades* series provides the answer to Freud's famous query 'what does a woman want?' He claims:

> What a woman wants, as expressed by the extraordinary success of *Fifty Shades of Grey*, the fastest-selling book of the 21st century – with almost 100 percent of those sales made to post-feminist women in developed countries – is whippings, floggings, spankings, canings, paddlings and every imaginable form of sexual humiliation and pain inflicted by icily sadistic, ultra-domineering men (2012).

Barber's oversimplification of the publishing phenomenon perpetuates the disparaging idea that women all want the same things romantically and sexually, and furthermore that what 'women want' in pornography and fiction is what they want in real life. It is possible that this is Barber's misguided attempt at irony, but as a reviewer for a national newspaper, this 'irony' is still sexist, and comes much too close to what many people genuinely believe.

Despite the problematics of these assertions, Barber is definitely not alone in these assumptions. Feminist critic Katie Roiphe builds on this logic in her *Newsweek* cover story on *Fifty Shades* for which the headline reads: 'The Fantasy Life of Working Women: Why Surrendering is a Feminist Dream'. She asserts that the popularity of *Fifty Shades* and other media depicting submission demonstrates a clear desire for women to be dominated in their sex lives, because they are ostensibly overwhelmed with how much power and responsibility they now have in their careers (Roiphe 2012). Although some women reading *Fifty Shades* may indeed be sexual submissives not all of them are, and you do not have to be sexually submissive to enjoy this work of fiction. These criticisms are predicated on an assumption that women are incapable of consuming fiction *as fiction*, and they strip away the readers' agency to simply read without blindly replicating. When this same logic is applied to many genres of typical straight men's pornography the assertions are often horrific, as we have seen in Robin Morgan's statement that 'pornography is the theory, rape is the practice' (Sarracino & Scott 2008: 173). Some of the most popular genres of men's pornography focus around fantasies that many of the viewers would never think of pursuing in real life, yet when analysing pornography many critics make the assumption that people only consume the pornography that they wish to enact. As sex educator and psychotherapist Keiko Lane explains 'pornography invokes a suspension of disbelief. It asks us to project ourselves into the experiences of others we witness, to try to imagine how those experiences would feel, and whether we want to enact them' (2013: 172). Sometimes we consume pornography and decide that it does or does not reflect a desire we want to act out. Similarly, although the *Fifty Shades* books may demonstrate types of sexual fantasies in which individual women wish to indulge, they do not necessarily demonstrate 'what they want' in real life.

The books do, on the other hand, examine Ana's 'wants' from her sexual and romantic relationship. Christian refuses to participate in sexual acts that Ana does not either consent to or explicitly request. She frequently refuses Christian's advances when she is uninterested or not ready, and he makes it very clear to her that she holds the power and control in their relationship (James 2011: 278). This would, if anything, demonstrate that women are invested in enjoying sexual fantasies of power via reading about sexual submission. Although, I do feel compelled to say at this point, that if Ana did enjoy giving up her agency for sexual pleasure that would also be fine, because this is fiction.

One of the most interesting aspects about many criticisms of the *Fifty Shades* series is that the text actually predicts and addresses them. Ana has many internal discussions with both her 'subconscious' and her 'inner goddess' which reflect a new spin on the trope of the devil/angel on the shoulder. Ana's inner goddess is depicted as a young beautiful, happy woman who tends to come out in moments involving sexual arousal or play, whereas her subconscious is depicted as an older, judgmental woman in half-moon spectacles who asks Ana to question the more wanton desires of her inner goddess. Sometimes both women gang up on Ana to criticise her for enjoying herself, notably when she is being spanked and reveling in the experience. The two characters are a way for James to personify Ana's combined enjoyment and confusion of both Christian's bondage practices and their general dom/sub roles. For example, throughout the first book her inner goddess frowns when she submits to Christian, but dances when she disobeys him. After the first time she is spanked by Christian, Ana is both aroused and confused. After spanking and sex Christian pulls down Ana's sweatpants in order to rub some baby oil on her to help with the swelling, and her subconscious quips bitterly '*up and down like a whore's drawers*' to which Ana comments 'in my head I tell her where to go' (James 2011: 195). There are many moments like this in which Ana confronts her internal evaluators, and the portion of her audience whose blatant condemnation slips and segues into slut-shaming of Ana's desires. Christian also confronts the shame and judgement that Ana puts on herself. He often comes out to tell her 'don't judge yourself' (James 2011: 176) and when she admits that she feels ashamed about enjoying being spanked he tells her 'don't waste time on guilt and shame' (James 2011: 206). James preempts readers feeling conflicted about their personal enjoyment, and not only mirrors that conflict but offers some consolation via character dialogue. The inner goddess and the subconscious function as an easy way for James to make Ana's thoughtful desire and navigations of agency clear to her readers, which makes the fantasy more accessible.

Depictions of abuse and BDSM

People from all ends of the political spectrum have taken issue with *Fifty Shades* in some way, be it for its depiction of women, its depiction of BDSM, its status as 'literature', or just its general popularity – it is truly a disparaged text. One protest of the series was organised by Clare Phillipson who runs a charity for victims of abuse. Phillipson called for women to bring her their copies of the book so that she could burn them in protest (BBC 2012). She insists the series is 'an instruction manual for an abusive individual to sexually torture a vulnerable young woman' and that Christian does 'horrific sexual things' to Ana (Flood 2012). Although Phillipson's opinion of the text might seem extreme, many others agree with at least the base assertion that the books depict some type of abusive relationship (Evans & Kane 2013; Casey 2012; Gold 2012).

The types of problematic assertions that Phillipson and others make when they describe Ana and Christian's relationship as 'abusive' are only worsened by the insistence that reading about a fictional 'abusive' relationship will create more abusive relationships in the real world. This line of thinking is almost identical to the previously mentioned classic anti-porn argument 'porn is the theory rape is the practice', only in both cases the woman is still the victim. The logic being that consumption of porn by men and women will lead to more sexual violence perpetrated towards women overlooks the ways that rape culture is created in real life (i.e. the Steubenville rape trial in Ohio, the suicide of Amanda Todd in British Columbia, or more general cultural norms such as victim blaming, sexual repression, slut-shaming etc.) by placing the blame on fictional scapegoats within pornography. This logic and rhetoric is very similar to the argument that blames video games, not gun control laws or bullying, or other systemic problems, for school shootings in the United States. The idea that there is a connection between these fictional books and abusive relationships not only trivialises the seriousness of abuse, but it can also inadvertently perpetuate a culture of victim-blaming by assuming that women want and/or seek out abusive relationships in the same ways that they seek out supposed 'narratives of abuse'. This logic is a type of victim-blaming that focuses the attention and blame on the women writer and readers of these texts instead of the real life abusers of women.

There are also criticisms of the series that involve questions about how the BDSM community is negatively or inaccurately represented. Although I understand these complaints, this is a fictional, pornographic and therefore unrealistic depiction of BDSM. Nowhere has James claimed that the story at hand is in anyway representative of all (or any) BDSM arrangements. In fact, Ana and Christian's relationship is actually extremely uncharacteristic because Ana comes to the relationship with no sexual or BDSM experience whatsoever. In my opinion the choice to make her inexperienced was a mechanical (one may even say literary) decision made because pornography involving more experienced sub/doms would not be as arousing for readers who have not been introduced to the culture, whom I speculate are the books' target audience. Ana is being introduced to the culture and its props and scenarios so that even a reader who knows nothing about 'kinky' sex will not feel alienated by the text. The primary motivation of this text is to arouse, and therefore the story is going to take the form that is most effective in accomplishing these ends.

Many have stated that the *Fifty Shades* series makes a distinct and direct connection between the assumed sadomasochistic tendencies of Christian Grey and his mental instability due to a history of child abuse (Roiphe 2012). For all that James at no point implies that all members of the BDSM community are mentally ill, she does very clearly make this illness a part of Christian's story. The confrontation with Christian's past, and Ana's conviction that it has something (or everything) to do with his sexual preferences, is by far the most problematic element of the narrative from my perspective, as it can be read as a type of pathologising of BDSM. Christian confesses, halfway through *Fifty Shades Darker*, that he believes he is indeed a sadist; he claims, in a matter-of-fact way, that he derives pleasure from whipping women, and he believes it is because the women he selects as his submissives resemble his neglectful dead mother (James 2012a: 233). Tristan Taormino, author of *The Ultimate Guide to Kink* (2012), explains that she takes issue with Christian's character because 'there is an assumption that the reason he's kinky is because… he had a rough childhood' and that furthermore 'there's this assumption that there's this one-to-one correspondence, which in real life there isn't' (in Mayer 2012). Many others have agreed with Taormino's position, and up until midway through *Fifty Shades Darker* I held this same concern. Taormino argues that the query of 'why do people enjoy the lifestyle?' is not really a question that can be answered because 'people are so different in their turn-ons, turn-offs, fantasies, fetishes, kinks, and their sexuality is so individual' (in Mayer 2012). Everyone's sexual preference is individual, but the real question here is: are readers internalising these arguably negative ideas about BDSM? I think the answer to this question is implicit in the culture and fandom surrounding the novels. There is an implied curiosity on behalf of the reader to attempt to participate in some dom/sub or bondage play after reading the novels if it tickles their fancy in the right way; many have cited an increase in profits from sex shops around the world attributed to readers wanting to either try out bondage or toy play after reading the series (Martin 2013; Fletcher 2011). The BDSM play of the novel is not treated as something for only those who have a tortured past like Christian, but something that can be for everyone, including Christian. I'm not saying that all women read these novels as an intro to BDSM; like I argued above, reading the books does not translate directly into replicating their scenarios, but consumption of pornography more broadly, as a type of safe sexual exploration, often leads to people determining what sexual acts they are and are not interested in (Lane 2013).

However, later on in the second book, James confronts the issue of pathologising BDSM head-on through the character of Dr. Flynn, Christian's therapist. Ana asks him about Christian's self-described sadism, worrying that 'he has needs which [she] can't fulfill' (James 2012a: 291). Dr. Flynn instead confirms that Christian is 'not a sadist' (James 2012a: 271) and then replies at length:

> That's no longer recognized as a psychiatric term. I don't know how many times I have told him that […] Christian just thinks the worst of any given situation. It's part of his self-abhorrence. Of course, there's such a thing as sexual sadism, but it's not a disease; it's a lifestyle choice. And if it's practiced in a safe, sane relationship between consenting adults, then it's a non issue. My understanding is that Christian has conducted all of his BDSM relationships in this manner (James 2012a: 291).

This conversation between Ana and Dr. Flynn suggests that James was well aware that if she was going to continue to use Christian's past as the narrative trope that was keeping the two characters apart, she was going to have to give some sort of exposition, in order to bring light to Christian's behaviour. Readers may have come to the book with the assumption that BDSM is usually the result of mental instability, but the narrative instead shows the ways that BDSM is the healthy outlet through which Christian heals and expresses his sexuality even though he had previously conflated his interest in BDSM with his mental instability and childhood abuse. This chapter of the series highlights that (as Taormino explains above) there is not a one-to-one solution for why Christian enjoys the BDSM lifestyle. It is Dr. Flynn's informed opinion that brings the reader a more complex and accurate description of Christian's unique sexual and personal identity.

Pornographic tactics and pornotopia

What I find most useful when trying to think about pornography as a genre with specific constraints and functionality is Steven Marcus' concept of 'pornotopia'. Like utopia, pornotopia is a 'no place', and this lack of place is what allows it to take on the life that it does. Every aspect of pornography is constructed as a tactic to either build or create sexual arousal and therefore everything exists solely for the purposes of sex. As Marcus explains, pornotopia does not exist in any location, and (very importantly) does not even exist within the confines of literature; it instead 'truly exist[s] behind our eyes, within our heads' (1977: 268). In pornotopia, the sun rises and sets only so that sex can take place and people exist for similar reasons: 'all men in it are always and infinitely potent; all women fecundate with lust and flow inexhaustibly with sap or juice or both' (1977: 273). Christian and Ana very much live in a pornotopia, in which money is never an obstacle. The series runs the gambit of pornographic scenarios; the pair have sex on Christian's desk, in the bath, in a hot tub, in the shower, in a hotel, on a grand piano, on a pool table, in his childhood bedroom, in his parents pool house, on a boat, in a plane, in an elevator, etc. The scenes usually involve brief foreplay, which includes occasional spanking or restraints, and always ends with world-shattering near-or-exactly-simultaneous orgasms. In a world of brand new cars, private aircrafts, a full time staff, and fully stocked sex playrooms, sex is *always* an option. The depiction of capitalism within the text is in many ways as pornographic as the sex itself because of its wish fulfilling tendencies. Money in this pornotopia is very literally infinite.

Throughout the novel James uses various pornotopia scenarios and characterisations as what I will refer to as pornographic tactics. The most obvious of these tactics lie in Ana's sexual innocence and virginity, which allow for not only an accessible entry point to the narrative, but an exciting (no matter how forced) mode of identification for the reader. Ana's innocence allows readers to relive and rewrite the excitement and possible disappointment of their first time through a virginity fantasy that is a fabulous encounter full of many long and glamorous orgasms. Ana's excitement for sex and her initial resistance to Christian's 'kinkery' creates a tension in the text that plays with the readers' desires. The reader is anticipating not only the sex scenes, but also the kinky sex scenes. Christian and Ana are playing sexual games of anticipation and power struggle with the reader as much as each other in order to create sexual tension that will further arousal. This same tension is created through Christian's inability to be touched where his scars are, therefore Ana is constantly longing to reach out and claim that which is forbidden. The narrative is all about building tension and then dismantling it which allows for the book to be extremely explicit while still somehow always leaving something to be desired. Ana's pain and her confused resistance to it also become a pornographic tactic (James 2011: 195). Her pain quickly becomes about much more than just Christian's sexual desires. The pain and her conflicted feelings about her arousal from that pain give her reason to resist Christian which provides the narrative with its primary conflict and tension that keeps the narrative going for three lengthy books.

Despite the fact that *Fifty Shades* fits so snugly into the broader genre of pornography it also pushes its boundaries in many ways as well. The sex scenes found throughout the series are an assorted mix of stereotypical porn scenarios and romance novel sexual fantasies that make sex seem easy and perfect – as is expected in pornography – contrasted with extremely realistic and candid conversations about sexual acts, bodily fluids, and pregnancy. In one scene, when things became erotic, I assumed that the fact that Ana was currently having her period would be ignored, as it often is in pornography. Yet James successfully made the scene more erotic, because Ana has her period. Christian and Ana engage in some mild foreplay and Ana eventually begs Christian for sex. Christian quickly and directly asks her when she started bleeding and Ana replies that her period began the previous day, to which Christian replies with a simple 'good' and tells her to hold onto the sink:

> I'm bending down. He reaches between my legs and pulls on the blue string… what! And… gently pulls my tampon out and tosses it into the nearby toilet. Holy fuck. Sweet mother of all… Jeez. And then he's inside me… ah! (James 2011: 298).

After their earnest sex scene they collapse in a heap, in which Ana is cradled in Christian's lap. After recovering from her orgasm she notices that she is bleeding on him: '"I'm bleeding", I murmur. "Doesn't bother me", he breathes' (James 2011: 299). Ana recounts to the reader that 'he's standing there, naked, gloriously naked, with my blood on him' (James 2011: 299). I was shocked and delighted by the profoundly intimate and sex/body positive nature of this scene that plays with the realities of menstruation while still maintaining the pornotopia illusion.

James pushes the boundaries of pornotopia frequently by writing sex scenes that include shaving pubic hair (James 2012b: 53) or pregnancy (James 2012b: 507–511). In many ways I saw these more 'realistic' elements acting in odds with the indulgence of pornography and of the idealistic pornotopia. In pornotopia there is no risk of pregnancy and there are no periods, but these concessions of realism actually seemed to function as a means of pornographic persuasion. I hypothesise that this realism, and this female perspective on sex, might actually be enticing readers by showing sex that is pornographic, while still being recognisably relatable to their own lives that are likely also punctuated by pills and periods.

Returning to the question of Christian's abuse as a child and subsequent mental anguish, these are also elements of the narrative that have nothing to do with the more 'pornographic' elements of the book. If anything they are in direct contradiction of them. Upon discovering that a four year old Christian almost starved to death by spending four days alone in a room with his dead mother, the reader is likely not going to feel aroused. Furthermore when the reader finds out that all of Christian's previous submissives supposedly resemble his mother, the reader is also likely to feel turned off. These moments may be hard to reconcile because the possible revulsion the reader feels at these moments can both be an example of the text's failures as pornography, and of its successes as a novel. As a novel these connections seem quite interesting, but as pornography they get in the way of its true purpose. James also does work to undo many of these more problematic story lines. Near the very end of *Fifty Shades Darker* Ana sneaks into Christian's childhood bedroom and inspects a photo of his mother. She quickly discovers that, although the mother looks very much like Christian, she looks absolutely nothing like Ana, other than being a brunette (James 2012a: 368). After this realisation, Ana, and likely the reader, have again reconciled their once confused sexual feelings about Christian Grey and can rejoice both when the couple return to the bedroom, and Christian gets down on one knee and presents Ana with a ring.

Conclusions

Many criticisms of the series, and similar criticisms of *Twilight*, quickly and eagerly strip the agency away from not only the female characters but also the readers by assuming that they are passive in their consumption of the narratives. Detractors shame Ana's character for wanting this type of sexual interaction, and further shame the female readership for being aroused by such 'un-feminist' material (Roiphe 2012). Within the text Ana's subjective thought process is open to the reader. She describes herself, countless times, as both enjoying and understanding the power exchange between herself and Christian. In one particular instance she describes:

> With one swift thrust, he's fully inside me. I groan loudly, gutturally, and revel in the fullness of his possession. He puts his hands on mine on top of my head, his elbows hold my arms out and down, and his legs pinion me. I am trapped. He's everywhere, overwhelming me, almost suffocating. But it's heavenly too, this is my power, this is what I do to him, and it's a hedonistic, triumphant feeling (James 2011: 245).

In this moment the reader sees Ana illustrating and translating what kinky sex feels like to her, to millions of other women (and men), in both an accessible but suitably complex manner. She describes how it turns her on to be trapped and how that consensual 'trapping' translates into a sense of empowerment. Readers can, hopefully, understand more fully their own feelings about sexual power exchange, and comprehend their understanding of how empowerment and feminism can fit into the context of BDSM. As readers, instead of stripping Ana's power away from her in these moments, we should instead be more willing to perceive and recognise the enjoyment and agency that she does have within these sexual scenes, which is so uncommonly depicted in any media. Many cite the fact that Ana is not fully sexually submissive as a failing of the text to accurately depict a BDSM relationship. But Ana, by the end of the series, has in my opinion, become a full-blown switch (i.e. someone who is comfortable moving fluidly through or alternating between both sub and dom roles). Ana is very involved in her sex life with her husband and very enthusiastic about the BDSM aspects of it although she prefers to refer to it as 'kinky fuckery'. It is worth noting that to my knowledge the position/identification of switch is never offered to Ana throughout the series, possibly because, much like bisexuality, the identification of switch is often criticised or marginalised as imaginary or fence sitting.

After the last vanilla sex scene of the series Ana lies on top of Christian and thinks of: 'Images of us together, in the playroom; the Tallis, the table, on the cross, shackled to the bed […] I love his kinky fuckery—our kinky fuckery. Yes. I can do that stuff. I can do that for him, with him. *I can do that for me*' (James 2012b: 502). Ana is the one who forces Christian back into the playroom after her brush with death in *Fifty Shades Freed*. Ana explains their relationship in the last words of the series (before the epilogue) saying 'I'm in this for the long haul. I love this man: my husband, my lover, father of my child, my sometimes Dominant… my Fifty Shades' (James 2012b: 505). Christian too has become, not quite a switch (although he did live much of his life as a sub), but a 'sometimes dominant', an identity new to him that is appreciated by Ana. Maybe these scenes make people uncomfortable because they do not adhere to the traditional roles associated with

BDSM and bring up questions of when kinky-fuckery becomes 'legitimate' BDSM play. Is James troubling the boundaries of BDSM? Or is she affecting its legitimacy within normative culture? Is making BDSM normative a threat to the community? Who has the privilege or cultural capital to partake and be accepted into BDSM culture? What financial or cultural restraints may hold someone back from partaking? Is the 'Red Room of Pain' (Christian's Playroom) a financial fantasy for James and her readers as much as a sexual one? This discussion of James, and *Fifty Shades* is not about what has, and has not, been done. It is about what has been seen and read on a mass scale and what has now been normalised in the popular conscious of the millions of readers of this text. James is straddling two worlds; in the sexual normative and vanilla world her text is quite transgressive and controversial, in the world of BDSM and erotic fiction it is quaint and for some, too normative. It is not everyday a text can come along that is so powerful that it not only captivates, but offends people of so many different walks of life.

References

Barber, J. (2012) 'What Fifty Shades of Grey taught us about publishing'. *The Globe and Mail*. http://www.theglobeandmail.com/arts/books-and-media/what-fifty-shades-of-grey-taught-us-about-publishing/article6580566/.

BBC (2012). 'Fifty Shades book burning call by abuse charity'. *BBC News*. http://www.bbc.co.uk/news/uk-england-tyne-19354560.

Boog, J. (2012) 'The lost history of Fifty Shades of Grey'. *GalleyCat*. http://www.mediabistro.com/galleycat/fifty-shades-of-grey-wayback-machine_b49124.

Bosman, J. (2014) 'For 'Fifty Shades of Grey,' more than 100 million sold'. *The New York Times*. http://www.nytimes.com/2014/02/27/business/media/for-fifty-shades-of-grey-more-than-100-million-sold.html?_r=0.

Casey, K. (2012) 'Is 'Fifty Shades of Grey' dangerous?'. *Forbes*. http://www.forbes.com/sites/crime/2012/06/23/is-fifty-shades-of-grey-dangerous/.

Cox, D. (2010) 'Twilight: the franchise that ate feminism'. *The Guardian*. http://www.theguardian.com/film/filmblog/2010/jul/12/twilight-eclipse-feminism.

Evans, C. M. & Kane, A. (2013) '50 Shades of Grey trilogy normalizing child sex abuse'. *American Thinker*. http://www.americanthinker.com/2012/09/50_shades_of_grey_trilogy_normalizing_child_sex_abuse.html.

Fletcher, C. (2012) '50 Shades under the tree means surge for sex toy sales'. *Bloomberg*. http://www.bloomberg.com/news/2012-12-12/50-shades-under-the-tree-means-surge-for-sex-toy-sales-retail.html.

Flood, A. (2012) 'Fifty Shades of Grey condemned as "manual for sexual torture"'. *The Guardian*. http://www.theguardian.com/books/2012/aug/24/fifty-shades-grey-domestic-violence-campaigners.

Gold, T. (2012) 'Twilight is not feminist: it's female masochism'. *The Guardian*. http://www.theguardian.com/commentisfree/2012/nov/16/twilight-not-feminist-sado-masochism.

Hamer, M. (2012) '50 Shades of anti-feminism'. *iVillage*. http://www.ivillage.com.au/50-shades-anti-feminism/.

James, E.L. (2011). *Fifty Shades of Grey*. Waxahachie, TX: The Writers Coffee Shop Publishing House.

James, E.L. (2012a) *Fifty Shades Darker*. Waxahachie, TX: The Writers Coffee Shop Publishing House.

James, E.L. (2012b) *Fifty Shades Freed*. Waxahachie, TX: The Writers Coffee Shop Publishing House.

King, D.L. (2012) 'Is Fifty Shades erotica?' In L. Perkins (ed) *Fifty Writers on Fifty Shades of Grey*. Dallas: Bella Books.

Lane, K. 'Imagining possibilities'. In T. Taormino, et al. (eds) *The Feminist Porn Book*. New York: The Feminist Press.

Marcus, S. (1997) *The Other Victorians*. New York: Basic Books.

Martin, A. (2013) 'Fifty Shades of Sex Shop: Sexual fantasy for sale.' *Sexualities* 16 (8): 980–984.

Mayer, A. (2012, July, 11) 'Fifty Shades of Grey Critics slam bondage stereotypes'. *CBC* News.

Roiphe, K. (2012) 'Working women's fantasies'. *Newsweek*. http://www.newsweek.com/working-womens-fantasies-63915.

Sarracino, C. & Scott, K. (2008) *The Porning of America*. Boston: Beacon Press.

Tan, C. (2012) 'Fifty Shades of Stories'. In L. Perkins (ed) *Fifty Writers on Fifty Shades of Grey*. Dallas: Bella Books.

Taormino, T., et al. (2013) 'Introduction: The politics of producing pleasure'. *The Feminist Porn Book*. New York: The Feminist Press.

Williams, L. (1989) *Hard Core*. Los Angeles: California University Press.

Sara Johnsdotter

Written Fantasies: A Case of Language-Induced Sexual Excitement

Introduction

What is the role of language in sexual fantasising and efforts to stimulate sexual excitement? Sexual fantasising, and the enactment of fantasies in pornography, is usually associated with visual imagery, and written erotica is currently under-researched (Paasonen 2010: 138). Indeed, language has an important role to play in sexual fantasy, judging from the worldwide popularity of internet archives of written erotic stories.

There seems to exist 'a general scholarly unwillingness to address bodily reactions to texts' (Paasonen 2010: 147). This is enigmatic in light of the fact that the main motivation behind reading erotica and other arousing texts is the desire to create such carnal effects. It is not difficult to find scholarly work on 'sex' or 'body' in language, but very hard to find work on 'language in the body' – that is, studies on embodied sex-related language, or more generally on the relation between sexual sensations and language. Research questions could potentially cover areas such as the role language plays for desire and arousal. How are certain erotically loaded words embodied, and what processes are at work when 'dirty talk' or written erotica create physical reactions in the form of sexual arousal? How important is language in sexual fantasies?

In this chapter I will explore the role of language in sexual fantasising through a discussion of a specific case: the invention of *female cum* in amateur written erotica. I intend to show that the linguistic form of this phenomenon carries a special capacity to elicit sexual arousal and may serve as an example of the inherent power of language to create bodily responses of sexual excitement.

Sexual words

Taboo words are emotionally charged and conspicuous, and they have the ability to arouse people more than other categories of words. A phenomenon of interest in this context is how taboo words, among them those with sexual content, are cognitively stored. At a neural level they seem to stand out, as shown by the fact that many aphasia patients retain their ability to use taboo words while other linguistic faculties are lost (Eilola & Havelka 2010: 135), and swearing is salient in some forms of Tourette Syndrome (van Lancker & Cummings 1999). In most people's subjective experience, taboo words are more emotionally charged in one's native language than in languages learned later in life, as has been validated in experimental research (e.g., Harris, et al. 2003). These words' specificity is also demonstrated through the potential of 'dirty talk' (*lagnolalia*) to heighten sexual pleasure (Harris 1995, Cameron & Kulick 2003).[1]

When it comes to written pornography, certain words that are taboo in the vernacular are especially eroticised.[2] The emergence of written pornography in Great Britain in the second half of the 19th century shows a process where curse words were systematically used to blend 'dirtiness' and eroticism (Sigel 2000: 395). Until that point in time these words (such as *cunt*, *prick*, *fuck*, and *bugger*) had had other connotations; for instance, 'cunt' had until then, with a bawdy ring to it, designated a part of a woman's body. Now, "cunt" no longer connotes a place, but becomes a place that a man chooses to "fuck"' (2000: 407). Vernacular words adopted from the lower classes were eroticised in pornographic works among the male upper class, where they circulated out of reach of censoring authorities. These 'dirty' words became increasingly nasty and arousing: as a method to speak of pleasure in ways that other contemporary discourses were unable to do due to censorship (Sigel 2000: 411ff).

The word spelled 'cum' – in contrast to the word spelled 'come' – is exclusive of erotic or pornographic contexts and has been around since the 1970s.[3] In most dictionaries the word is described as follows or similarly: as an intransitive verb, 'to experience orgasm' and as a noun, 'semen ejaculated during orgasm', both forms marked as 'vulgar' and 'slang'. Thus, the prevailing understanding is that

---

1 Cameron and Kulick (2003) report about a campus-wide sexual consent policy to prevent rape at Antioch College in Ohio in the 1990s, in which verbal consent was required for each act during a sexual encounter. A follow-up found that many women spoke of better (more exciting, more varied, and more pleasurable) sex as a result: 'They found themselves talking much more explicitly than they had previously been wont to do about specific sexual acts, and they claimed this enhanced the experience of sex' (2013: 37).

2 The different uses of the words *pornography* and *erotica* will not be discussed in this chapter, and I will use the terms interchangeably. Paasonen (2010) suggests that the two terms can be described by their respective narrative dynamics: 'The realism of porn is achieved through dedication to recording the details of bodies and acts, while erotica is characterized by a certain kind of emotional and sensual realism' (p. 151). She admits that the categories are overlapping and have leaky boundaries. For a discussion with key references, see Eshghi (2012).

3 Online Etymology Dictionary, *etymonline.com*.

'cum,' when used as a noun, refers to discharge from the male body only.[4] I have found two exceptions; both are online dictionaries being frequently updated by their users. *Wiktionary* lists two meanings of the noun 'cum': both 'male semen' and 'female ejaculatory discharge.' In the *Urban Dictionary* several entries out of 133 list 'cum' as referring also to female liquids.[5]

I searched for occurrences of female 'cum' in fiction through Google Books. The first female 'cum' I was able to find is dated 1991, in a book by Red Jordan Arobateau with the title *Hobo Sex*, and then there is no trace of it for several years. Suddenly, starting in 2005, several erotic publications use the word 'cum' to refer to female fluids (e.g., Stalwart 2005, Longren 2006, recent publications include Tumbles 2014, McIntyre 2014). Obviously, there is a semantic shift in the word at some point in the first years of the 21st century. The first occurrence in the Urban Dictionary is from 2003: '*A male or female orgasm resulting in sometimes unexpected amounts of love juice spurting vociferously*' (posted by the signature PetePole). Several other entry authors testify to the existence of female 'cum' in later dictionary entries.

Female cum in my corpus of written amateur erotica

I investigated the use of the word 'cum' and especially 'female cum' in a corpus of a little more than five hundred erotic stories, or two million words. The stories were collected in March 2013 from the Internet archive *Literotica*.[6] This archive of hundreds of thousands of erotic stories was established in 1998 (Paasonen 2010: 139). *Literotica* is a well-attended website: during the last six months in 2013 the website of *Literotica* had between 2.4 and 2.6 million unique visitors every month in the U.S. alone.[7]

I collected stories to reach a million words from the category 'Erotic Couplings', and half a million words each in the categories 'First Time' and 'Non-Consent/ Reluctance'. The stories were analysed using Wordsmith Tools 4. I investigated the occurrence of female cum in this corpus using the search string 'her cum' in order to find the references to female bodily fluids. I sorted out the examples in

---

4 E.g., *The American Heritage Dictionary of the English Language, Flick – Dictionary of Sexual Terms, Oxford Reference Online, NTC's Dictionary of American Slang and Colloquial Expressions, Sex Slang* (Dalzell & Victor 2007).

5 At *urbandictionary.com*, 11 May 2014.

6 Some parts of this chapter have already been published in Johnsdotter (2011), based on a pilot study with a corpus of half a million words.

7 Statistics from the company Compete, which provides site statistics at *compete.com*.

which the expression referred to the verb (such as 'Do you think we should let her cum?') and focused on the ones where 'cum' was a noun.[8] A few examples:

> Tara lay on the bed, wet with her sweat and her cum all over. The greasy pussy juices dripping down her crotch mixed with my spittle.
> ('36 Hours of Pleasure', *Erotic Couplings*)

> Soon, her orgasm subsided and Ken picked Melissa up and pushed her onto the bed on her back. He smiled and slowly pushed her legs open as he observed her owned pussy, with mingled combinations of her virginal blood and her cum flowed down her pussy lips.
> ('A Cheerleader's Cherry', *First Time*)

> As Jake leaned forward, it must have changed the angle just enough, and he hit something, and that something made her expectantly shoot her cum all over him. It came so fast, so hard; it scared the hell out of Rebecca, never having really orgasmed with such a force before. ('A Chance Worth Taking – Rebecca', *Non-Consent/Reluctance*)

Traditional 'cum,' that is, male ejaculate, is a mix of prostatic fluid from the prostate gland and semen from the gonads which is expulsed through the urethra (Peate 2003). Even though the actual spermatozoa only make up 1% of the fluid (Lilja & Malm 1994: 77), its ability to play a crucial part in the human reproductive process is what makes it irrefutably different from any sexual fluid emanating from the female body.

So what does the female 'cum' refer to in the erotic stories of the corpus? The stories offer examples of female 'cum' referring to both *lubrication* during sexual arousal and *ejaculation* co-occurring with or resulting from orgasm. Here are two examples of when 'cum' is obviously about lubrication:

> Richard could tell that Molly was enjoying this, as her cum dripped onto his face even before he started.
> ('A Bowl of Cherries', *Erotic Couplings*)

> Her cum and Cliff's oral attentions had her quite wet but the cockhead was big and she groaned around Cliff's cock as George fed her cunt several inches of his big dick.
> ('A Better Life for Lauren Ch. 02', *Non-Consent/Reluctance*)

---

8 Some uses are ambiguous, such as 'feeling her cum on his tongue' ('A Blue Dream'), in which 'cum' can potentially be both a verb and a noun. Limiting the search to the string 'her cum' was a strategy to reduce the number of hits. The word 'cum' alone renders more than 2,000 hits.

In other stories the word appears to describe wetness emitted during orgasm:

> I slammed my cock into her hard and held it as her pussy gripped me tightly. Her cum soaked my cock as she exploded into a mind numbing orgasm.
> ('A First for the Ages', *First Time*)

> When she came her whole body seemed to lift itself off the bed and remain suspended in the air. She couldn't breathe, think, or recall anything she may have said. All she saw were explosions of light behind her clenched lids. All she felt was rapid shots of heat and electricity erupt from her veins. Her cum was an avalanche of liquid steam that cascaded over Chad's fist and onto his face.
> ('A Bastard and a Slut', *Non-Consent/Reluctance*)

Generally speaking, a woman's vagina is lubricated as a result of sexual arousal. The fluid that works to lubricate is the neurogenic transudate, which emits from the vaginal walls and is produced immediately when sexual arousal begins (Levin 2007: 46).

Apart from lubrication, female wetness during sex may have to do with ejaculation: women as well have prostatic tissue and may ejaculate. Estimates vary between 14% and 54% of all women (Gilliland 2009: 123). Female ejaculate leaves the body through the urethra but should not be confused with urination and incontinence at orgasm (Zaviačič & Whipple 1993, Whipple & Graziottin 2006, Gilliland 2009). There is also the possibility that, in fact, all or most women ejaculate: the secretion of many, or most, women back-fluxes into the bladder rather than being 'shot' through the urethra and out of the body (Levin 2007: 47).[9]

The existence of lubrication of the vagina during sex seems to have been unproblematised from an ideological perspective. The often rather blunt descriptions of its function, such as 'For women, an increase in vasocongestion produces vaginal lubrication, which obviously facilitates sexual interaction' (Laan & Janssen 2007: 283) remain undisputed. In contrast, statements about female ejaculation have brought on critical voices. Among them is the philosopher and political scientist Shannon Bell, who wrote the essay "Feminist ejaculations" in 1991. She gives an account for how female ejaculation was discussed by Greek and Roman ancient scholars (who pondered whether female fluids played a role in reproduction or not, or if they contributed to pleasure only), the 17th-century anatomist Regnier

9 Santamaria (1997, in Levin 2007: 47) investigated urine samples before and after orgasm. A secretory product, prostate-specific antigen (PSA), was found in the post-orgasmic urine in 75% of the women in the study group, but not in their pre-orgasmic sample. It remains unclear, however, whether this marker for a prostate ejaculation (i.e., PSA in the urine after orgasm) stems from arousal or orgasm (ibid., see also Gilliland 2009).

de Graaf (who stated that the discharge from the female prostate causes as much pleasure in women as in men), and by modern scholars. Somewhere on the way the idea of a female ejaculation was dropped and forgotten:

> Since female ejaculatory fluids did not contain 'seed', these fluids were left without a word to describe them. The apparent solution was to drop the notion of a female 'semen', which simultaneously meant the loss of the concept of female ejaculation (Sevely & Bennett 1978: 17).

When pornography developed in 18th-century England, it mirrored the medical discourse, which was still seeing the body in humoral terms (regulated by the four humours phlegm, yellow bile, blood, and black bile), and sexual fluids were regarded as ingredients in this larger humoral system (Peakman 2012). Pornography displayed those aspects of bodily functions that were expected to be controlled and contained by civilised people, and bodily fluids were at the centre of the erotic material. Loss of vaginal fluid, and also female ejaculations, were seen as natural. 'Indeed, in erotica, female ejaculations were positively fêted', Peakman asserts (2012: 58); excessive vaginal secretions were enjoyed and depicted as an obvious sign of sexual proclivity (p. 60).

In the 19th century, instances of female ejaculation were linked to disease and eventually pathologised (Bell 1991: 156–157). Beside scattered references to the existence of female ejaculation, the phenomenon was mainly denied or ignored from 1950 and the subsequent decades. Masters, Johnson, and Kolodny, as late as in 1982, claimed that female ejaculation is 'an erroneous belief' and associated it with 'urinary stress incontinence' (Bell 1991: 159, see also Gilliland 2009: 122). In a study inspired by phenomenology, thirteen women who regularly ejaculate described their experiences. Even though most women eventually ended up in feelings of acceptance, or acceptance tinged with resignation, it was not unusual to have felt deeply embarrassed about what many women had understood to be urination during sex (Gilliland 2009). Sharon Bell does not seem very surprised that the academic field at large has downplayed female ejaculation; the key question, according to her, is why feminist scholarship has silenced the ejaculating female subject (1991: 162ff). She suggests that this failure to speak out has to do with reluctance to see similarities between female and male sexual functioning: 'Ejaculate – fluid that shoots, fluid that sprays – has been given over to the male body. To accept female ejaculate and female ejaculation one has to accept the sameness of male and female bodies' (1991: 162–163).

This visible – *palpable* – wetness is highly eroticised in written erotic narrative, whether in the form of lubrication or ejaculation, as shown in the quotes from the erotic stories above. The eroticisation of this visible sign of sexual pleasure will be further examined with the help of insights from film studies, where arousing devices in the pornography genre have been discussed for some time.

Maximum visibility in filmed pornography

Film scholar Linda Williams has analysed hardcore pornographic cinema in terms of the 'frenzy of the visible': 'the very impetus for the invention of cinema was precisely that it seemed able to register the previously invisible hard-core "truth" of bodies and pleasures in a direct and unmediated fashion…' (Williams 1999: 30). She quotes Michel Foucault's idea that we feel pleasure in 'knowing' pleasure, in that sense pornography and its antecedents aim at revealing the mysteries of sexual pleasure. They are attempts to reach the intrinsic truths of sexual bliss. In a historical perspective, pornography has been a male genre; therefore, the secrets of female sexuality, its 'confession', have been the focus of attention.

The irony, says Williams, is that while it is quite easy to represent male pleasure and climax in visual media – through erection and ejaculation of semen – signs of female sexual pleasure are elusive. In women, orgasm takes place in an 'invisible place' (1999: 49), and in mainstream film pornography female pleasure is primarily expressed through extensive moaning and groaning. Moans and cries of pleasure are heard from men too, but they are not as loud and dramatic as those produced by women (Williams 1999: 123, see also Jackson & Scott 2007: 106f, and Potts, 2000: 66). In absence of physical, visible evidence of female pleasure and its peak, such as erection and ejaculation of sperm, the female actors have to try to convince the audience, through displays of audible 'evidence', that they are in fact being immensely pleasured. The cinematic medium has a limitation here that does not apply to written erotic narrative, where female pleasure and climax can be given evidence through a linguistic account.

Consequently, the strength of the film medium to reveal the 'truth' of female sexual pleasure – its ability to 'objectively' represent realistic sex acts – is at the same time its weakest point, in its failure to make visible invisible female pleasure. Deborah Shamoon describes how this limitation is overcome in Japanese erotic comics for women, in which female pleasure is depicted through genre-standardised devices. The women in these drawn comics are 'dripping with juices' (2004: 88): 'the wet vagina serves as a proof of the woman's arousal and a demand for satisfaction […] the wetness is typically overdetermined. Fluids gush forth in a tide of unbridled sexual excitement in the many repeated close-ups' (2004: 91). There is an evident parallel between the Japanese women's erotic comics and the Internet erotic stories in that they picture female arousal and pleasure with abundant wetness, and neither media sets any limits to such a representation – or to exaggerations. Just like drawings allow for representing things impossible to capture on film, written narrative offers the same opportunity.

There is a genre within pornography, in which female ejaculation is celebrated and fetishised (and often manipulated before the camera). However, the ejaculating woman rarely appears in mainstream film pornography, and where such films and videos exist, they are usually produced by women (Straayer 2004: 235). It is hard to say why film pornographers have avoided exploiting the ejaculating women to a greater extent, and any suggestion must remain a conjecture. One hypothesis is that eroticisation builds upon polarity between the sexes: 'The very definition of the sex act is premised on socially constituted bodily difference, and heterosexual desire and pleasure are generally both represented and experientially understood in terms of gender polarity' (Jackson & Scott 2007: 96; see also Straayer 2004, Williams 1999: 30, and Bell, 1991). In the current scientific discourse, the female and male sexual organs are usually defined in terms of passivity and activity. The vagina is the receiving, passive part, while the penis ejaculates and discharges (Braun & Kitzinger 2001: 224). We may assume that this perceived difference between the sexes is exactly what people learn to experience as sexually arousing, and, hence, the difference *per se* is eroticised. Another possible explanation for the lack of ejaculating women in mainstream film pornography might be that most women do not ejaculate in a visible manner. Consequently, the ejaculating woman would appear to be an exaggerated figure to the general audience due to lack of personal experiences. And yet, 'ordinary people' may describe female ejaculation as the optimal orgasm: in an interview study about orgasm a female informant valued female ejaculation ('coming like a guy') over an orgasm without ejaculation (Potts 2000: 64).

'Real' vs. faked female sexual pleasure and the effortless orgasm

In cinema the audible moaning is the most salient sign of female pleasure, while in written erotic narrative, as well as in the Japanese erotic comics for women, the wetness and fluids play the most important role. This is not only a result of the fact that written narrative and comics are silent media: acoustic expressions can still be represented (in my corpus of erotic stories, there are twenty-odd-letter words to convey these sounds). The crucial aspect here is that *the body does not lie* (Cameron & Kulick 2003: 15). While the general view is that men cannot fake or hide an orgasm, a well-known concern in at least Western societies is that women may fake orgasm (Roberts, et al. 1995,

Cameron & Kulick 2003: 15ff, Jackson & Scott 2007: 106ff).[10] The noise in film pornography, however loud, may still be faked noise. In contrast, the visible wetness in Japanese comics and all female cum flowing in Internet erotic short stories represent pleasure in ways that are seemingly 'undeniable.' Bodily fluids cannot be faked; thus, when described or depicted, they bear witness of 'true' pleasure and 'real' orgasms. They are, to speak in Foucault's terms, 'involuntary confessions' (Williams 1999: 50). Faked female orgasms are not sexually arousing, while 'real' female pleasure and climax are.

A sensate body – a body physically able to feel – is not enough to feel sexual desire and pleasure. What is needed is the embodied ability to decode bodily sensations, as well as cultural and social conventions of signification or, in other words, a shared sense of erotic meaning (Jackson & Scott 2007: 100f, Cameron & Kulick 2003: 15). There is some variation when it comes to exactly what people are sexually aroused by; yet, sexually explicit descriptions in images and words have a general potential to result in arousal (Laan & Janssen 2007, Hardy 2008). 'Cum' is genuinely erotically loaded. Further, when used in the context of female pleasure, it borrows a feature generally associated with male ejaculation: an appearance of orgasm as being straightforward and uncomplicated, almost effortless. As noted by Jackson and Scott, 'within heterosexual relations, women's orgasm has conventionally been seen as more problematic, elusive and mysterious than that of men' (2007: 96, see also 103ff, and Potts 2000), and, in Western popular constructions of heterosexuality, female orgasm requires performance skill on the part of the male (ibid., Cameron & Kulick 2003: 16). When 'cum' is used to describe the female climax, it connotes a physical sensation so strong its culmination cannot be held back – as analogous to how the male orgasm is usually constructed. Therefore, 'female cum' is more arousing than the usual 'female wetness' and orgasm, which may rather be associated with prolonged efforts and perhaps even frustration. In short, the word 'cum' connotes an unavoidable release that is not preceded by wearisome toil. Therein lies its explosive potential to create sexual arousal in sexual fantasising. In addition, with the unique spelling of the word 'cum', signalling pornography, this arousing capacity is not only about language, but *written* language.

10 In many societies other sexual scripts might be at play. For example, it is reported from Sudan that women generally are expected to *hide* signs of sexual pleasure: 'If the woman has an orgasm, she tries to not show it, and if she is unable to control her reaction, she denies that it was brought on by sexual ecstasy' (Lightfoot-Klein 1989: 89).

Eroticisation of female bodily fluids – a feast of consumption

In mainstream pornography the male discharge in the form of 'cum' is highly eroticised, as shown by so-called money shots in filmed porn and the porn subcategory of facials.[11] Like in 18th-century pornography (Peakman 2012), bodily fluids in today's written erotica are eroticised through their transgressive nature, at the opposite end of that which is civilised and under control. Bodily fluids can also be categorised as taboo in the purity-and-pollution order suggested by social anthropologist Mary Douglas: to create order in a chaotic world, we classify some things as dirty, polluted, dangerous, or taboo while other things are labelled as clean, pure, and safe – and bodily fluids are among the 'polluted' and tabooed things (Fischer 2011: 40.). The focus on female cum in erotic narrative is then in itself a transgression of a taboo.

In my corpus, there are occurrences in which female cum is described as something the protagonist sees ('in bed, wet with her sweat and her cum all over') or feels through penetration ('her cum soaked my cock'), but many occurrences describe female cum in a context of oral sex ('her pussy flooded my mouth with her cum'), and with an emphasis on smelling or tasting – a feature which is considerably more difficult to depict in filmed pornography:

> … and the sweet tang of her cum on his mouth drove him mad.
> ('A Better Life Ch. 1', *Erotic Couplings*)

> He quickly moved his tongue to her inner parts and licked her cum into his mouth. She tasted salty and sexy.
> ('A Bedtime Story', *Erotic Couplings*)

> I used my tongue to strip the thick cum from her fingers as I sucked and swallowed. Candi giggled and began to slide her fingers in and out of my mouth as I swallowed her cum… I closed my eyes, revelling in the taste of Candi's juices…
> ('A Bit of Christmas Candi Ch. 2', *Erotic Couplings*)

Some stories paint pictures of cunnilingus even more strongly in terms of *consumption*:

> He removed his fingers and licked her again, lapping up her cum as fast as she came.
> ('A Basic Instinct Ch. 02', *Non-Consent/Reluctance*)

---

11 Money shot: 'The moment in a pornographic film where the male subject of the scene in question ejaculates; so named because it is often considered the most important part of the film, and often an actor who is unable to provide the shot goes unpaid' (*Wictionary*). Facial: 'A sex act of male ejaculation onto another person's face' (*Wictionary*).

… he felt the first waves of her orgasm crashing over him, the flood of her release filling his mouth and flowing down his chin. His name echoed through the room as he held her tight to his lips, his tongue pressing down on her clit, his lips closed tight around her swollen pussy. Sucking, drinking her cum, lapping up every sweet drop, and not stopping there for one second…
('A Birthday Surprise', *Erotic Couplings*)

I kissed and licked her fingers, tasting her sweet nectar. Her cum was thick on her fingertips and I revelled in its oily, sweet taste. It was the perfect dessert to end a perfect evening.
('A Boss, A Mentor, A Lover', *Erotic Couplings*)

Within psychoanalyst tradition there have been associations made between cunnilingus and cannibalism (Coleman 1935, Khan, 1973). According to Freud, infantile pre-genital sexuality comes with some cannibalistic features, which aim at aggressively incorporating the object 'and obtaining mastery over it' – oral sex would stem from this sexual organisation in our psyche (Kahn 1973: 294, a later psychoanalyst who asserted that there are also tender and sensual dimensions to oral sex). In vernacular or slang the theme of consumption stands out in the linguistic sexual metaphor of 'eating', or 'eating someone out'. According to Wiktionary, one of the meanings of *eat* is 'To perform oral sex on someone' [transitive, informal, vulgar], and the example sentence offered is '*Eat me!*'

A search on 'eat' in the corpus renders 216 hits. Many of these refer to real food – like steaks or dinner or cake – but many (close to a hundred) refer to cunnilingus:

He sure seems to love my body, he feels me and kisses me all over, sucking on my nipples, feeling my breasts, kissing up my legs, which I spread so he can get at me, and then eating me. It's almost like he does eat me, fingering me, licking me, sucking on my clit, almost biting it.
('A Big Appetite', *Erotic Couplings*)

Some occurrences explicitly make associations with food:

I was willing to eat a gallon of that nasty cunt cheese to get what I wanted.
('A Day of Many Firsts', *First Time*)

Your pussy is fucking wet, baby. Mmmm, I want to taste it. I want to eat you up like a juicy peach.
('A Big Weekend Surprise', *Erotic Couplings*)

According to Wiktionary and also Urban Dictionary, 'eating' is about oral sex performed on either sex. However, only one story in my corpus uses the verb in a reciprocal sense ('After, we fool around a while and eat each other and then fuck'; 'A Big Appetite', *Erotic Couplings*). Very few occurrences are about 'eating' in the fellatio sense – here is one example out of six hits in four different stories:

> Now it was her turn to greedily eat every drop and continue to lick and suck until he pulled it out.
> ('A Bewitching Night', *Erotic Couplings*)

In three stories sperm is consumed, but through cunnilingus. There is a tendency for *eating* in relation to female genitals and *sucking* in relation to male:

> So she asks me all about how it feels when you eat me and when I suck you.
> ('A Blossoming', *First Time*)

> We both know you loved sucking my cock and we both know you're gonna love having me eat you out.
> ('A Bastard and a Slut', *Non-Consent/Reluctance*)

Both *cock* and *dick* collocate more strongly with *suck* than *clit*, *nipple* and *tits*.[12] *Pussy* is far down in the list of collocates and *cunt* even further down. There is a strong relation between *eat* and *pussy*, while the male genitals are not even on the list of collocates of *eat*. *Lick* collocates strongly with both *pussy* and *cock*.

To summarise, female cum in these narratives is almost exclusively used in a positive and appreciative sense, closely associated with delightful consumption. The *eat* metaphor stands out in relation to female fluids, demonstrating their capacity to provide a greater sexual intensity in transcribed fantasies.

Written depictions of the female cum: authorship and readership

Since the 1970s the word spelled 'cum' (meaning 'semen' only) has been used widely in written erotic narrative for its ability to sexually arouse the readers. Being genre specific –with few exceptions, the word is not used outside pornography – it has a special potential for signalling eroticism. When now used to designate also female fluids, it is reasonable to assume that the purpose and the function of the usage is the same: to arouse sexual excitement. Traditionally, the pornographic field has been dominated by male producers and consumers. How can we understand the linguistic invention of 'female cum' in relation to

---

12 Collocation is about how words or terms co-occur more often than would be expected by chance.

the classical discussion about the 'male gaze'? A male heterosexual writer and reader may enjoy the description of female pleasure in the form of abundant cum: herein lies the undeniable evidence of a woman's non-fakeable sexual bliss. In the words of Williams, 'in most pornography, the woman's body is solicited, questioned, and probed for secrets that are best revealed when she herself is not in control' (1999: 50). This feature was prominent also in 18th-century pornography:

> Part of the erotic value of the body lay in its interpretation as a humoral body. Although control over bodily fluids was imperative in a civilised body, the very fact that female fluids were portrayed as so free-flowing depicted 'uncivilised' women with 'impolite' and embarrassing bodies. [...] Despite (or more likely, because of) the fact that these women's bodies were embarrassing and uncontrolled, they were nonetheless exciting (Peakman 2012: 65).[13]

We can thus assume that the 'male gaze' is pleased by the existence of cum emanating from female bodies. However, is it reasonable to assume that there is no 'female gaze' there to appreciate the presence of female cum when a female person reads erotic stories, or that she would not make use of it when writing? There is no way to know for certain whether the authors of specific erotic stories in the Internet archives are male or female. The stories are generally published with a signature that hints at a certain gender of the author, and the general impression is that both women and men are active writers. Lately there has been a 'democratization of pornography' (Hardy 2008: 61), where private citizens engage in 'horizontal' communication. Written erotica, in contrast to audio-visual pornography, is often authored by women (Paasonen 2010: 139), and sex blogging, often anonymous, is heavily dominated by women (Attwood 2009). Paasonen (2006) cites Nikunen, who has criticised the assumption that the consumer of pornography is necessarily male, an assumption that situates women in the realm of the 'chaste look', as detached from the influence of porn (Paasonen 2006: 415). The same could be said about assumptions that women are not authors of pornographic narrative.

---

13 The quote goes on: 'But most importantly, at the same time, women's bodies that expressed copious sexual fluids were both happy and healthy bodies (albeit uncivilised) as opposed to the sick bodies of their over-ejaculating male counterparts' (2012: 65). Here Peakman refers to the masturbation panic (reinforced by the medical society) in the 18th and 19th centuries.

Some stories in my corpus are coarse throughout the whole plot, while others mix 'dirty words' with a more traditionally romantic or 'soft' framing, like in this example: 'her pussy .... glistened with her cum, her flaps looked like rose petals, opening to the sun' ('Hot Summer Nights', *shorteroticstories.com;* in Johnsdotter 2011: 183) or this example:

> ...to worship a masculine, confident man and be relished and cherished for your femininity......in return...? Let's play, baby......hard..! Softly.....gently.....wildly....let's learn each other's movements...teach me how to fuck you, babe... ('In Hot Water', *lushstories.com*; in Johnsdotter 2011: 190).

While it is true that one's biological sex does not determine the nature of one's discourse (Hardy 2001: 448, see also Sonnet 1999: 175), styles may harmonise with established gendered conventions to a higher or lesser degree. Many of these erotic stories seem to aim at satisfying a female reader, irrespective of the authentic gender of the author.

If faking orgasm is as common as stated (e.g., Roberts, et al. 1995), then most women are familiar with the experience of having faked sexual climax at some point, and thinking of that situation is probably not arousing. In contrast, a description of a woman who is truly – *undeniably* – aroused or orgasming (proven by her producing cum) will have the potential to elicit arousal. The Japanese erotic comics for women is a genre of manga that grew out of romance comics for teenage girls; that is, it was never a sub-genre of porn for men. In this genre, aimed at creating arousal in *women*, the male body is almost excluded in the drawings: it is the female body and its signs of arousal that is on display to arouse the sexual desire of the female reader (Shamoon 2004). As noted by Shamoon, we cannot assume a male gaze from the fact that it is the female body that is in focus of the depiction of sexual pleasure: 'what may appear visually similar can, in the context of different audiences and different generic expectations, have radically different meanings' (2004: 83, see also Eshghi 2012). Consequently, while undoubtedly pornographic media have a tradition of pertaining to a male world, many of the contemporary expressions are created by and for women. Part of these representations may be about women enjoying to display the signs of female pleasure, possibly also in the form of adopting a new term, and concept, such as female 'cum.'

Female cum paints a picture where female pleasure is about loss of control. While losing control, a woman 'cumming' also plays an active part in the sense that she *produces* something and, possibly, even ejaculates. These phenomena are active and contrast to the traditionally passive role ascribed to female sexuality. A feminist reading would perhaps suggest that the existence and celebration of female cum is a concession to discourses that value the male as norm – the male sexuality as active, producing, ejaculating. For instance, Annie Potts (2000, in a 'feminist deconstruction of the heterosexual orgasm') understands a female informant's statements about her orgasms with ejaculation in this way:

> The most significant experience (female ejaculation) is valued perhaps precisely because it comes closest to Maggie's understanding of the male orgasmic experience (*coming like a guy = ejaculation*). 'Orgasm', on the other hand, is associated with 'physical contractions' and less 'moisture'. Thus, male orgasm – as perceived by Maggie – is inadvertently privileged over the 'standard' female orgasm, which lacks ejaculation. In addition, it is only the male heterosexual experience of sex that allows Maggie to articulate and understand 'coming' (Potts 2000: 64–65; italics in original).

Seen from this perspective, female cum is but a pathetic replica of male orgasm, and focusing on it is underpinning male-centred versions of sex. Another kind of feminist reading is the one presented by Shannon Bell (1991), in which she argues that women's (sometimes latent) ability to ejaculate is about power over one's body, and she claims that ejaculation is a way for feminists to 'appropriate and reclaim the female body' (1991: 163). The crux of the matter seems to be whether female pleasure is, or ought to be, construed in terms of sameness or difference in relation to male sexuality.

Female cum in sexual fantasy

These discussions about cultural, social, and ideological constructions of female sexual pleasure take place among scholars. Meanwhile more popular representations of female sexual pleasure are being formed; for instance, in the form of the spread of the linguistic innovation of 'female cum' in erotic narrative. According to linguist Andreas Blank, an innovation of this kind must execute a 'good cognitive performance' (Blank 1999: 62). When it comes to the spread of the word 'cum' to describe female fluids during sex, we can note that the word in its new context indeed performs a complex cognitive task: it may refer to both lubrication and ejaculation; it speaks simultaneously of excitement, desire, pleasure, orgasm, and loss of control; it is, because of its historical use in pornographic contexts, loaded with a potential to arouse sexual excitement. Possibly, it was created to fill a lexical gap and create symmetry in descriptions of male and female pleasure. The blurredness of the word's exact meaning points in that direction: it remains unclear whether the word, when used for women's fluids, primarily describes lubrication or ejaculation, or both. Obviously, the semantic shift in this word is not mainly about finding ways to describe reality as exactly as possible, but to serve the probably most important purpose of erotic texts, namely to create sexual arousal.

This invention of 'female cum' may be seen as an example of 'linguistic resources that people use to animate desire' (Kulick 2003: 136, see also Cameron & Kulick 2003: 106ff). A strength of a concept such as 'female cum' is that it overcomes the dilemma of the woman possibly faking pleasure during sex. When the word is used in erotic narrative, the reader is supposed to be convinced that authentic and undeniable female pleasure is described. Borrowing from connotations of male 'cum,' it implies unrestrained and effortless pleasure. In this respect, written erotic narrative may accomplish something that mainstream filmed pornography fails to do. This accomplishment – giving a convincing depiction of female sexual pleasure, condensed in the word 'cum,' and overcoming the dilemma of the faked female orgasm – might be enjoyed by both female and male writers and readers. Using 'cum' to describe the results of female pleasure in fantasised scenarios is indeed a linguistic resource that is used to create desire and sexual excitement. How well the word describes the physiological realities in the world outside of the narrative is of secondary importance in comparison with this efficacy.

References

Arobateau, R.J. (1991) *Hobo Sex.* Oakland, CA: Red Jordan Press.

Attwood, F. (2009) 'Intimate adventures: Sex blogs, sex "blooks" and women's sexual narration'. *European Journal of Cultural Studies* 12(1): 5–20.

Bell, S. (1991) 'Feminist Ejaculations'. In A. Kroker & M. Kroker (eds) *The Hysterical Male: New Feminist Theory*. Basingstoke: Macmillan Education.

Blank, A. (1999) 'Why do new meanings occur? A cognitive typology of the motivations for lexical semantic change'. In A. Blank and P. Koch (eds) *Historical Semantics and Cognition*. Berlin, New York: Mouton de Gruyter.

Braun, V. & C. Kitzinger (2001) 'Telling it straight? Dictionary definitions of women's genitals'. *Journal of Sociolinguistics* 5(2): 214–232.

Cameron, D. & Kulick, D. (2003) *Language and Sexuality.* Cambridge: Cambridge University Press.

Coleman, S.M. (1935) 'Oral erotism in paraphrenia.' *The British Journal of Psychiatry* 81: 203–204.

Dalzell, T. & Victor, T. (2007) *Sex Slang*. London: Routledge.

Eilola, T.M. & Havelka, J. (2010) 'Affective norms for 210 British English and Finnish nouns'. *Behavior Research Methods* 42: 134–140.

Eshghi, S. (2012) *Female Authorship and Implicit Power in Women's Erotica: Japanese "Ladies' Comics" and Fifty Shades of Grey*. M.A. thesis in Asian Studies, The University of British Columbia. *https://circle.ubc.ca/handle/2429/43745*

Fischer, N.L. (2011) 'Purity and pollution: Sex as a moral discourse'. In S. Seidman, N. Fischer, and C. Meeks (eds) *New Sexuality Studies*. London: Routledge.

Hardy, S. (2001) 'More black lace: Women, eroticism and subjecthood'. *Sexualities* 4(4): 435–453.

Hardy, S. (2008) 'The pornography of reality'. *Sexualities* 11(1–2): 60–64.

Harris, D. (1995) 'Dirty Talk.' *The Baffler* 7: 91–97.

Harris, C. L., Ayçiçegi, A. & Gleason, J.B. (2003) 'Taboo words and reprimands elicit greater autonomic reactivity in a first language than in a second language'. *Applied Psycholinguistics* 24: 561–579.

Jackson, S. & Scott, S. (2007) 'Faking like a woman? Towards an interpretative theorization of sexual pleasure'. *Body and Society* 13(2): 95–116.

Johnsdotter, S. (2011) '"The flow of her cum": On a recent semantic shift in an erotic word'. *Sexuality and Culture* 15: 179–194.

Khan, M.R. (1973) 'Cannibalistic tenderness in nongenital sensuality'. *Contemporary Psychoanalysis* 9(3): 294–302.

Kulick, D. (2003) 'Language and Desire'. In J. Holmes & M. Meyerhoff (eds) *The Handbook of Language and Gender*. Oxford: Blackwell.

Laan, E. & Janssen, E. (2007) 'How do men and women feel? Determinants of subjective experience of sexual arousal'. In E. Janssen (ed) *The Psychophysiology of Sex*. Bloomington: Indiana University Press.

Levin, R.J. (2007) 'The human sexual response: Similarities and differences in the anatomy and function of the male and female genitalia: Are they a trivial pursuit or a treasure trove?'. In E. Janssen (ed) *The Psychophysiology of Sex*. Bloomington: Indiana University Press.

Lightfoot-Klein, H. (1989) *Prisoners of Ritual: An Odyssey into Female Genital Circumcision in Africa*. New York, London: The Haworth Press.

Lilja, H. & Malm, J. (1994) 'Sperman' [The Sperm]. In B. Fredricsson & Å. Pousette (eds) *Andrologi* [Andrology]. Stockholm: Almqvist & Wiksell Medicin.

Longren, R.J. (2006) *What You Can Do for Me: Erotic Stories*. The United States: Lulu.com.

McIntyre, B. (2014) *Collection of Lesbian and Exotic Stories*. CreateSpace Independent Publishing Platform.

Paasonen, S. (2006) 'Email from Nancy Nutsucker: Representation and gendered address in online pornography'. *European Journal of Cultural Studies* 9(4): 403–420.

Paasonen, S. (2010) 'Good amateurs: Erotica writing and notions of quality'. In F. Attwood (ed) *Porn.com. Making Sense of Online Pornography*. New York: Peter Lang.

Peakman, J. (2012) *Mighty Lewd Books: The Development of Pornography in Eighteenth-Century England*. Basingstoke: Palgrave Macmillan.

Peate, I. (2003) *Men's Sexual Health*. London and Philadelphia: Whurr Publishers.

Potts, A. (2000) 'Coming, coming, gone: A feminist deconstruction of heterosexual orgasm'. *Sexualities* 3(1): 55–76.

Roberts, C., et al. (1995) 'Faking it: The story of "ohh!"'. *Women's Studies International Forum* 18(5–6): 523–532.

Sevely, J.L. and Bennett, J.W. (1978) 'Concerning female ejaculation and the female prostate.' *Journal of Sex Research* 14(1): 1–20.

Shamoon, D. (2004) 'Office sluts and rebel flowers: The pleasures of Japanese pornographic comics for women.' In L. Williams (ed) *Porn Studies*. Durham: Duke University Press.

Sigel, L.Z. (2000) 'Name your pleasure: The transformation of sexual language in nineteenth-century British pornography'. *Journal of the History of Sexuality* 9(4): 395–419.

Sonnet, E. (1999) '"Erotic fiction by women for women": The pleasures of post-feminist heterosexuality'. *Sexualities* 2(2): 167–187.

Stalwart, V. (2005) *The Erotic Adventures of American Glory: Book One*. The United States: [no editing company].

Straayer, C. (2004 [1993]) 'The seduction of boundaries: Feminist fluidity in Annie Sprinkle's Art/Education/Sex'. In P.C. Gibson (ed) *More Dirty Looks: Gender, Pornography and Power*. London: BFI Publishing.

Tumbles, T. (2014) *Hostage Take Over: Erotic Stories*. Resounding Wind Publishing.

Van Lancker, D. & Cummings, J.L. (1999) 'Expletives: Neurolinguistic and neurobehavioral perspectives on swearing'. *Brain Research Review* 31: 83–104.

Whipple, B. & Graziottin, A. (2006) 'Orgasmic disorders in women'. In H. Porst & J. Buvat (eds) *ISSM Standard Committee Book, Standard Practice in Sexual Medicine*. Oxford: Blackwell.

Williams, L. (1999) *Hard Core: Power, Pleasure, and the "Frenzy of the Visible."* Berkeley: University of California Press.

Zaviačič, M. & Whipple, B. (1993) 'Update on the female prostate and the phenomenon of female ejaculation'. *The Journal of Sex Research* 30(2): 148–151.

Deborah Blizzard

Making the Fantasy: Consumption, Relationships, and the RealDoll

'Didn't I tell you, you're the only one who can see me like this'.
- Emmy, the mannequin, to her human lover, Jonathan.
Mannequin, 1987[1]

'Those are nice, huh? And they're not real, so they'll last forever'.
- Lars, the human, to Bianca the doll, as she is given flowers.
Lars and the Real Girl, 2007[2]

'Real women can make you happy or unhappy. RealDolls can make you only happy'.
- Client suggested slogan for RealDolls.
Testimonial from the RealDoll Website, 2014[3]

In multiple cultures worldwide evidence of dolls as both representations of humans and companions to humans are identifiable. In some cases the doll may be totemic, or an object to deliver messages to others. In still other cases dolls may be used as protection against evil spirits or unwanted conditions. Dolls are frequently companions to children – entities to attach love and dreams. Although the precise uses of dolls and their multiple meanings vary, in all situations dolls reflect and even help to define the morals and politics of their context. Intriguingly in some cultures dolls have taken on a unique role in human-doll relationships where the doll is not only a social companion but is also a highly sexualised one. Although dolls have been used to achieve both benevolent and malevolent deeds, the sex doll stands somewhere in between moral claims of acceptability and inappropriate expression. Like the dolls before it and those in production today, dolls (sex- and otherwise) are many things, but at its core they are an invitation into a new way of knowing and interacting within a complex world.

The pursuit of sexual freedom and fulfilment is a driving factor for many individuals. How such fulfilment is attained varies depending on multiple constructed social norms including morality, access, and legal parameters; therefore what is normal and enjoyable to one person may not be to another.[4] Unlike other

1 IMDb. (1990–2014). http://www.imdb.com/title/tt0093493/?ref_=fn_al_tt_3.
2 IMDb. (1990–2014). http://www.imdb.com/title/tt0805564/?ref_=nv_sr_1.
3 Testimonials (June 9, 2014). https://secure.realdoll.com/june-9th-2014/.
4 On social construction, e.g., Restivo 1994, Blizzard 2007, Hess 1997.

personal issues that are disarming (and in this case frequently disrobing), sexuality practices that lie at the cultural margins of normality are often matters of taboo – not openly discussed (except in rare cases) and potentially a topic of ridicule and voyeurism. Although the sex doll may seem a unique and relatively benign fetish, for some it also raises a multitude of questions regarding how it may affect human-to-human relationships as well as how we frame claims of culturally defined beauty and sensuality.[5]

Although in most Western contexts it is the concept of love that is desired, its reality and attainment can be both questionable and problematic (e.g., Schafer 2008). Far from the hetero-normative concept of marriage in which a man and woman fall in romantic love and live as a socially accepted couple, many individuals do not aspire to, cannot attain, or actively avoid such a relationship. Individual differences in sexualities, partner preference, and even geographic location may make the realisation of this concept of romantic love impossible. Within these limits, sexual and social companionship can be difficult for some, and the doll may be a realistic alternative to, and even preferential to, human-to-human companionship.

Normalisation of the doll in popular culture

Human companionship, as a commodity, is not new. Across cultures and time, arranged marriages, prostitution, and arguably the legal state of matrimony itself demonstrate that companionship can have a figurative or a literal price.[6] However, unlike the purchase of human companionship, the purchase of the doll allows its owner to create the doll's presumed personality and to live out multiple fantasies of emotional and physical expression. Although feminists and gender theorists have critiqued the sex trade and other forms of the commodification of human sexuality, often these explorations turn toward the trade of the human body; fewer have analysed how the sex doll and its *representation* as the human

5 Although this chapter focuses on dolls, some work has been done on 'statue love' which dates back to the times of Pygmalion. For a detailed analysis of these ancient artefacts see Smith, M. (2014). *The Erotic Doll: A Modern Fetish*. New Haven, CT.: Yale University Press and Ferguson, A. (2010). *The Sex Doll: A History*. Jefferson, N.C.: McFarland & Co.

6 The ability to buy the sex partner as a doll runs in cultural parallel with the ability to buy *human* companionship. A comparison can and should be made between sex dolls and online dating or mail order brides (including the often demeaning and objectifying terms utilised to describe them). Although beyond the scope of this chapter, a potential answer lies in how we envision sexuality, consumption, and objectification.

body may symbolise the role and position of women (and to a lesser extent, men) in our culture. The social processes of normalisation of actions and artefacts and the socialisation of humans to accept them becomes important: what once seemed odd, different, or even immoral, can now be seen as acceptable, reasonable, and worthy. The combination of more realistic dolls and the greater access to them and increasing awareness of them, make today's doll an exotic commodity that may enhance the ability to fulfil a fantasy while also acting as a reflection of what aspects of sexuality and sensuality are valued within a given environment.

Dolls, as sexualised companions, have a long history and depending upon how one defines the doll, the precise dates and examples will vary. However, many reports on the history of the sex doll indicate that it is within the 17th century where sailors were known to use cloth to create female-like forms where the sex doll of today begins to take shape. These figures termed '*dame de voyage* in French, or *dama de viaje* in Spanish' with created anatomies were crude yet useful devices on long voyages (Beck 2014, np, see also Ferguson 2010). As time continues, so too does the quality of dolls, and by the 20th century dolls such as inflatable blow-up dolls are available for purchase in pornography magazines and by the 1980s are available for purchase in adult stores. In the cases above the dolls were minimalistic representations of women: sewn together with rough material or inflatable plastic; however, they did serve a purpose, and those who used them likely did so knowing quite well that the artefact was more of a physical receptacle than an object to which a sexual and sensual – even social – relationship might evolve (e.g., Ferguson 2010).

In recent years advancing technologies within doll manufacturing and increased social media with access to films, television, blogs, documentaries, and newspaper and magazine articles about sex dolls, have made the dolls better-known and socially accepted – at least within some segments of popular culture.[7]

7 Beyond the Doll becoming more identifiable, other approaches to Doll subcultures are identifiable. As reported in *The Independent* (7 January, 2014), Channel 4 is creating a documentary, 'Secrets of the Living Dolls'. In this documentary the issue is not men with dolls, but men as dolls. The men share a unique hobby: they wear masks to look like dolls and interact as dolls. Ellen Jones writes: 'Therein lies the inherent contradiction of a film like *Secrets of the Living Dolls*. If, as the film's participants suggested, masking is no big deal and just a hobby like any other, then why make a film about it? And if it's more complicated, then why not take the time to dig deeper and discover what makes it so?' She continues, 'I must admit to finding this documentary troubling. Not because of the masking itself – which seems a harmless, if pricey, way to get your kicks – but because of what it says about society's

Communications expert George Gerbner argues that the more we see and interact with televised images and narratives, the more readily we accept these and similar images and narratives into our daily lives, a process outlined in his work on 'cultivation theory' (Gerbner 1969). Summarised by O'Guinn and Shrum, 'cultivation theory posits that heavier viewers of television will have beliefs about the social world that are more consistent with televised social representations than will light viewers. To the heavy television viewer, the real world becomes more like the TV world' (O'Guinn & Shrum 1997: 280). Expanding Gerbner's approach to other forms of visual media, it appears that the ability of the dolls to be part of cultural narratives may be the first steps toward bringing them into daily life while normalising their existence and socialising humans to accept them within our cultural context. A question emerges, are these dolls really becoming more noticeable through popular culture? A review of recent popular culture sightings of the dolls, literal and figurative, leads to a resounding yes.

To illustrate, in the 2006 article 'Flexible friendship' in the British magazine METRO, author Lisa Scott presents two owners of dolls (in this case the popular RealDolls): one a bisexual woman, Wanda; and the other a heterosexual man, David. Both are in committed relationships with real humans, but also both experience sexual companionship with their respective dolls that allow them to live out fantasies without hurting their human companions (e.g., cheating or straying from a commitment). Although David is clear that the main use for his doll is sexual gratification, Wanda seems more lost within her fantasy of being able to be intimate with 'the most beautiful woman in the world' as well as being able to share a deep connection to the artistic rendering that becomes the doll (Scott 2006). As Scott investigates the reasons why the dolls are used, she makes an intriguing observation: '[although] they are used mainly as sex aids [...] they are also popular with film-makers, artists and scientists' (Scott 2006: np). In this light Wanda's words are revealing, 'I didn't buy Roxanne out of sexual frustration', she says. 'I desired one in the same way one might wish to own a beautiful painting or sculpture' (Scott 2006: np).[8] Wanda sees her Doll as a work of art, and a review of some doll websites (e.g., RealDoll) and buyer testimonials frequently echo similar views.

Although some critics may dismiss such comments as hyperbole and argue that the doll is less a work of art for a collector than an erotic object for an

obsession with physical perfection and sexual availability.' http://www.independent.co.uk/arts-entertainment/tv/reviews/secrets-of-the-living-dolls-channel-4--tv-review-9042439.html.

8 Scott, Lisa. (22 Februrary, 2006) 'Flexible Friendship' *Metro*. http://metro.co.uk/2006/02/22/flexible-friendship-21056/.

owner, it is notable that some artists including renowned photographer Helmut Newton[9] and surrealist painter Salvador Dali[10] have used dolls and mannequins within their art, reflective of Pygmalion themes within literature.[11] Although some artists may bring a high-end framing to the doll or mannequin, it is the popularisation of the doll in films and television that are making them more familiar to the average viewer. To illustrate, the BBC documentary 'Guys and Dolls' follows four men who live with dolls, and Allison de Fren's 'The Mechanical Bride'[12] documents the multiple histories and stories of the desire to create the perfect woman through mechanical means. The television show *Sons of Anarchy* ran a plot line where dolls were featured and *My Strange Addiction* similarly featured a segment, 'Doll Love Lasts Forever', which similarly to 'Guys and Dolls' chronicled the life of one man's experience with his doll. Although documentaries and one-off plot lines on television shows do help to introduce the doll to a larger audience, it is the ability of mainstream films to bring the dolls into theatres and homes world-wide that are more apt to normalise the doll. Two films of particular note are *Love Object* (2003) and *Lars and the Real Girl* (2007).

---

9 According to Anthony Fergusson's history of sex dolls, renowned 20th century photographer Helmut Newton, known for his often risqué images, presented photos with dolls as the topic within *Playboy Magazine*; however, the images were seen as too unsettling and the magazine did not to publish them (cf., Mori 1970, Ferguson 2010: 46). In his autobiography Newton writes, 'My preoccupation with store dummies, dolls, etc., began in 1968, when English *Vogue* published my first series of photos with these dummies. It showed a favourite model of mine, Willie Van Rooy, confronting a store dummy… creating a kind of Doppelgänger' (Newton 2003: 222, photo titled *Der Dopplegänger*).

10 Beck, J. (6 August, 2014) 'A (straight, male) history of the sex doll'. *The Atlantic*. http://www.theatlantic.com/features/archive/2014/08/a-straight-male-history-of-dolls/375623/.

11 For an excellent discussion of technofetishism, dolls, mannequins, surrealism, and multiple genres of science fiction, see Allison de Fren (2009) 'Technofetischism and the Uncanny Desires of ASFR (alt.sex.fetish.robots)', *Science Fiction Studies* 36(3): 404–440.

12 According to the synopsis offered on the official website of 'The Mechanical Bride', the work demonstrates that 'The desire to bring the perfect artificial woman to life is as old as Pygmalion, but new technologies are making its realization ever more likely. Limning the border between fantasy and reality, this provocative and eye-opening documentary journeys from the outer limits of science fiction—visiting classic scenes of fembots in film and television—to the state of the art in artificial companions—from life-sized silicone love dolls to humanoid robots'. http://www.mechanicalbride-movie.com/index.html.

Based upon mainstream film awards as an indication of popular familiarity, of the two movies noted above, *Lars and the Real Girl* likely had the largest impact on viewers.[13] In the film a man lives in a small, remote northern town in the U.S. Living a relatively reclusive life, Lars orders a doll for companionship, Bianca. As the plot unfolds, the small community in which Lars and his family live, including friends, a kind doctor, and local business people, become accustomed to Bianca and see the social improvement in Lars, as well as enjoy the fantasy of Bianca. Bianca is not short on friends, rides to the mall, and eventually gains employment and is elected to the school board. Similar to other human-human relationships Lars and Bianca demonstrate through the fantasy the trials and tribulations of a relationship: love, jealousy, and negotiating boundaries. As a story, *Lars and the Real Girl* shows a tender side of Lars' social and psychological fragility and the ability of Bianca and those who support them to help Lars find his own humanity through his experiences with Bianca.

In this light the images and rhetoric contained within television, film, and art converge in critical analysis of the role between fantasy and reality as exemplified by the sex doll.[14] When considering the experience between a human and doll, it becomes evident that today's fiction may become tomorrow's reality (cf., O'Mahony 2002, de Fren 2009). Where has this imagination, this collective

13 Released in 2007, *Lars and the Real Girl* appeared in mainstream theatres and grossed nearly six million USD in box office sales, $4.5 million worldwide, and $5.5 million in DVD sales ('The Numbers: where Data and the Movie Business Meet'. http://www.the-numbers.com/movie/Lars-and-the-Real-Girl#tab=more (28 October, 2014). It was nominated for multiple international, national, and local awards and reviewed heavily. The notoriety of being nominated and in some cases winning a well known award cannot be underestimated in helping to bring the film – and its contents, a doll – to public light and consumption. The film was nominated for Best Writing for the Academy Awards and Best Actor by the Golden Globes and Screen Actors Guild. (IMBd. http://www.imdb.com/title/tt0805564/awards (28 October, 2014). *Love Object*, on the other hand, was released in 2003 and only grossed $6,028, a far cry from *Lars and the Real Girl*. However, unlike *Lars and the Real Girl*, *Love Object* does not appear to be suited for mainstream viewing. Identified as a drama/horror/romance by IMDb. http://www.imdb.com/title/tt0328077/, it did receive five awards and two nominations for the work, albeit from lesser-known (in popular culture) competitions including the Fangoria Chainsaw Awards and Woodstock Film Festival. http://www.imdb.com/title/tt0328077/awards. For a brief discussion of these two films, see also de Fren (2009: 411).

14 For an examination of technosexuals and robotic renderings of women, see de Fren 2009.

consciousness and unconscious brought contemporary Western Culture and what are its implications for gender? Here I explore two issues relevant to the increasing familiarity and normalisation of the sex doll as exemplified by one of the industry's leaders, RealDoll. First, how does the doll represent and create the sexual fantasy of its purchaser; and second, as the dolls become more prevalent, how might they limit the definitions and framings of human beauty and sensuality, notably that of women?[15]

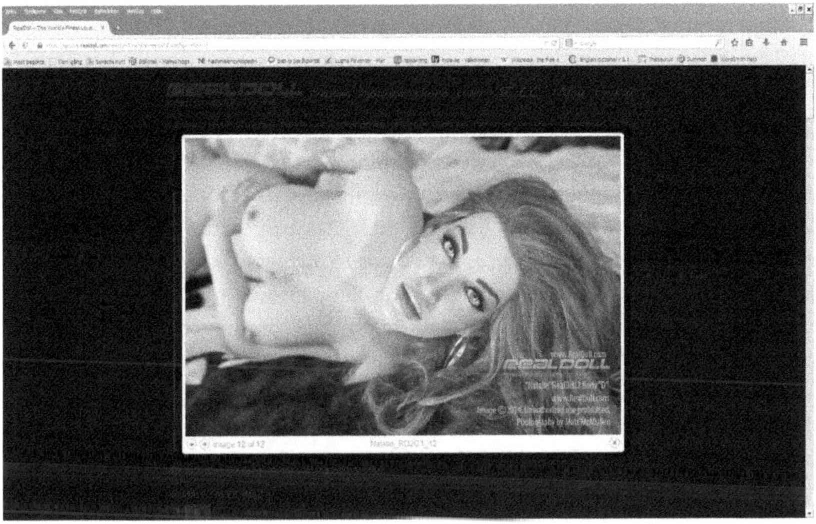

The RealDoll: creating the ideal

First unveiled by Abyss Creations LLC in 1996, the RealDoll is a creation merging Hollywood artistry and erotic toy knowledge that today sells approximately 200–300 dolls per year.[16] The RealDoll website promotes itself as 'the home of the world's finest love doll' on the market, and it very well might be so: most of the dolls are made to order, and with artists rendering beauty and technicians

15 Although there are male sex dolls (or some in the design phase), the female forms greatly outnumber the males. The shear diversity of female dolls as opposed to the few males may suggest a further entrenchment of power inequities already noted in gender studies analysis.

16 Beck, J. (6 August 2014). 'A (straight, Male) History of Sex Dolls'. *The Atlantic*. http://www.theatlantic.com/features/archive/2014/08/a-straight-male-history-of-dolls/375623/.

creating a life-like body, this full-size companion is unique.[17] These mannequin-style partners are intended to bring sexual pleasure to the user by creating the feel and look of a 'real' person (cf. Mori 1970).[18] Although the idea of a human experiencing sexual fantasies with a doll may at first blush appear unsettling, in fact a closer examination reminds us that humans having sexual relations with non-humans is not new (e.g., Ferguson 2010). From bestiality to blow-up dolls, sex toys or devices, to computer simulation and stimulation, humans have crossed multiple culturally constructed boundaries of sexual acceptability though rarely without cultural, political, or religious critique.

The dolls are designed to evoke an emotive identity, read outward as expression by its partner (cf., Levy 2007). Although the doll is not human it can stimulate very human emotions within its owner. The doll is the figurative receptacle of the emotions put into it as well as the literal receptacle of human touch and fluids that evoke and signify human arousal. It is not just a doll; it is its own Otherness. Certainly the doll is not human, but it may be near-human to its partner if the partner infuses it with personality, and emotional and perceived agency that can only be read by its human lover or companion. From a technoscientific and gender studies view, these dolls, through their similarities and differences, offer a unique opportunity to examine how we are recreating ourselves by identifying how and what parts of the human should appear and feel to others (e.g., Haraway 1991). At the same time, these developments usher in a new era in which individual sexual fulfilment may come at a cultural price of further objectification of the female body.

The purchase of life-size dolls for erotic human partnerships is one of the newest examples of sex in the marketplace. The doll takes the purchaser into a world that blurs 'reality' with 'fantasy'. And although reality and fantasy constantly collide in sexuality and daily life (e.g., daydreams) the acquisition of a doll may further promote consumptive and capitalistic approaches to the objectified

---

17 RealDoll Website. https://www.realdoll.com.

18 Mathematician and roboticist Marharhu Mori (1970) believes that there is a disconnect that affects individuals when looking at robots. He asserts that when the robot appears just life-like enough that it is the subtle *differences* that create a state of unsettlement: it looks almost real enough to 'pass' until something reminds us that it is not human. Here, we enter the 'Uncanny Valley'. As the dolls become more human-like we are apt to enter Hori's 'Uncanny Valley', in which fantasy and reality blur and once through we may come to accept these dolls as representations of how the ideal woman might look and act. On the uncanny, see also Freud, et al. (2010).

body. The ability to normalise the fantasy and to make it real is the promise of the doll; the body is one that can be purchased and made into what the buyer wants. In fact, the webpage for the RealDoll explicitly states its intent to the potential buyer: '*If you've ever dreamed of creating your ideal woman, then you have come to the right place*'. What, then, is the ideal?

Making the fantasy real: what is available

Before further articulation of the RealDoll, it is important to note that while it may have been one of the first to gain notoriety in popular culture, it is not the only doll currently available. Though the sex doll industry may be a niche market, it is also large, and similar to other competitive global markets, there is an emerging style of doll; nevertheless, various sexual aspects of the dolls (as promoted by the companies that produce them) do differ.

Although a handful of companies, primarily in the U.S. and Japan, are creating high-end, often silicon-based dolls with articulating joints, a few of the dolls bring a distinct aspect to the race to create the best doll. Beyond RealDoll, two of the companies worth note are the Japanese company Axis Honey Doll and the U.S.-based Truecompanion.com. Though not the first doll to incorporate audio into the doll, the Honey Doll is the world's first doll with a built-in MP3 player that is programmed to respond with erotic sounds when certain parts of the body are touched. More intriguing is that it is also possible for the user to program his or her own voice (or for that matter someone else's voice) into the doll to further the realism of the experience.[19] Beyond the audio, Axis has concentrated on the importance of fellatio with the doll. Ferguson explains, 'Honey dolls has also focused attention on the oral sex capability of the dolls. This involves the use of a medical product known as elastomer rather than silicone, which allegedly allows for a much greater resistance to tearing' (Ferguson 2010: 54).

One of the newest competitors to the RealDoll, Truecompanion.com, unveiled Roxxxy in 2010. Depending upon which iteration the purchaser selects, Roxxxy comes with a base personality, a personality made to order, or five preprogrammed personalities.[20] The website describes the preprogrammed personalities aptly:

---

19 Softpedia. 'Japanese Company Intros Next Generation of Sex Dolls. Love Moaning Included' (August 13, 2007). http://news.softpedia.com/news/Japanese-Company-Intros-Next-Generation-of-Sex-Dolls-Live-Moaning-Included-62539.shtml.

20 To be clear, as with all technological advancement, each doll goes through different iterations in development – some of which spin off into different styles available within the company. For example Trueconmpanion.com boasts three forms of Roxxxy: one,

Frigid Farrah – She is reserved and shy
Wild Wendy – She is outgoing and adventurous
S&M Susan – She is ready to provide your pain/pleasure fantasies
Young Yoko – She is oh so young (barely 18) and waiting for you to teach her
Mature Martha – She is very experienced and would like to teach you![21]

Douglas Hines, founder of the company that builds Roxxxy, believes that sex can only take the lover to a certain point, after which the owner will want to have a conversation with the doll. And, with the ability of Roxxxy to receive updates over the internet to increase her vocabulary and presumed awareness of the contemporary world that she and her owner share, the fantasy of her learning about the owner and his or her interests becomes quite realistic. With preprogrammed personalities the dolls may both assist users in living out their fantasies while at the same time the preconceived notions of what words and activities should be expressed within the personalities are necessarily limited by the programmer and any forthcoming data uploads. Thus the programming of a voice to express personality may both enhance the fantasy by making the doll seem more real while at the same time its limited vocabulary and knowledge may implicitly hinder the imagination and fantasies of the owner.

Although Honey Doll and Roxxxy have a share of the market (as do other dolls and companies not named here), the RealDoll still stands as one of the industry's best-known dolls.[22] Since its unveiling in 1996, the RealDoll has also undergone multiple iterations and advances, all of which reflect the presumed and learned desires of the purchasers and are suggestive of the future of continued doll manufacturing (e.g., a RealDoll is on display in the *Museum of Sex*, New York City, NY).[23] It is the longstanding familiarity of the RealDoll that makes it an industry leader and thus merits it to be the doll at the centre of this examination.

Roxxxy Pillow, is the head and torso of the doll that can be stored within a pillow for ease of movement and heightened discretion; Roxxxy Silver, like Roxxxy Pillow, offers 'sex talk, but also comes with arms and legs; and finally, Roxxxy Gold offers all that Roxxxy Silver does, but is also able to listen and learn about her partner; she is also able to be downloaded with distinct personalities.' Truecomanion.com (n.d.). http://www.truecompanion.comhttp://www.truecompanion.com/shop/faq.

21 Truecompanion.com (n.d.). http://www.truecompanion.com/shop/faq.

22 For an excellent list of high-end dolls on the marketplace and the differences between them, see Chapter Three, 'The Great Leap Forward' in Ferguson, A. (2010). *The Sex Doll: A History*. Jefferson, N.C.: McFarland & Co.

23 http://www.museumofsex.com.

As noted above, as the RealDoll has gained recognition and as technologies have evolved, there are now multiple styles of RealDoll available for purchase, including the Classic, RealDoll 2 (RD2), Boy Toy, and the Wicked Doll. Each style blurs the lines of reality and fantasy in multiple ways, and depending upon the desires of the purchaser one style may be more appropriate than the other. To understand how purchasers select and experience their dolls, the following section examines the RealDoll website and testimonials of purchasers to better identify how the RealDoll fulfills and impacts multiple approaches to sexual fantasy. Following this examination, the chapter problematises the RealDoll as a potential simulacrum to real women and asks what that might mean for the future of human-human relationships. Finally the chapter offers concluding thoughts on the role and implications of the RealDoll within a social context.

What purchasers see: making the fantasy come to life

Depending upon the fantasy and the preferred ways to attain gratification through the doll the purchaser may select one style of doll over another. The selection process is both reflective of the fantasy and limits the abilities for the user to achieve them; therefore closer examination of the dolls is necessary. It is also important to note that RealDoll holds customer privacy closely; thus when examining the website as an indication of what is available for purchase and how buyers react to their dolls it is limited to a controlled website as a portal into a world of sexuality, sensuality, and fantasy. The website necessarily sells its products with emphasis on quality and the rhetoric reflects the ability of the doll to assist the buyer in realising his or her fantasy. Similarly the testimonials are sent in by the purchasers through the company website, and it is reasonable to assume that not all testimonials are posted or that all are as complimentary as the ones that the browser of the site may find available. Nevertheless, the rhetoric of the website and the testimonials chosen to reflect the identity of the company do tell an important story of what the doll promises the buyer.

Perhaps the best recognised RealDoll is the RealDoll Classic.[24] The RealDoll website describes the Classic:

24 For individuals interested in the Classic, there are two options: purchase one already configured or create your own. Intriguingly, the already configured ones are not characterised by a numbering system, but by names of real women such as Stacy, Mellissa, and Stephanie.

> The one that started it all. Our female dolls are the most lifelike and enjoyable sexdolls that you can buy anywhere! With holes in all the right places and with the FaceX system, the possibilities are endless.
>
> The female RealDolls feature our patented Face-X System which allows you to have multiple interchangeable faces for one body. View our photo galleries to see which faces pair best with which bodies. We offer 16 standard female faces and 10 bodies. You can customize your doll with any of our standard options or have a doll made to match any you see in the gallery.[25]

It is intriguing that there are more potential faces than bodies, but for some owners who have a proclivity toward a certain body type but fantasise about multiple women, the Face X system (ability to remove the head and attach a different one) may offer the alternative needed to have social and sexual relationships with multiple women (and with a general price of 5–10,000 USD, may make the cost of multiple faces more tolerable than multiple bodies). In essence, the appearance of the partner (facially) can be changed to reflect the mood and fantasy of the buyer. And, the faces are unique. Eye colour (including veins), and lip, eye showdown and liner colours, are just a few of the ways to customise the face. While the body may remain constant, the malleability of the face to evoke different readings of the doll as a social agent within a relationship is considerable and may offer greater breadth to the possible fantasies explored by the purchaser.

Although the Classic is the one that 'started it all', technological development and imagination have led to the RD2. According to the company, the RD2 is the outcome of more than seventeen years in the industry and like its predecessor, the Classic, it is the ability of the purchasers to customise the doll and the simulation of real skin and even skeletal system that help to lay claims of coming closer to the reality of the fantasy:

> RealDoll 2 features advanced weight reduction without sacrificing the feel of the doll, two patented styles of interchangeable faces (Magnetic face and full head style FaceX systems), 7″ deep removable mouth inserts, optional removable vagina inserts for ease of hygiene and maintenance, and an ever expanding line of faces and bodies continually added to the RealDoll2 collection to expand your future options.
>
> Coupled with engineering improvements in our skeleton system, including stainless steel parts and tooled aluminium fingertip guards, these new dolls have developed a great reputation and set new standards in the doll industry. And only with the patented Realdoll FaceX system can you easily purchase future faces to *create an entirely new persona* for your doll in seconds [my emphasis].[26]

---

25 Website for the classic RealDoll. https://secure.realdoll.com/select-realdoll-classic/.
26 RealDoll (2014) Abyss Creations. https://secure.realdoll.com/select-realdoll-2/.

A new addition to the RealDoll line is the BT doll or 'Boy Toy'. These dolls are more petite, under limited production, and when the dolls are sold out the production will not resume. In many ways they are the ultimate collectable for the doll collector. The company advertises: 'Hand crafted using cutting edge materials, these posable silicone dolls are designed with fun in mind. Boy Toy Dolls are lightweight, easy to maintain, and made of an exclusive, all new Platinum silicone material. They have features that cannot be found on any other doll in the world, and yes, of course, they are anatomically correct!' They continue: 'We currently offer three BoyToy doll series at this time: The Boy Toy Celestial ("BT3") Series, Boy Toy Seasons, and Boy Toy C Series.'[27] Although three styles are available, the continuity within the line is their petite size and that, similar to the other RealDoll lines, the BT doll is customisable and promises high quality to the owner. Most intriguing is that one of the artists at RealDoll is specifically named as *the artist* to render the beauty; thus if an owner has purchased a doll or is aware of the industry artists' reputations, he or she may be familiar with the craftsmanship afforded in these limited production dolls.

Finally, the Wicked Doll is the outcome of a business collaboration between Abyss Creations LLC (RealDoll) and Wicked Pictures™ to bring a simulation of a publically known real woman (in these cases actresses in the adult film industry) into a person's home (currently six women are modelled into the doll form). The company is clear about its desire to allow everyone who wishes to 'have a porn star ready and waiting for you every night!' and the dolls come with special bonuses including a 'current DVD of the featured actress, a 1 year membership to wicked.com, an autographed photograph of the actress and a bottle of perfume chosen by the actress'.[28] Unlike the fantasy of building your own doll as seen in the Classic, RD2, and Boy Toy, the Wicked Doll promotes a different fantasy: the ability to take an already familiar woman who has been placed in storylines created by another person's fantasies and bring that person out of the magic of film and into the reality of a home. According to the site the dolls are 'completely realistic representations of the Wicked Girls'. They continue:

> Each of these dolls has been created using cutting edge technology to replicate every detail of these well known actresses, from digital scanning to silicone casting of fine details like skin texture on the hands and feet. The line has debuted with dolls of jessica drake and Alektra Blue...[29]

---

27 Boy Toys Dolls (2014) Abyss Creations. https://secure.realdoll.com/boy-toy-dolls/.

28 Wicked Doll website. https://secure.realdoll.com/wicked-realdoll-home/.

29 Wicked RealDoll (2014) Abyss Creations. https://secure.realdoll.com/wicked-realdoll-home/.

Here the Wicked Doll offers a unique entry into fantasy: she is a known woman, a commodity, whose likeness is purchased for the pleasure of the owner. Pornography expert Peter Lehman reminds readers that the narrative structure and 'star system' is fundamentally different within pornography than other film genres (Lehman 1995: 5). In pornography, the star often plays himself or herself, and as he reflects on his earlier work (1993), Lehman argues, 'porn does not maintain the classical distinction between the actor and the fictional character' (Lehman 1995: 5). Thus, when purchasing the Wicked Doll it may lead to the fulfilment of fantasies directly aimed at the persona created by real women in the adult film industry rather than at an imagined or other fictional character.

As an object, purchased and owned by its users, the RealDoll inhibits a world of different possibilities, but two common themes within the testimonials are the enjoyment of being with the doll and the beauty within the art of the doll. In some cases, the sexuality and sensuality of the human-doll relationship is that it allows the fantasy of the perfect person borne out in the eyes of its beholder. The doll can literally be everything to an owner who sees within it the attainment of a touchable fantasy and dream companion. Or as one satisfied customer explains, his doll is the greatest achievement since the moon landing.[30] While hyperbole for most, the exuberance with which he frames and sees his doll is striking.

The owners of dolls (as reflected in the testimonials posted by the company) express an exuberance and awe of the dolls they purchase. In fact one owner, Frank, compared himself to a Frank Lloyd Wright client:

> Since receiving my doll I feel like the Frank Lloyd Wright client who so loved their house that they did not want to leave it.
>
> Enough cannot be said about the extent of realism to my doll. Photos do not convey the impact of see[ing] this doll with your own eyes sitting on your own furniture. I enjoy having a glass of wine while admiring her sitting nude on a chair.[31]

It is within the merging of the art and the technological customisation that people can live out their fantasies with objects of desires.

Another testimonial, from an artist, attests to the craftsmanship of his doll and how even his 'shrewd eye' notes the detail within the doll. The owner explains:

> To tell the truth I am sort of blown away by this doll. Stormy Daniels. How lifelike she is… please give my best to the artists who made this. I am an artist myself, and I have a bit of a shrewd eye. This is the utmost superior work, a purchase I would make again.[32]

---

30 Testimonials. (July 30, 2014) https://secure.realdoll.com/august-18th-2014/.

31 Testimonials. (August 13, 2014) https://secure.realdoll.com/august-13th-2014/.

32 Testimonials. (September 25, 2014) https://secure.realdoll.com/september-15th-2014/.

Stormy Daniels is both a partner and a piece of art. Intriguingly, the doll can both assist in achieving fantasies and its craftsmanship allows the artist-owner to be assured of the quality and attention to detail that other artists put into making Stormy special.

When exploring the testimonials on the RealDoll website, it is also intriguing that the process of ordering the doll may require multiple phone calls and other forms of communication between the purchaser and the company. This back-and-forth appears to facilitate a form of relationship not only with the dolls but also with the company that creates them. Many of the testimonials actually identify members of the RealDoll team by name and express gratitude for their services and, in the case of the artists, amazement at their talent. To illustrate, one owner writes, both stressing the doll as a work of art and acknowledging the skilful work of RealDoll employees:

> This great work of art that you folks at abyss have created, has to be the coolest investment that I have ever made. matt you are one talented guy, and Annette was great to work with over the phone when ordering or answering my questions. thanks so much for all your hard work, my doll is one wicked cool lady.[33]

The openness of the company and talent within the company that purchasers continually stress in their testimonials may actually help minimise a sense of taboo or marginalisation for the purchasers, who, while engaging in practices not readily accepted by many, are able to potentially find some sense of comfort and community as they realise their fantasies.

Still another case offers further insight into the ability of the owner to use the doll to fit within an already existing lifestyle. The purchaser of Mellissa writes the company, 'She is everything I expected the most perfect doll I have ever had she will be able to display my retro clothes collection very well'.[34] Two points become clear: she is not the first doll and she will play a role in assisting the owner to take further pride in another part of his identity – a collector of retro clothes. Collectors of objects often feel a great sense of pride in their collections and show them off in their homes and even at public events such as conventions. Here the doll is not only a doll but also the embodied human likeness to show off yet another part of the purchaser's identity. Similarly, another owner writes in regarding his or her doll that she is 'fun to dress' and sends in a photo of the doll for the company to view.[35] The doll is wearing a wedding dress.

33 Testimonials. (August 15, 2014) https://secure.realdoll.com/august-14th-2014/.

34 Testimonials. (August 21, 2014) https://secure.realdoll.com/august-21-2014/.

35 Testimonials. (August 18, 2014) https://secure.realdoll.com/august-18th-2014/.

Although most dolls are representations of feminine ideals and female physiology, increasingly companies such as RealDoll are serving customers who desire male dolls (male dolls account for approximately 1/10 of RealDoll purchases and come with fewer customisable parts).[36] While many gender scholars are most concerned with objectification of the female body (based upon well documented statistics of violence against women through sexual and domestic abuse), it is also important to recognise that, when considering the attainment of fantasies, both men and women with multiple sexual identities may find assistance through a doll (on violence and abuse, e.g., Kimmel 2014). Although concerns over objectification usually trend toward the female body, and thus are a primary concern of this work, one testimonial written by a woman about her doll offers intriguing insight into the multiplicity of ways to customise a doll to render the fantasy possible.

In this case, a woman who is engaged to a man writes the company to elaborate upon how happy she is with her doll, a replica of the British character Sweeney Todd. Her fantasy of Todd comes alive through the doll. Her testimonial is long and passionate with some words in all capitals and a redundancy of the word 'amazing' running throughout. She conveys her joy over her Sweeney Todd RealDoll:

> A-MAZE-ZING!!! Abyss Creations is the bomb!! Truly A-MAZE-ZING art!! Awesome!!!

She continues:

> …words fail me except this: HE IS A-MAZE-ZING!!!! The level of detail!! He looks soooo incredibly real!!! I had him customized to match the look of someone I admire that I am obsessed with Sweeney Todd!! And the team who worked on him got him to look just like him!![37]

Also intriguing is that she ordered two versions of the face: one clean-shaven and the other showing beard stubble or '5 o'clock shadow'. Such an order may suggest the fulfilment of her fantasies with her imagined ideal of Sweeney Todd to more accurately reflect either the imagined time of day in which the fantasy is played out (i.e., if she is enacting a fantasy mid-day she may want Todd clean shaven) or the ability of the fantasy to change the reality of the time of day in which the fantasy is played out (e.g., although it may be mid-day she may

---

36 Beck, Julie. (6 August 2014). "A (Straight, Male) History of Sex Dolls" *The Atlantic*. http://www.theatlantic.com/features/archive/2014/08/a-straight-male-history-of-dolls/375623/.

37 Testimonials (June 26, 2014) https://secure.realdoll.com/june-26th-2014/.

fantasise it is evening and thus prefer the stubble of facial hair). Perhaps he has been traveling and has not had time to shave? The reality of a man's facial hair changing overtime can become an important element in making a fantasy become a reality. Regardless of the specific fantasy, the different readings of the face of the same character, Sweeney Todd, may help her to live out her fantasies with greater authenticity to presumed reality.

Objectification and consumption of the human

Although humans have sexual fantasies, how they immerse themselves within those worlds differ. Daydreams, pornography, poetry, and open relationships are but a few examples of well known and often utilised vehicles for realising the fantasy and bringing it to a form of life or other reality to pleasure humans. Another lesser known, though increasingly popular, artefact that is being added to the options of tools to engage in fantasy and role play are the RealDolls and others like them. Although their cost may make them out of reach for many, the increasing availability of different technologies and materials (as well as ways to bring them together, such as interchangeable parts or sectioned out pieces that are more relevant to the buyer) may make the attainment of one of these dolls more possible in the future. However, as a simulacra or other form of copy, the RealDoll is also problematic in that it is purchased, created, and has no will of its own. *As a doll* it is an inanimate artefact; but, *as a partner* in some form of social relationship (even if it is only instigated and played out by the human, cf. Levy 2007) it may pose some intriguing, if not unsettling, questions for current and future developments in human-human relationships. Notably, the dolls most often replicating the female form will likely have implications for how real women live within and under socially constructed ideals of beauty and sensuality.

Dolls are intriguing artefacts (e.g., Ferguson 2010, Wood 2002). From a young age, humans often identify dolls as representing a safe place to share dreams, hopes, and love. In fact, the idea that a doll would turn on its owner, partner, or friend has been the topic of many horror films and stories that keep both children and adults up late at night listening to creaks under the bed or in the closet. But in general, and ideally, dolls are calming artefacts and the relationship between the owner and his or her doll is one that only the human knows until he or she shares it with others. What is intriguing, however, is that while the human has the relationship with the doll, the doll does not express a self-determined will (though some companies such as Trucompanion.com are working on weak AI to simulate a sense of independence within the doll). Put simply, the doll is always compliant to the needs and desires of its owner. This is not surprising; all dolls and inanimate objects lack free will, but the question does emerge: as these dolls become more realistic, and humans and communities slowly begin to normalise their existence within life experiences, how might the lack of free will of a sexual partner affect implicit and explicit beliefs in sexual consent?

Another concern that is brought to light in an examination of dolls is the fact that they are made to order perfection. Returning to the RealDoll website, '*If you've ever dreamed of creating your ideal woman, then you have come to the right place*' creates excitement and hesitation. What makes the ideal? Although the dolls are becoming physically realistic (though exaggerated body parts are certainly not realistic), it does offer one pause to ask what aspects are the most admired in the ideal woman? For example, cultural narratives often identify femininity as fulfilled through attaining motherhood or being a caretaker to a family.[38] But if this is part of the ideal woman, the doll, at best, can only fulfil parts of the narrative. Although science fiction and fantasy may bring Stepford Wives into conversations about creating the ideal woman, often when such storylines are pursued they are not with exuberance to the future but with cautionary hesitation. Here, the dolls both entrench and problematise the myth of idealised femininity and womanhood.

Beyond biological and psychological framings of the ideal woman as expressed above, the concept of making the ideal partner creates a precarious situation: beauty is not universal and is often unattainable. The RealDoll offers the purchaser the opportunity to choose from the items that the company believes are most important in beauty and customisable female perfection. Such beauty might be unattainable by real women who may judge themselves against the doll as a measure of beauty. Similar to concerns long echoed by social critique of the fashion industry and the 'beauty myth', will these dolls, *en masse*, limit the ways in which women and prepubescent and pubescent girls see themselves and how far might they go to simulate the dolls that ironically are built to, at some base level, simulate them (Wolf 2002, see also Bordo 2004)?

And finally, perhaps most concerning is the method through which the construction and deconstruction of the doll and its ability to have interchangeable parts such as faces as well as disembodied parts including heads, arms, legs, and torsos, build upon a longstanding concern over the ability of humans to objectify women into pieces of a whole and disembody them in art, entertainment, and reality (e.g., Duden 1993, Casper 1998). The disembodied view of humans is that

38 For critiques of feminine ideal requiring motherhood, see Blizzard (2007), Casper (1998).

the parts are more than the sum of the whole and that some parts are more important than others. As noted in critiques of advertising, often only parts of bodies are shown (e.g., breasts, torso, thighs) and often the face is not seen or considered relevant. Some critics of the disembodied and objectified body argue that not seeing the body as a whole suggests an overall lack of acceptance of the body and person within it. The ability to see a woman as only breasts or other erogenous zone only minimises the meaning of the entire woman, including her mind.

Concluding thoughts

When examining the increasing familiarity of the doll, notably the RealDoll, it becomes clear that the ability to live out personal fantasies may come at a cultural price of both limiting and enhancing fantasies by limiting definitions of beauty and sexuality. Within the last twenty years the development of sex dolls has not only become lucrative, but it is also increasingly prevalent in popular culture. Although sexual freedom and the fetishes it sometimes musters is not in itself worrisome, the slippery slope of accepting these dolls as representations of the ideal woman is culturally significant (cf. Harding 1995, Kilbourne 2000). The ability to buy a sexual partner has expanded from the streets of urban areas to 'socially camouflaged' wooden boxes delivered to any front door (Maines 1998). Within this context we find a double-edged sword: how do individuals balance sexual freedom to choose a doll as a companion with the potential cultural implications of further entrenching sexual inequalities?

As the RealDoll has gained prominence, it has utilised technological advances that assist purchasers of the doll to live out sexual and sensual fantasies in multiple ways. From the Classic Doll where one can purchase a pre-designed doll or customise the doll to the RD2 and Boy Toy that offer a lighter body, better internal structure, and further refinement in what can come in a special order, the dolls offer purchasers the fantasy of what an ideal should be, including the ability to change the face as necessary to attain such idealism. Alternatively, the Wicked Doll offers a buyer the chance to bring in an already crafted ideal of beauty and sexuality as represented through the actresses in Wicked Entertainment™ films and bring them home to live out their own fantasies already suggested or primed by the adult film industry. Making the social link to the Wicked Doll even more real and more human-to-human is that the doll comes with a signed picture of the actress and a selected bottle of perfume chosen by the actress, suggesting how she might smell to the buyer.

The RealDoll is many things to many people. To the buyers it may be a vehicle to make fantasies come true. To the creators they might represent the cutting edge of adult erotic toys and the ability to craft the ideal partner. And, to social theorists and gender scholars they may be problematic representations of beauty and commodification of the human body. Where is the balance and what do multiple genders, societies, cultures, and individuals stand to gain and lose as these dolls become more prevalent? There is no clear answer; however, what is clear is that as humans continue to find creative and provocative ways to fulfill and build social and sexual fantasies, everyone affected (which is *everyone*) should be aware, alert, and compassionate to the individual and communal outcomes of these developments.

References

Beck, J. (2014) 'A (straight) male history of sex dolls'. *The Atlantic*. http://www.theatlantic.com/features/archive/2014/08/a-straight-male-history-of-dolls/375623/.

Blizzard, D. (2007) *Looking Within: A Sociocultural Examination of Fetoscopy.* Cambridge, Mass.: The MIT Press.

Bordo, S. (1993) *Unbearable Weight: Feminism, Western Culture, and the Body.* Berkeley: University of California Press.

Casper, M. J. (1998) *The Making of the Unborn Patient: A Social Anatomy of Fetal Surgery*. City: Rutgers University Press.

Cowan, R. S. (1983) *More Work for Mother: The Ironies of Household Technology from the Open Hearth to the Microwave*. New York: Basic Books.

de Fren, A. (2009) 'Technofetishism and the uncanny desires of ASFR (alt. sex. fetish. robots)'. *Science Fiction Studies* 36(3): 404–440.

Duden, B. (1993) *Disembodying Women: Perspectives on Pregnancy and the Unborn*. Cambridge, Mass.: Harvard University Press.

Ferguson, A. (2010) *The Sex Doll: A History*. Jefferson, N.C.: McFarland & Co.

Freud, S., McLintock, D. & Haughton, H. (2003) *The Uncanny*. New York: Penguin Books.

Gerbner, G. (1969) *The Analysis of Communication Content: Developments in Scientific Theories and Computer Techniques.* New York: Wiley.

Haraway, D.J. (1991) *Simians, Cyborgs, and Women: The Reinvention of Nature.* New York: Routledge.

Harding, S. (1995) '"Strong objectivity": A response to the new objectivity question'. *Synthese* 104(3): 331–349.

Kilbourne, J. (2000) *Can't Buy My Love: How Advertising Changes the Way We Think and Feel.* New York: Free Press.

Kimmel, M.S. (2011) *The Gendered Society*. New York: Oxford University Press.

Lehman, P. (1995) 'Revelations about pornography'. *Film Criticism* 20(1–2): 3–16.

Levy, D. (2007) *Love + Sex with Robots: the Evolution of Human-Robot Relations*. New York: Harper Collins.

Maines, R. (1998) *The Technology of Orgasm: "Hysteria," the Vibrator, and Women's Sexual Satisfaction*. Baltimore, Md: The Johns Hopkins University Press.

Mori, M. (1970) 'The Uncanny Valley'. *Energy* 7(4): 33–35.

Restivo, S.P. (1994) *Science, Society, and Values: Toward a Sociology of Objectivity*. Bethlehem, Pa.: Lehigh University Press.

O'Guinn, T. C. & Shrum, L.J. (1997) 'The role of television in the construction of consumer reality'. *Journal of Consumer Research* 23: 278–294.

O'Mahony, M. (2002) *Cyborg: The Man-Machine*. London: Thames & Hudson.

Schafer, G. (2008) 'Romantic love in heterosexual relationships: women's experiences'. *Journal of Social Science* 16(3): 187–197.

Smith, M. (2014) *The Erotic Doll: A Modern Fetish*. New Haven, CT.: Yale University Press.

Wolf, N. (1992) *The Beauty Myth: How Images of Beauty Are Used against Women.* New York: Anchor Books.

Wood, G. (2002) *Living Dolls: A Magical History of the Quest for Mechanical Life.* London: Faber and Faber.

Pernilla Ouis

The Politics of Sexual Fantasies: The Inversion of Sexual Fantasies in Orientalism and Occidentalism

Sexual stereotypes of the Other

How can a sexual fantasy have political implications? And, vice versa, can political circumstances influence certain sexual stereotypes of the Other? The West has been accused of constructing an Eroticised Other within the discourse of Orientalism. The veil, in particular, seems to evoke certain sexual fantasies with political connotations: The *unveiling* of the Oriental woman can be regarded as a classic Western sexual fantasy, as well as a symbolic colonial conquest of the territory of the Other. The seductive and decadent odalisque in the harem is another element in the fantasy of the East that can be contrasted to the Victorian puritan sexual morality in the colonial age. These figures of sexual fantasies and what may be labelled ethnopornography have had certain political implications, such as, according to Said's (1978) influential analysis on Orientalism, the conquest and submission of the Other.

In the present chapter I will elaborate on the Western colonial sexual fantasy of the Orient. Furthermore, I will discuss whether or not this representation was purely a fantasy, and whether the representation of Oriental sexuality had any factual basis at all. Also, I will describe ideas of the sexualised and immoral Occident that exist in the Orient today. In the postcolonial age, the idea of an Oriental and an Occidental sexuality seems to have been inversed: The promiscuous Oriental has become the puritan, while the formerly so civilised, controlled, Christian coloniser has become the one with a decadent and bestial sexuality. This postcolonial discourse on Western sexuality will be put within its political context of Islamism, which in its turn produces another sexualised stereotype of the Other; i.e. the promiscuous Westerner in the discourse of Occidentalism. Shereen El Feki elegantly explains this inversion in the introductory chapter of her book *Sex and the Citadel: Intimate Life in a Changing Arab World*:

> And the West, once praised by some in the Arab world for its hard line on same-sex relations, is now seen by many as a radiating source of sexual debauchery from which the region must be shielded. Perceptions, however flawed, are shaped by position. Western

> view of Arab sexuality, and vice versa, have shifted in part because attitudes within their respective societies have also changed (El Feki 2014: 10–11).

The aim of this chapter is to discuss how the sexual fantasy about the Other – regardless who – plays a crucial role in the 'clash of civilizations' (Huntington 1996) between the West and 'the rest', and how sexual stereotyping is used by both sides. The usual mode in this process is to ascribe various negative characteristics to the Other and, hence, when norms and values change within a society, this imagined stereotype must also change in order to fit.

The veil and the colonial gaze

Perhaps the most important trigger in the male Westerner's sexual fantasy is the veiling of Muslim women. To go *behind* or *beyond the veil* is a recurrent theme in Western writings about the Orient, prominent among both male and female travellers since the colonial age. For the Westerner, the *unveiling* is about gaining access to the forbidden, and in this way to be able to conquer and subdue the Other. It has been a prioritised colonial struggle to unveil Oriental women, often under the paroles of modernity, liberty, and gender equality. However, the failure to unveil them has likewise caused frustration, aggression, and sexual fantasies by the Western colonisers. This particular mix of annoyance and sexuality is an important element in Orientalist discourse.

The theme of the Western erotisation of the Orient and the colonisers' frustration caused by the veil has been scrutinised by Malek Alloula (1986). He has analysed French postcards depicting colonised Algerian women in his work *The Colonial Harem*. The favourite motif of these postcards was veiled Algerian women showing their private parts, dating from the three first decades of the 20th century. Alloula argues that the French colonisers in general, and particularly in this case the photographer, were provoked by veiled Algerian women who could observe without being observed:

> These veiled women are not only an embarrassing enigma to the photographer but an outright attack upon him. It must be believed that the feminine gaze that filters through the veil is a gaze of particular kind: concentrated by the tiny orifice for the eye, this womanly gaze is a little like the eye of the camera, like the photographic lens that takes aims at everything (Alloula 1986: 14).

Veiled women caused a particular kind of irritation for the French photographer, as he was being prevented from accomplishing himself as *gazing*. Hence the photographer must 'unveil the veiled and give figural representation to the forbidden' (ibid.). For this purpose, the photographer arranged photo sessions in studios with unveiled, colonised women, often using prostitutes as models, to cope with this 'double violation'. The photos become a kind of 'symbolic revenge' according to Alloula. The women often exposed their breasts while lifting the veil in these postcards. Alloula focuses on the emotions of the photographer to a great extent, but the popularity of the postcards must be put in its colonial context and into a more generalised analysis. The erotic contrast between nudity and the Muslim completely covering clothing is still a recurrent theme in so-called burka-porn, a specific category on porn sites. The contrast between covered and uncovered is still alluring and a powerful sexual fantasy.

In the context of Victorian Puritanism, however, the phenomenon of veiling caused annoyance on many levels. Surprisingly, veiled Muslim women were accused of sexual immorality despite their fully covering dress. In particular, Western *women* noticed the freedom of these women, probably compared to their own restrictions. Lady Montagu wrote about Turkish women in 1763 that, because they were fully covered, these women could not even be recognised by their 'jealous husband' in the streets, concluding: 'This perpetual masquerade gives them entire liberty of following their inclinations without any danger of discovery' (Montagu 1763 (2): 34). Lady Elisabeth Craven (1789: 205) wrote similarly: 'I think I never saw a country where women may enjoy so much liberty, and free from all reproach, as in Turkey' (quotes also in Schick 1999: 224–225). Hence, this presumed freedom was interpreted as a chance for Oriental women to be promiscuous and immoral. Therefore the veiling was met with contempt, rather than with the interpretation that this mode of dressing could be seen as a good and liberating strategy.

According to Pratt (1992: 166–167), the term *feminiotopia* is used to denote 'idealised worlds of female autonomy, empowerment, and pleasure'. The feminotopia of the Other was an important part of the Orientalist discourse, and veiling stimulated fantasies of such utopian worlds in which Oriental women were in power, enjoying and pursuing their sexual desires. Such worlds were definitely threatening to the Victorian gender order. Thus Islamic gender segregation in the colonial time was viewed as threatening since it supposedly gave women power (to be compared with how the same segregation and the veil is today seen as nothing but oppressive for women). The most prominent feminiotopia was of course the harem.

The harem: within the forbidden sexual space

Apart from the veil marking a forbidden, eroticised space, the idealised harems were another important colonial sexual fantasy. Schick (1999) elaborates on the relation between sexuality and spatiality in his book *The Erotic Margin*. He defines the mythical Orient as the space of eroticised otherness, the *Libido Loci*. Schick explains the colonial meaning of the harem:

> Setting an erotic story in a harem thus deploys pre-established connections between sexuality and the Orient, conjuring an exclusively female space filled with compliant and desirous naked women, a taboo place in which the vicarious entry of the reader or viewer evokes all the excitement of the forbidden (Schick 1999: 53).

The harem is both a Libido Loci and a feminiotopia. Schick points out that powerful sexual fantasies are set in harem contexts: Marquis de Sade situated his excesses in *The 120 Days of Sodom* (originally written in 1785, first published in 1904) in 'Turkish-style beds' (What is special about them?, asks Schick) and other sadomasochistic stories in harems. Flaubert (1869) named a brothel *La Turque* in a novel (Schick 1999: 54). To produce sexualised spaces of otherness is to bring order to the geopolitical balance dictated by the hegemonic powers, according to Schick: 'Describing difference – or, more accurately, constructing socially significant difference – serves to construct the norm itself, an important function of xenological erotica' (ibid.: 65). These sexual fantasies fit into a larger scheme of colonialisation, subjugation, and the construction of the Orient.

Alloula's (1986) analysis of French postcards could serve as a good example of this particular political sexual fantasy. The postcards often depicted women imprisoned in their own homes, leaving the Western man on the outside. Accordingly, the outside/inside dualism becomes spatial categories that combined form a place for the fulfilment and non-fulfilment of sexual desire. When the photographer/coloniser has access to the inside, he 'has penetrated the harem, the most powerful expression of the symbolic overcoming of the obstacle' (ibid.: 26). He gets access to the Oriental feminiotopia with all its women willingly accepting every kind of sexual activity. The odalisque is 'the very symbol of the harem, its highest expression', according to Alloula (ibid.: 74). She is a hidden, mysterious, and submissive sexual slave, who becomes available to and symbolically penetrated by the coloniser.

The harem is a space of total sexual freedom in the Western mind: 'A universe of *generalized perversion* and the *absolute limitlessness of pleasure*, the seraglio does appear as the ideal locus of the phantasm in all its contagious splendour' (Alloula 1986: 95, italics in original). The presumed abundance of women in addition to the absence of men in the harem was a particularly erotic circumstance, stimulating elaborations on sapphism. The lack of phallus adds to the sexual frustration of the Western man, and must be compensated for by his associations to various perversions in the harem setting, according to Alloula, who concludes that the harem fantasy 'underscores its polysexuality, to zoophilia and other vices, one can now add female homosexuality' (ibid.: 96).

However, any sexual fantasy must be put in its historical, social, and cultural setting. Fantasies do not emerge in a void. Said (2003[1978]) argues that fantasies about the erotic Orient must be understood in relation to colonialism and the strict regulation of sexuality in the West at the time:

> We must as well recognize that for nineteenth-century Europe, with its increasing *embourgeoisement*, sex had become institutionalized to a very considerable degree. On the one hand, there was no such thing as "free" sex, and on the other, sex in society entailed a web of legal, moral, even political and economic obligations of a detailed and certainly encumbering sort. (...) so the Orient was a place where one could look for sexual experience unobtainable in Europe. Virtually no European writer who wrote on or traveled to the Orient in the period after 1800 exempted himself or herself from this quest: Flaubert, Nerval, "Dirty Dick" Burton and Lane are only the most notable. (...) What they looked for often – correctly, I think – was a different type of sexuality, perhaps more libertine and less guilt-ridden (Said 2003[1978]: 190).

Orientalism is primarily about creating an image of the excellent and flawless self in relation to the Other and what the self is not. The notion of the morally good sexuality in the colonial age created a counter-image of the immoral and perverse sexuality of the Other. The sexual lives of the West were for the bourgeoisie perhaps much more regulated compared to what they observed in the Orient.

Western erotica of the Orient

Many prominent Orientalists devoted themselves to translating classical Arabic texts, some of which had erotic content. Sir Richard Burton ('Dirty Dick', see quote above) translated *The Arabian Nights: Tales from a Thousand and One Nights* in 1885 and (from the French translation) *The Perfumed Garden* in 1886. Burton's translation from 1886 has been accused of not being correctly translated from the Arabic original, but having inserts of Burton's own sexual fantasies and other non-Arabic sources (Colville 1999). However, Burton found the French translation incomplete due to the censoring of some passages of homoeroticism, and started working on yet another translation that he called *The Scented Garden*. This translation was never published because his wife burned it after his death in 1890 due to its explicit erotic content. This incident is perhaps symptomatic of the clash of Western puritanism with the alleged Oriental sexual freedom.

But not only Burton used his own sexual fantasies while ascribing them to the Orient: false erotica (including fictitious Oriental imprints) soon became a new genre of literature in the colonial age. One classical example of this genre is the novel *The Lustful Turk* (or *Lascivious Scenes from a Harem*), first published anonymously in 1828. The publisher William Dugdale was prosecuted in 1857 for obscenity in the book. The novel became widely spread after 1893, however, when it was reprinted by Dugdale. The book is based on 'letters' from an English woman to her friend, telling her story as a captive and sex slave in a harem, including scenes of rape, anal sex, threesomes, and lesbianism.

The Oriental man was depicted differently from the Western man in this erotic literature. The Other was omnisexual, and the male Other portrayed both as effeminate but still a rapist, a despotic oppressor of women. The female Other was depicted *both* as a threat and a rape victim. In the translator's preface to the Swedish translation of the Arabic version of *The Thousand and One Nights* (Östrup 1928), the Oriental man is commented upon. He displays an 'unmanly' behaviour as he becomes sick when he falls in love, according to the translator. Östrup (1928: 13–14) comments: 'Instead of acting and fighting, which to our aesthetic mind is the precondition for that one would feel sympathy for him, he sits down and complains [...] the Oriental (man) is persevering in his passion but has only seldom independent will power and decisiveness' (my translation). The effeminate, weak, and often homosexual man is a recurrent theme in Oriental erotica of the time.

The boom in translations of erotic literature from the Orient into European languages during the colonial age meant in practice that Oriental literature classified as *ars erotica* (in Foucauldian terminology) was understood as *scientia sexualis* in the West:

> Tales about Arabian women engaging in sexual intercourse with, say, bears or monkeys, not to mention each other, were thus viewed not as humorous, or allegorical, or didactic, or whatever their original audiences might have thought of them, but as true accounts of sex in the Orient (Schick 1999: 188).

Schick (1999: 230) concludes: 'in this study I have argued that sexuality played an important role in the construction of Europe's spaces of otherness [...] In turn, these spaces of otherness were instrumental in helping Europe to signify itself, that is, define its own identity and place in the world'. These sexual fantasies played an important political role in the era of colonialism. The colonial sexual fantasies encompassed the submission of Oriental women and the attempt of going behind the veil and penetrate into their private space and conquer them.[1] The harem was depicted as a space of uncontrolled promiscuity, lesbianism, and the absence of 'real' men controlling women, contrasted to the Victorian notions of sex for procreation and a 'civilised' sexuality. The Oriental man was feminine and unmanly.

Even today, in the genre of so-called Sheikh Romance in the escapist Romance genre, a somehow different ideal of the Oriental man – the desert sheikh – is present (Jarmakani 2011). He is 'dark and desirable, but not too dark; masculine and powerful, yet willing to surrender to love' (Taylor 2007: 1034). The sheikh romances reveal a *masculinised* Other man, an alpha-male hero. Again one can discern that the sexual fantasies of the Other have political implications: The white woman is the object of the sheikh's desire, and in the end, when he surrenders to her love, he becomes a civilised and modern man. Hence, he is united with the West through the white woman, and 'the differences and dangers can be controlled and neutralised' (ibid.: 1045), while she 'completes the export of American values by marrying the sheikh' (ibid.). Thus, Western *women*, both as fictive heroines and as readers of sheikh romances, might play an important part in current imperialism.

Oriental sexualities

But what can we really know about sexuality in the Orient during the colonial time? Can the representations described here all be dismissed as sexual stereotypes and fantasies about the Other? For instance, what about the harems – did they ever exist as depicted by the colonisers? Fadwa El Guindi is an anthropologist who has done extensive historical and anthropological research on the veil in Islam. She argues that the English/European word harem (stress on the first syllable) is a distortion of the Arabic word *harim* (stress on the second syllable) that derives from the root *h-r-m* (note: Semitic languages are based on a root of three consonants), which means 'sacred' (i.e. the word *haram* means forbidden or taboo). Harim means basically *both* to the women of a household and to their space with connections to sacredness and inviolability. She refers to the Egyptian feminist Huda Shaarawi who describes the harem as a place of household management, social relations, and political discussions rather than 'a locus of sexual orgies' (El Guindi 1999: 56). El Guindi refers to the harem as a space of 'sacred privacy'. Thus, exclusively female space existed, but with completely different connotations from those of the colonial, imagined harem.

1 This is analogous to the explanations of (male) rape of females of the enemy in war (see for instance Eriksson Baaz & Stern 2009).

The Harem Bath (date unknown). By Austrian artist Ernst Rudolph (1854–1932).

Furthermore, Said (see quote above), in spite of his brilliant analysis of the corrupt and unfair picture of the Oriental, recognises that the Orient was *in fact* more sexually liberal than the West in the colonial age. It has been difficult, however, to find presumably neutral descriptions of the facts of Oriental sexuality in the colonial age. Some domestic manuscripts have been translated, but can one trust translations? Perhaps a manuscript in Arabic that is alleged to be from the 13th century can help us. It was written by the physician Al-Sayyid Harun ibn Husain al-Makhzumi, and is said to be found in a private collection. It was translated into Swedish in 1970 under the title *Njutningens källor* (English: 'The Sources of Pleasure'). One might speculate that this manuscript could be fiction in the genre of Western Oriental erotica, but the translator assures its authenticity. It is remarkably outspoken in regards to sexual issues. For instance, it states that 'the woman, just like the man, is gifted with her own organs for intercourse and reproduction. She was created to feel pleasure and not simply submit to copulation for reproduction, as some false prophets have preached. God has blessed the lustful, responsive woman and during the intercourse she should give and take pleasure in equal measure' (al-Makhzumi 2004[1970]: 20, my translation from the Swedish)

A large part of the book is an elaboration on the categorisation of different types of women based on their behaviour during the orgasm, i.e. the wild one, the one who always moves, the begging one, the wondering one, the talkative one, the full-blood, the strange one, the hungry one, the sobbing one, and the tormented woman. The existence of an erotic harem is taken as a matter of fact in this book. The doctor/author also elaborates on the physical appearances of breasts and vaginas, as well as various descriptions of intercourse positions and techniques. The book communicates a picture of Oriental sexuality that corresponds well to the Orientalists' representations. So, is this a colonial fantasy, or rather a realistic report of a contrasting sexuality?

The accuracy of Western sexual representations of the Orient is to some extent also confirmed in the book *Sexual Life in Ottoman Society* by Sema Nilgun Erdogan (1996). The harems discussed are the ones of the Ottoman Sultans, and the author states: 'The mystery of the Harem has always been an up to date topic for some Western writers. They tried to picture this fabulous establishment mainly with their imagination' (ibid.: 9). Although the Westerner is blamed for using imagination rather than fact, since he was not let into the existing harems, Erdogan perhaps unintentionally accepts and confirms the Orientalists' view. The book, which is based on authentic documents, actually reveals a similar picture of the harem to the Orientalist one. It could be argued that the major fault of the Orientalists was that they generalised what might have happened in the palaces of the Sultans to the whole of the Muslim population. *Sexual Life in Ottoman Society* also discusses homosexuality and dancing boys, referred to as 'passive homosexuals', and states that their dance 'was erotic and provoked the sexual desires of the spectator' (ibid.: 73). The feminine and homosexual Oriental man was, as discussed previously, a part of the Oriental erotica and in Erdogan's book his existence is taken as a matter of fact.

Other writings from the Orient confirm the picture of a more liberal view of sexuality in general and homosexuality in particular. An example is the famous *The Rose Garden* (*Gulistan*) by Sheikh Muslih-uddin Sa'di Shirazi, a Persian classic from 1258, which also includes homoerotic stories. It is interesting to note the forgiving attitude of Allah in the text, such as: 'See the generosity and kindness of God. The servant has committed sin and he is ashamed' (Shirazi 1258). In *The Ring of the Dove: A Treatise of the Art and Practice of Arab Love* (written around 1022) by Ibn Hazm, the author, who was an important Islamic scholar, elaborates on sin. He argues that man has two extremes, reason and lust:

> These two contrary natures are the poles in a man; they are two of the body's various faculties, by means of which the body acts; they are so to speak a pair of screens, upon which fall the rays emanating from those wonderful, lofty, sublime substances (Ibn Hazm 1953[1022]: 230).

Oriental sexuality is difficult to grasp, and it is an easy mistake to conflate written fiction with facts in the interpretation of historical sexualities. Sexualities are social constructions, based on cultural and collective fantasies, as well as interpretations of lived experiences. So what is fact and fiction in this case? Maybe the answer is not that complicated. In the anthology *Islamicate sexualities*, Brad Epps, scholar of Romance languages and literature, states what is perhaps the most obvious interpretation regarding Western colonial sexual fantasies: 'These fantasies take the fairly well-trodden path of nostalgic celebration of the relative permissiveness and freedom of Arabic sexuality – relative, needless to say, to Western sexuality' (Epps 2008: 132). An exaggeration of that which differs from one's own taken-for-granted world is often all it takes to create a fantasy of the other. Or is it simply that the exotic – the different – is somehow so alluring and interesting that it becomes the erotic (Bem 1996)? However, Epps problematises his own statement regarding the (im)possiblity to categorise different sexualities of the East and the West altogether (see discussion below).

Postcolonial deconstructions: the example of the veil

In postcolonial writings, the discussed sexual fantasies have been criticised and deconstructed for justified reasons. Alloula's book has throughout a tone of indignation:

> What I read on these cards does not leave me indifferent. It demonstrates to me, were that still necessary, the desolate poverty of gaze that I myself, as an Algerian, must have been the object of at some moment in my personal history. Among us, we believe in the nefarious effects of the evil eye (the evil gaze). We conjure them with our hand spread out like a fan. I close my hand back upon a pen to write *my* exorcism: *this text* (Alloula 1986: 5, italics in original).

Alloula wants to challenge the evil eye (i.e. the colonial gaze) with his writing. The postcolonial strategy is about deconstructing the image of a barbaric Oriental sexuality, as well as the oppressiveness of the veil. Several contemporary Muslim writers defend the veil and tend to deconstruct Western accusations. Katherine Bullock, an Australian convert to Islam, writes in her book on the veil that it is essential to unpack 'the notion of veil as oppressive' (Bullock 2002: 18). She, correctly in my opinion, notes that the veil has much more important symbolic connotations in the West than being, simply a garment: 'The veil was the metaphor for the entire Middle East. So even if the topic at hand was a discussion of other aspects of Muslim customs and manners, the veil could be invoked as shorthand for the disabilities that Muslim men and women faced because of their religion' (ibid.: 18). Yegenoglu (1998) argues that the veiled Oriental woman is the iterative element par excellence. The veil threatens Western power and supremacy and must be penetrated and lifted: physically in the sexual fantasies, geographically by colonial rule, and philanthropically by modernists and feminists. If the unveiling of Muslim women was an imperialist and modernist project, supported by the West and the Muslim elite, the re-veiling in the last decades is a sign both of postcolonial awareness and Islamist political identity. The new veiling could basically be understood as resistance against the West, either formulated in Islamic terms or not (El Guindi 1999). This re-veiling is, on the other hand, interpreted in the West as a provocation against sexual liberalism and individual freedom.

The Western critique against the position of women in the Orient has been addressed in the postcolonial project. An example of such deconstruction is the book *Veiled Half-Truths: Western Travellers' Perceptions of Middle Eastern Women* (Mabro 1991), where the colonial image of a passive veiled woman is scrutinised. Veiled women were perceived as sex objects, incarnating the mystery of the Orient. Mabro puts it bluntly about these women: 'they may not all be as exotic and beautiful as Western fantasy has depicted them' (ibid.: 4). In an anthology of more than 700 pages on *Feminist Postcolonial Theory: A Reader* (edited by Lewis & Mills, 2003) one of six parts of the book is on the theme 'Harem and the Veil'. Yengenoglu sums up postcolonial constructions of the veil and Oriental sexuality, and argues convincingly that the unveiling ambitions should be seen in the context of the disenchantment and longing for transparency of Enlightenment, aiming at knowledge and power. But the Muslim woman refused to be subjected to this Western agenda, as she insisted on observing others without being seen herself. In this sense, veiling is about rejecting the role of being an object of Western knowledge and supremacy. Hence, the veil has a political importance in postcolonial discourse as a more general example, but sexual issues are implicit in the analysis of the veiling.

In postcolonial writings on the veil, Lord Cromer has been given a symbolic role. He was the British Agent and the Consul-General of Egypt 1883–1907, working actively for the 'elevation' and (thus) unveiling of the Egyptian woman. At the same time, he was the founding member and president of the Men's League for Opposing Women's Suffrage in England. He incarnates the colonial endeavour of liberating the Other woman, while being blind to the oppression of women by the colonisers themselves 'at home'. The same argument can be raised against female travellers in the colonial age, wearing tight corsets and other 'oppressive' clothes while trying to liberate Muslim women from their veils. In Sayyid's (1997) deconstruction of the Western fear of Islamic fundamentalism, he asks the justified question why the enforcing of women wearing the veil is considered as an articulation of fundamentalism, when the forced *unveiling* of them is not. He notes that apparently 'control is only exercised when it is a restriction' (ibid.: 9). He concludes that there is an assumption of an 'essential' woman that is unveiled, and that veiling is a violation of these women's subjectivity. Sayyid's analysis is a typical example of the postcolonial decentring of the West.

Islamism and the promiscuous Occident

The rejection of a notion of the lustful Orient has been most effective in the Islamist movement, which emerged and spread in the late 1970s, inspired by the revolution in Iran. The rejection of this sexual stereotype was not the only effort, but also to create a contrasting image: the image of a truly decadent and sexually immoral Westerner. This is a recurrent theme in Islamist publications, and coincides with the sexual liberalism of the West during the late 20th century. The Islamist movement is anti-Western, and sexuality plays an important role. Inglehart and Norris (2003) argue that the supposed clash of civilisations does not regard issues of democracy and human rights, but a clash in the view of women and sexuality (see Ouis 2009). This is the 'true clash of civilizations', and of course symbolic sexualities, i.e. fantasies, are of uttermost importance.

The roots of the supposedly new sexual puritanism in the Orient, as an opposition to the West, can, according to Joseph A. Massad (2007), professor of Modern Arab politics, be traced to the Arab intellectual elite. In a historical process, the puritanism of the colonisers was accepted and internalised in the modernizing ambitions among Arabs, but turned against the West as it became more sexually liberated:

> Victorian notions of appropriate and shameful sexual behavior and its civilizational dimensions would rank high in the thinking of these Arab intellectuals, not least because such notions were the basis for judgment not only of non-Europeans but also the late *European* Romantic art, literature, and poetry constituting the "Decadent movement", which was often condemned as "degenerate", especially on account of its sexually explicit motifs, including sadism, incest, sodomy, and lesbianism, and identified as "barbaric" and "primitive" in sensibility (Massad 2007: 15, Italics in original).

An example of Arab intellectuals' attempts to formulate their own sexuality is found in Abdelwahab Bouhdiba's book *Sexuality in Islam*, first published in French in 1975. According to Massad (2007: 144 ff) the book is a hallmark of the Arab post-1967 period, and exposes an approach that, according to Massad, is both 'semi-Orientalist' and 'secular feminist'. Boudhiba (1998[1975]) identifies Islam as feminist, while he considers Arab society misogynistic. However, the author is negative towards the sexual liberalism he witnesses in the West during this period:

> A new danger lies in wait for the Arabo-Muslim societies: the ethical void, cretinization through sex, systematic infantilization. The negation of traditional references is certainly a necessary stage in our history, but the negation of those references is still a reference. The great risk is precisely non-reference. The easy models of sexual behaviour, imported from North America or Europe, relentlessly diffused through mass media, do not help us to find much meaning in sexuality (Boudhiba 1998[1975]: 244).

Western sexuality is a 'joyless, savourless, colourless eroticism that is no more than bestiality' (ibid.: 247). Boudhiba accuses Arab men of searching for the 'anti-wife' in the dancer, film star, or prostitute, adding: 'The sexual act is becoming facile, brief, straightforward and joyless' (ibid.: 243). The solution to this sexual disease is found in Islamic marriage and in the sexual pleasures to be expected in the hereafter for believers (see Carlbom, this volume), a mantra to be repeated in the Islamic movement to come. Western sexuality is thought to be deprived of its myths and taboos, while Islam gives positive meaning to sexuality in its organisation of public-private, lawful-unlawful. Here we can see a typical example of the contrasting, political sexual fantasy constructed in the East about Western sexuality. This fantasy is not an erotic dream about the Other; rather it is a negative and depressing picture of boring and cold sexual acts performed for selfish reasons only.

One of the chief ideologists of the Islamist movement, Abul A'la Maududi (sometimes spelled Mawdudi) published his influential book *Purdah and the Status of Woman in Islam* already in 1939, a book that has been reprinted numerous times. His work is perhaps the standard for how Western sexuality is depicted within Islamism. He explains the sexual problematics in the West with the fact that women are economically independent. He asks the rhetorical question: 'Why should a woman who wins her own bread, supports herself economically and does not depend on anyone for security and maintenance, remain faithfully attached to one man only for the sake of satisfying her sexual desires?' (ibid.: 13). He goes on: 'Especially, when the concept of moral equality has cleared her way to all obstacles for satisfying sexual desires freely, why should she forsake the easy, pleasure-giving and alluring way of satisfying them and choose the antiquated way that is not only laden with responsibilities but demands sacrifices also?' (ibid.: 13). Now, perhaps Maududi underestimated the power of the ideology of romantic love (Giddens 1992) in the West in conserving sexual monogamy. But for him, gender equality, economic equality, and the free intermingling of the sexes explain the dreadful immorality of the West, a development Maududi witnesses with great disgust. Again we find the depressing view of moral decay and unsatisfied men and women in the West:

> In the absence of any moral restraint this urge is satisfied with increasing keenness and both the sexes begin to show off and display their physical charms without any consideration for decency. This tendency sometimes touches nudeness. … To satisfy this extraordinary sexual urge they are ever busy inventing and designing new ways: The nude pictures, sexual literature, love romances, nude ballroom dancing, sex-inciting films, all are means of intensifying the same fire which the wrong social system has kindled in every heart. To save their faces, they call it "art" (Maududi 1990[1939]: 14–15).

However, a justified question is whether Maududi's description is a 'fantasy' or whether it is just his own interpretation of the Western reality he experienced, an interpretation just as valid as anybody's? Of course his understanding is influenced by his religious and cultural background, but most representations might have some connection to reality (Brante 2001).

The Islamist fantasy of Western sexuality is not a fantasy that aims at evoking any erotic emotions. It has mainly political dimensions: that of a warning directed to fellow Muslims against the so-called 'Westoxication' that in their view denotes the 'sickness' that the secularists have caught. However, since such a massive campaign is needed to keep the believers on the right path, this implies that Western sexuality is alluring and attractive. In addition to this political function, their sexual fantasy is also a strategy for degrading the Westerner. It is definitely an expression of Occidentalism, a theme elaborated by Buruma and Margalit:

> The West is the main target of the enemies of idolatry, even though Islamist political activism is often directed at the oppressive regimes in nominally Muslim countries. One reason for this is the idea of arrogance, manifested in Western imperialism, that is seen as an infringement of the rule of God. The other is about the breaking of sexual taboos – that is, about the West as the main corruptor of sexual morality (Buruma & Margalit 2004: 126–127).

The Western response to the Islamists' accusations is that the Western (contemporary) liberal sexuality represents a healthy and sound one. How did this change come about? The sexual liberalism in the West that developed changed the Western view of sexuality tremendously. In a comparative analysis, Glover and Marklund (2009) analyse how the sexualisation of Sweden in the 1950s and onward was associated with modernity and progress, while the same sexualisation of the Orient was not, but rather the opposite. They argue that the *Sweden-sex nexus* constructed a Northern Other. In the perceived Swedish sexuality, sex became associated with gender equality and rationality heading towards sexual democracy, and incorporated the future of the West and new sexual ideals. These modern values seem in general to be prevalent in the contemporary West. The Islamists, on the other hand, are being accused of being driven into terrorism out of sexual frustration (only). This is a popular explanation to the 9-11-attack that circulated in Western mass media afterwards (for a summary of the debate, see Scaribey 2009).

Foucault reassessed and final reflections

Thus, an inversion of imagined sexual identities can be discerned: the lustful and promiscuous Oriental has become a sexually frustrated puritan from the Western perspective, while the Westerner has become decadent and promiscuous in the view of the Orientals, or at least of the Islamists. I argue that these sexual fantasies have political origins, as well as functions. Massad (2007) has perhaps best identified the historical process of this inversion, by pointing out how the colonial accusations of sexual immorality were internalised by the pro-modern Arab intelligentsia. To be modern, was to accept the coloniser's view on sexuality:

> In adopting this Weltanschauung, Arab intellectuals also internalized the epistemology by which Europeans came to judge civilizations and cultures along the vector of something called "sex", as well as its later derivative, "sexuality", and the overall systematization of culture through the statistical concept of "norms", often corresponding to the "natural" and its "deviant" opposite (Massad 2007: 6).

The intellectual Arab movement that emerged at the turn of the previous century was self-reflexive, aiming at identifying certain elements in their own culture and religion (their 'backwardness') that were seen as obstacles to progress and modernity. This can be seen as an example of 'strong Orientalism', when the Orient accepts the Occidental description of themselves, resulting in 'how orientalism actually constitutes the Orient' (Sayyid 1997: 32). In this case, the accusations of sexual immorality made the Orient 'correct' themselves in regard to sexuality and adopt a more puritan ideal. However, when Western society during the 20th century became more sexually liberated, these Arab intellectuals began to distance themselves from Western sexual ideals and (lack of) morality. In my view, this aversion culminated in the Islamist discourse, as discussed above.

Several Muslim writers today tend to distance themselves from the Islamists' notion of Islamic sexuality, and acknowledge that these values were originally imported from the West. They argue that 'real' Islam is not misogynistic or repressive on sexual matters. For instance, Ilkkaracan (2002) argues that modernisation and nationalist ideologies had a more negative impact on women's sexuality than did Islam, while warning against the Islamic Religious Right. However, in her writings as well as in that of other Muslim activists (e.g., Barlas 2002, Kugle 2003), understanding is rather about what Islam *ought* to be, not how it is practiced by many Muslims and Islamists. In this case, the arguments are apologetic and normative rather than descriptive of what Islam is in regard to sex.

In this chapter, I have discussed the political connotations and the inversion of fantasies, as well as whether these fantasies might have some factual basis, or whether they are purely imaginary representations. From a postmodern perspective, such borders are almost impossible to uphold, or not even considered meaningful. Was the coloniser as puritan as postcolonial discourse suggests? Or is the Westerner as immoral and decadent as the Islamists believe? Perhaps the Oriental was just as licentious as the coloniser depicted him? And are the Islamists really advocating such a repressive sexuality that it even drives them to terror attacks out of sheer sexual frustration and the mentality 'they hate us for our freedom' (read: sexual freedom)?

Valerie Traub (2008: 20), professor of English and women's studies, questions Foucault's division of historical sexuality in *ars erotica* and *scientia sexualis*, and suggests that 'there must be other ways of producing knowledge about sexuality in history'. Foucault's dichotomy has had a great influence on the thinking and fantasies regarding Occidental and Oriental sexualities. Epps (2008) argues that we should even question Foucault's division between a repressive West and a permissive, erotic East. In a rather liberating way he expresses why the East-West division in sexuality must be abandoned altogether:

> ...for there and then, here and now, in the "East" and in the "West", *sexuality and its signs are ideologically charged.* To begin with, the idea that there "is" an Eastern sexuality and a Western sexuality – and that there "was" one in antiquity, the Middle Ages, or early modernity – is far from self-evident (Epps 2008: 132, my emphasis).

So, if we cannot discern any different, opposing types of sexualities in the West *contra* the East in reality, either historically or in the present, then all one can do is to discuss the *function* of the politicised sexual fantasies, keeping in mind that they are social constructions with political meanings. In this light, they are nothing but *fantasies*, and it is not relevant to ask about these fantasies' connections to reality, as reality does not in this case lend itself to dualistic categorisations. These fantasies are part of both sides' propaganda in the 'clash of civilizations'. A sexual fantasy is perhaps generally understood as something which invokes sexual arousal in the individual, but I have shown that these fantasies are also means of mobilising strong emotions against the Other. In this sense, the sexual fantasies discussed in this chapter can be used as powerful, psychological weapons. It is more complicated than the slogan 'Make love, not war', since fantasies about love-making can be used in the making of war.

References

Alloula, M. (1986) *The Colonial Harem*. London & Minneapolis: University of Minnesota Press.

Barlas, A. (2002) *'Believing Women' in Islam: Unreading Patriarchal Interpretations of the Qur'an*. Austin: University of Texas Press.

Bem, D.J. (1996) 'Exotic becomes erotic: A developmental theory of sexual orientation'. *Psychological Review* 103(2): 320–335.

Boudhiba, A. (1998[1975]) *Sexuality in Islam*. London: Saqi Books.

Brante, T. (2001) 'Consequence of realism for sociological theory-building'. *Journal for the Theory of Social Behaviour* 32(2): 167–195.

Bullock, K. (2002) *Rethinking Muslim Women and the Veil: Challenging Historical and Modern Stereotypes*. London: The International Institute of Islamic Thought.

Buruma, I. & Margalit, A. (2004) *Occindetalism: A Short History of Anti-Westernism*. London: Atlantic Books.

Colville, J. (1999) *Translation of The Perfumed Garden of Sensual Delight by Muhammad ibn Muhammad al-Nafzawi*. London: Kegan Paul International.

Craven, E. (1789) *A Journey through the Crimea to Constantinople in a Series of Letters from the Right Honourable Elisabeth Lady Craven, to his Serene Highness the Margrave of Brandebourg, Anspach and Bareith. Written in the Year 1786*. London: G.G.J & J. Robinson.

El Feki, S. (2014) *Sex and the Citadel: Intimate Life in a Changing Arab World*. London: Vintage Books.

El Guindi, F. (1999) *Veil: Modesty, Privacy and Resistance*. Axford & New York: Berg.

Epps, B. (2008) 'Comparison, competition, and cross-dressing: Cross-cultural analysis in a contested world'. In K. Babayan & A. Najmabadi (eds) *Islamicate Sexualities: Translations across Temporal Geographies of Desire*. Cambridge & London: Harvard University Press.

Erdogan, S.N. (2000) *Sexual Life in Ottoman Society*. Istanbul: Dönence.

Eriksson Baaz, M. & Stern, M. (2009) 'Why do soldiers rape? Masculinity, violence, and sexuality in the Armed Forces in the Congo (DRC)'. *International Studies Quarterly* 53: 495–518.

Giddens, A. (1992) *The Transformation of Intimacy*. Cambridge: Polity Press.

Glover, N. & C. Marklund (2009) 'Arabian nights in the midnight sun? Exploring the temporal structure of sexual geographies'. *Historisk tidskrift* 129(3): 487–510.

Huntington, S.P. (1996) *The Clash of Civilizations: Remaking of World Order*. New York: Simon & Schuster.

Ibn Hazm (1953[1022]). *The Ring of the Dove: A Treatise of the Art and Practice of Arab Love*. London: Luzac & Company.

Ilkkaracan, P. (2002) "Women, sexuality and social change in the Middle East and the Maghreb". *Social Research* 69(3): 753–779.

Inglehart, R. & Norris, P. (2003) 'The true clash of civilizations'. *Foreign Policy* 135: 62–70.

Jarmakani, A. (2011) 'Desiring the big bad blade: Racing the sheikh in desert romances'. *American Quarterly* 63(4): 895–928.

Kugle, S. (2003) 'Sexuality, diversity, and ethics in the agenda of progressive Muslims'. In Safi, O. (ed) *Progressive Muslims: On Justice, Gender, and Pluralism*. Oxford: Oneworld Publications.

Mabro, J. (1991) *Veiled Half-Truths: Western Travellers' Perceptions of Middle Eastern Women*. London & New York: I.B. Tauris & Co Ltd.

al-Makhzumi, al-Sayyid Harun ibn Husain (2004[1970]) *Njutningens källor*. Furulund: Alhambra Förlag AB.

Massad, J.A. (2007) *Desiring Arabs*. Chicago & London: University of Chicago Press.

Maududi, A.A. (1990[1939]). *Purdah and the Status of Woman in Islam*. Lahore: Islamic Publications Limited.

Montagu, M, Wortely (1763) *Letters of the Right Honourable Lady Mary Wortley Montagu: Written during her Travels in Europe, Asia and Africa, to Persons of Distinction, Men of Letters & in different Parts of Europe. Which Contains, among other Curious Relations, Accounts of the Policy and Manners of the Turks; Drawn from Sources that have been inaccessible to other Travelers*. London: T. Becket & P.A. De Hondt.

Ouis, P. (2009) '"Den verkliga kulturkonflikten?" Islamisk sexualmoralism i liberala Sverige'. *Socialvetenskaplig tidskrift* 3–4: 350–368.

Traub, V. (2008) 'The past is a foreign country? The times and spaces of Islamicate sexuality studies'. In K. Babayan & A. Najmabadi (eds) *Islamicate Sexualities: Translations across Temporal Geographies of Desire*. Cambridge & London: Harvard University Press.

Said, E. W. (2003[1978]) *Orientalism*. London: Penguin Books.

Sayyid, B. Salman (1997) *A Fundamental fear: Eurocentrism and the Emergence of Islamism*. London & New York: Zed Books.

Schick, I. Cemil (1999) *The Erotic Margin: Sexuality and Spatiality in Alteritist Discourse*. London & New York: Verso.

Scaribey, O. (2009) 'Does sexual frustration fuel Islamic violence?' *Beliefnet*. http://www.beliefnet.com/columnists/news/2009/11/does-sexual-frustration-fuel-i.php.

Shirazi, Muslih-uddin Sa'di (1258). *The Rose Garden (Gulistan)*. Downloaded at http://www.fordham.edu/halsall/pwh/sadi.html.

Taylor, J. (2007) 'And you can be my sheikh: gender, race, and orientalism in contemporary romance novels'. *The Journal of Popular Culture* 40(6): 1032–1050.

Yengenoglu, M. (1998) *Colonial Fantasies: Towards a Feminist Reading of Orientalism*. Cambridge: Cambridge University Press.

Yengenoglu, M. (2003) 'Veiled fantasies: cultural and sexual difference in the discourse of orientalism'. In R. Lewis & S. Mills (eds) *Feminist Postcolonial Theory: A Reader*. Edinburgh: Edinburgh University Press.

Östrup, J. (1928) 'Inledning'. *Tusen och en natt*. Malmö: Baltiska Förlaget AB.

Aje Carlbom

Blocking out Sexual Fantasies for a Fantasy of Eternal Sex: Islamist Views

Much has been written about Islam and sexuality during the last decade. Generally, many contributions focus on the differences between Western liberal conceptions of sexuality and the more conservative tradition prevalent in the Islamic world. Indeed, it seems to be the case, as Ronald Inglehart and Pippa Norris (2003: 65) argued in reply to Samuel Huntington's (1995) thesis of a clash of civilizations, that the most salient division 'between the West and Islam…concerns gender equality and sexual liberalization'. From data in the World Value Survey they concluded that values surrounding sexual relations is a more important divide between the two cultures than are democratic issues.

The following discussion is also grounded in the assumption that there are general differences between Islam and the West in matters of sexuality. However, my concern is not with Islamic ideas of sexuality seen in a general civilisation perspective. Here the issue is the status of sexual fantasies from an Islamic activist perspective. How do pious Muslims in the Islamic movement evaluate sexual fantasies? What kind of moral framework is used to interpret sexual fantasies? Further, what is at stake when pious Muslims argue for a certain stance towards sexual fantasies? What is argued in the following should be understood as a tentative discussion of an expanding field of research. Generally, several of the attitudes towards pornography formulated by Islamic activists can also be found among Western Christian fundamentalists and within the feminist movement. Islamic activists classify pornography in a negative way similar to Western Christian fundamentalists and radical feminists. The main difference – apart from the fact that Christian and Islamic activists regard pornography as a sin whereas anti-pornography feminists regard it as harmful to women (see for example Ahrold, et al. 2011, Berger, et al. 1990) – concerns the discourses used by these activists to evaluate and represent sexual fantasies and fantasies of sex. A Christian idea is that avoidance of sin (sexual fantasies) will lead to a Paradise where the believer is freed from bodily desires. The righteous Muslim (who blocks out sexual fantasies from the mind), will end up in a *pornotopia* where all carnal desires will be satisfied in infinity without any biological or social constraints.

Islam as an institution for sexual discipline

The discussion in this chapter is concerned mainly with normative Islamic thinking, and not much will be said about what actual Muslim believers actually do in their everyday lives. The data presented below is taken from the ongoing religious debate in the Islamic movement in which norms of how to practice Islamic ideals stand out as an important issue. Accordingly, the quotes below should not be seen as neutral statements of how Muslims in general think of Islamic norms. On the contrary, what is said is part of an ongoing struggle of influencing the hearts and minds of ordinary Muslims. This political work takes place both locally and globally, in Muslim contexts and in the West. The Internet is an important medium for this political activity (Sisler 2011). Those working to convince Muslims to act and think in a certain way are in the literature most commonly called Islamic activists or Islamists. The main difference between this category and other Muslims is that they are actively involved in a project to 're-Islamize society by encouraging individuals to practice Islam in daily life and to bridge the perceived gap between religious discourse and practical realities' (Clark 2004: 14). Islamic discourse categorises this work as *dawa* which, according to Tariq Ramadan (2002: 213), means that 'wherever a Muslim is, he or she is a witness of Islam's message, through his or her speech, behavior, and manner of dealing with people'. *Dawa* is mentioned in the Koran (14: 46) as 'God's "call" to human society to find in Islam the true religion' (Eickelman & Pescatori 1996: 35).

An important aspect of this ideological project is to try to control Muslims' behaviour by influencing their consciousness with norms constructed by Islamic ideas. This activity is grounded in the assumption that 'humanity cannot approach higher levels of nobility and virtue unless it is free from the dominance of blind carnal appetite', as Allie Haroun Sheik (2010: 3) formulates it. Since these activists perceive sexual conduct as one of the most central human activities, it is of great importance to impose a system of moral codes on Muslims in order to discipline their sexual desire in a certain way. As I have pointed out elsewhere (Carlbom 2012), Islamic activists opine that sexual desire can only have a lawful outlet within a heterosexual Islamic marriage. Sexual practice outside the social institution of matrimony is classified as *zina* [sin] according to *sharia* [Islamic law] and is therefore seen as unlawful (Ouis 2009). Generally, the internal political struggle between Islamic activists concerned with sexuality is about where to draw the moral boundary in matters of desire. How far can, or should, Muslims go in their physical and symbolic contacts with the other sex?

There is an old theoretical discussion about how to define religion. Many are familiar with the symbolic definition proposed by Clifford Geertz (2002 [1973]) where he argues that religion should be understood as a 'cultural system', and Emile Durkheim's way of seeing religion as a 'moral community called a Church' (1912 [1995: xxxiv]). Another way to understand religion, as it is constructed by Islamic activists, is to see their ideological work in terms of an activity to create what John Searle (2010) has called 'desire independent' reasons for action. Typical for social institutions, he argues, is that they provide humans with deontic powers, that is, for example, rights, authorisations, permissions, and duties, which are independent of our own individual desires (ibid.: 123). Seen in this light, the ambition of Islamic activists is to make other Muslims internalise an Islamic system of values in order to tame individual (sexual) desire in a certain way. As an imam in Sweden pointed out in an e-mail conversation with me: 'Muslims are encouraged to discipline their lusts and to avoid satisfying some of them in this world, regardless of whether it's about private parts or the pleasure of the stomach; by doing so, they will be rightly rewarded in the hereafter according to how they have strived'. Thus, if Muslims can control their own individual sexual and other carnal desires in their earthly life by making Islamic norms their own subjective morality, they will increase their chances to end up in Paradise where they will live an afterlife where they can, among other things, practice a sexuality free of social constraints and consequences.

Sexual fantasies from an activist perspective

It is common knowledge today that Islam, as a normative system, evaluates heterosexual sexuality as such in a positive way. As long as sexual relationships are consummated within legally stipulated boundaries, both men and women are encouraged to have sex. Thus, according to *sharia,* intercourse must take place inside a *nikah* [Islamic marriage]; if not, and if disclosed, there is a risk of punishment. As one of my informants puts it: 'To be unfaithful is regarded as a criminal act, it is very serious'. However, once sex takes place in the 'right place', and between the right people, Muslim men and women can do almost anything except practicing anal sex or having sex during menstruation. For instance, oral sex is a contested practice among religious activists but for some Muslims, such as my informant, it is accepted. As he says: 'I listened to a woman who called Yusuf al-Qaradawi and asked if it was allowed for her to practice oral sex on her husband. Qaradawi answered that he can suck you too. No problem. It is written in the Koran' (Carlbom 2012: 273).

For activists in the Islamic movement, sexual fantasies are regarded as a moral problem. The message from the activists is that Muslims ought to erase them from consciousness. The main problem with such thoughts seems to be that they may ultimately become a threat to marriage. Dr. Mufti Allie Haroun Sheik (2010) has devoted a paragraph in his book about Islam and sex to sexual fantasies. He warns Muslims against cultivating such thoughts. He contends that one of the problems nowadays is 'for a man to imagine that the woman he is making love to is not his faithful wife…but the scantily clad model, revealing more flesh than cloth' (ibid.: 186). Impressions like this can, he argues, lead to devastation, total ruin, resentment, hurt, destruction and separation (ibid.: 186–187). He concludes rather dramatically:

> Fantasy can never be the same as reality. This epidemic could create havoc in an otherwise peaceful and pleasant neighborhood. Marriages could collapse and homes broke when fantasies solely become instrumental in sexual gratification. Due to the exposure of all kinds of immoral filth and shamelessness in the form of films, videos, TV, plays, magazines, telephone lines and even newspapers, fantasy has become the common trend in modern times. This is completely forbidden and a major sin in Islam. It resembles adultery of the mind and heart (Haroun Sheik 2010: 188).

It is obvious that he sees much of contemporary symbolic production as threats to the possibility of constructing social cohesion in families and societies. His Islamic solution seems to be to put a ban on all sources that produce material for sexual fantasies since those 'pollute' the minds of pious Muslims in ways that may become catastrophic. The counsellor Dr. Abd Lateef Krauss Abdullah on OnIslam.net also sees pornography as a great problem for males. In an answer to a pious Muslim man who prefers porn to his wife, the counsellor says:

> You have opened the door to pornography and now you cannot close it. Pornography has become a major problem among the men in our community and we are getting questions in reference to it by the dozen. It is destroying marriages, families, and the lives of those indulging in it. On the surface it appears harmless because of our ignorance of psychology and how images – especially those of sex – get imprinted in our minds and create a suggestive effect on our *nafs* [Ego], stimulating a desire for something that is of course illicit.

The ambition to protect believers from profane inspiration of various kinds, is a common stance among religious fundamentalists of many creeds. For example, the representation of moral danger in the quote shows great similarities with attitudes found among Christian fundamentalists in the West. They also fear that 'the traditional family unit and the moral fabric of society' are at risk of breakdown because of pornography (Berger, et al. 1990: 31). Hence, 'moral persuasion' seems to be a common strategy among Christian, Jewish, and Hindu actors who practice a 'strong religion' (Almond, et al. 2003: 32, Carlbom 2003).

The same type of discussion is performed by religious specialists consulted by Islamonline.com, one of the most visited Islamic websites (Carlbom 2012, Sisler 2011, Svensson 2011). The *fatwa* department on this site has formulated what they call a 'ruling on sexual fantasies' as an answer to a worried letter from an anonymous Muslim woman. Her problem is that she has to fantasise about having sex with persons she does not know in order to 'feel satisfied', and she feels that this is a betrayal of her 'good and very religiously committed' husband. The woman is advised by the imam on Islamonline to avoid all external stimuli that can produce sexual ideas. The *fatwa* builds on a more complex argumentation. According to the imam on the website there is no harm in 'passing thoughts' of a sexual character; these are forgiven since 'they cannot be avoided' (IOL 2013). Sexual fantasies, however, become a problem when someone is 'dwelling on them,' and that means that a person will be called to account for them in front of God on Judgment Day (ibid.).

Furthermore, in order to convince the woman to let go of her behaviour, the Imam argues that sexual fantasies constitute a 'psychological disorder' if they dominate personal thinking to such an extent that someone cannot be sexually satisfied unless the fantasies are acted upon. There is also, according to the imam, a great risk that any person who frequently thinks about something develops a wish to fulfil the imaginations. Sexual fantasies, according to the imam, have their origin in so-called "kaafir lands"[1] where satellite channels send 'scenes of decadent societies,' and 'where there is no modesty and watching sex scenes is becoming a daily habit' (ibid.). This state of affairs, according to the imam, is 'obvious' for anyone who resides in such lands. In sum, the problem with sexual fantasies is that spouses will lose interest in one another (ibid.). Besides praying to God, the woman receives a *fatwa* suggesting different measures:

> Completely avoid everything that may provoke such fantasies, such as haram movies and TV shows which are shown on satellite TV, as well as avoiding reading stories that generate such fantasies. Focus on the present enjoyment instead of that which is absent. [...]. If each spouse focuses on the attractions of the other, they will not be distracted by fantasies of other things. Consult psychologists. There is nothing wrong with you going to a female psychologist or family doctor and ask her for advice (ibid.).

The main advice is that the woman should avoid all sources that stimulate sexual imagination. This advice is in line with how Mufti Haroun Sheik, cited above, reasons. Both of these sources give examples of how actors in the Islamic movement try to convince Muslims in general of the importance of following certain interpretations of Islam. Sexual fantasies, especially those coming from various

1 "Kaafir lands" is an Islamic expression used to denote lands or places dominated by unbelievers, generally people who do not believe in or practice Islamic dogma. For Islamic activists the Western world is such a place.

commercial media, are experienced as a threat to the wellbeing of pious Muslims individuals, their families, and the social order of society.

As pointed out above, my informant argued, with reference to Yusuf al-Qaradawi, that oral sex is an accepted sexual act when practiced with a legally wedded spouse. There are also those Islamic activists, however, who regard this sexual activity as morally disgraceful. For instance, this QA sequence took place at the Swedish website fatwarådet.se, a site dominated by a conservative religious outlook:

> *Question*: What is the verdict for the practice some call 'oral sex'?
> *Answer*: Allah has not allowed sexual relations [oral sex] for the man with his wife's mouth, never!
>
> And no one walks on this road except the one lacking moral character, even if he belongs to the Muslims, and it is also the case that they [Muslims] has taken this (habit) from non-believers by watching *pornographic movies* [my emphasis]. So it is obligatory for the Muslim woman to not allow her husband to do this.
> By: Shaykh 'Ubayd al-Jâbiri Hafidhahullâh

As we can see, this QA sequence establishes an associative connection between oral sex and pornography, which is said to be a habit among non-believers in pornographic movies, and therefore the Muslim woman is morally obliged to avoid the practice with her husband. The same stance towards films and other sexual representations is formulated by Ruqaiyyah Waris Maqsood (2000: 62) in the handbook *The Muslim Marriage Guide*. Several of her marriage norms are directed towards Muslim men and her angle is that sexual fantasies shown in porn movies are unrealistic and shocking for women. She argues that:

> Sexy and pornographic films are haram for Muslims. They are in fact not only degrading but dangerous, because they lead men to want and fantasize over very unrealistic sex. The women are actresses – their reaction to the men is not realistic at all but faked in order to please them. Many women would either feel nothing if these practices were indulged in, or would be shocked and upset (Maqsood 2000: 62).

In sum, the quotes above represent sexual fantasies and pornography as moral problems that should be dealt with in one way or the other. However, some Islamic activists also use concepts and terms from science when they advise Muslims to refrain from watching pornographic films. For example, the Swedish webpage Islamguiden.se argues that watching porn movies has the same effect on the brain as cocaine since it 'releases great amounts of dopamine which results in experiencing a "high", often leading to addiction' (Ghilan 2014). Porn scenes are allegedly uploaded in the brain's long-term memory and the 'dopamine reinforces the new connections with newly acquired sexual tastes, and the next thing taking place is the man asking his wife to engage in a sexual fantasy that was downloaded into his subconscious' (ibid.). Furthermore, since it is sexual fantasies from porn that reinforce the production of dopamine, the man will experience disappointment in sexual encounters with his own wife because this 'only one woman doesn't sound, act, or look the same as the ones downloaded into his mind' (ibid.).

Therapeutic solution

Obviously, some activists ground their Islamic perspective in the psychological discourse of 'porn addiction'. For instance, Heba Kotb (2004), perhaps the most famous Islamic sexologist in the Arab world, argues that pornography is 'absolutely Haram' (ibid.: 33). This is so, according to her, because it goes against what God mediated to humans as formulated in the Koran (24: 32, 32). Among other things, here it is argued that 'believing women…should lower their gaze and guard their chastity that they should not display their beauty and ornaments except what ordinarily appear thereof' (ibid.). Hence, for Kotb, to watch porn movies is to transgress an important moral boundary set up by Islam. Her main concern, however, is for 'those that have sadly fallen into pornography addiction' (ibid.). With inspiration from Alcoholics Anonymous she presents an Islamically grounded 12–step model in order to cure the addiction. The list emphasises that the solution should be about a complete surrender to God (ibid.). Kotb talks about porn addiction in general medical terms. However, it seems as though this discourse also has been picked up by Muslim persons who use it to diagnose themselves.

For instance, a man named Haythm directed a question to a counsellor on OnIslam.net, saying that 'my problem is that I am addicted to porn sites, masturbation for a long time now'. He has 'tried to give up many times in many ways', but has realised that 'I have sexual problems'. In the answer, the counsellor emphasises that Haythm is one of many who suffer from porn addiction and that this has serious consequences: 'Sexually addicted individuals will withdraw from their social relationships' and 'deny' their problems, as the counsellor formulates it. Haythm is told that if he continues doing this, it will 'affect your future relation with your wife' who will be 'hurt' and 'upset'. The counsellor suggests that he have his 'situation evaluated further by a professional therapist or counsellor'. Indeed, it seems as though the counsellor downplays a purely Islamic solution to Haythms online behaviour.

However, Islamic activists having the ambition to socialise Muslims into a certain Islamic normative thinking in regard to sexual fantasies should not be conflated with actually succeeding in doing so. During anthropological fieldwork in Cairo, Egypt, Maria Malmström (2009: 150–151) interviewed young Muslim women who watched pornographic movies in order to learn more about sex before they became involved in marriage. According to Malmström, the women did not regard watching the movies as a sensitive issue. On the contrary, 'they enjoyed watching movies like these and found them instructive' (ibid.: 150). She found that women of various ages took part of pornography from satellite TV and video movies. Also, men gathered to watch pornographic movies. Furthermore, John Borneman (2011: 237–239) has reported how young Syrian men gather to watch Internet porn. In a statistical study conducted in Indonesia, a Muslim majority country with strict anti-pornography laws, it was found that young men and women accept and consume pornography with the same frequency as in 'more sexually liberal and less religious countries with no or very few laws on pornography' (Hald & Mulya 2013: 991). These examples show the importance of making a distinction between what ordinary Muslims do and what Islamists want them to do, namely avoid all stimuli that can produce sexual fantasies in order to end up in Paradise.

Paradise and sex

The general cosmological reasoning among pious Muslims is that they live earthly life thinking of how to reach a pornotopic paradise and avoid a hell full of pain and suffering. Muslims often describe Islam metaphorically as the 'path' one must take in order to reach Paradise and evade the eternal fires of Hell. The general meaning of this is that a Muslim needs to follow the moral code of the Koran and the Hadiths in order to be assured a place in Paradise (see Figure 1).[2] Most pious Muslims live by these ideas and believe in the consequences that follow from not walking the straight path of Islam. As the Islamic sexologist Heba Kotb (2004: 36) formulates it: 'Your eyes will testify about what you looked at on the Day of Judgment. Remember that Allah is always watching. He is most Just and Merciful, and He rewards us for the good and punishes us for the bad we do'. Islamic activists and other pious Muslims operate within a quite simple cosmological model of the universe that can be illustrated like this:

2 The main source for pious Muslim practice is the Koran, and a second is the collection of empirical examples from the life of Prophet Muhammed in the Hadiths. These can be found in books put together by religious specialists.

Fig. 1

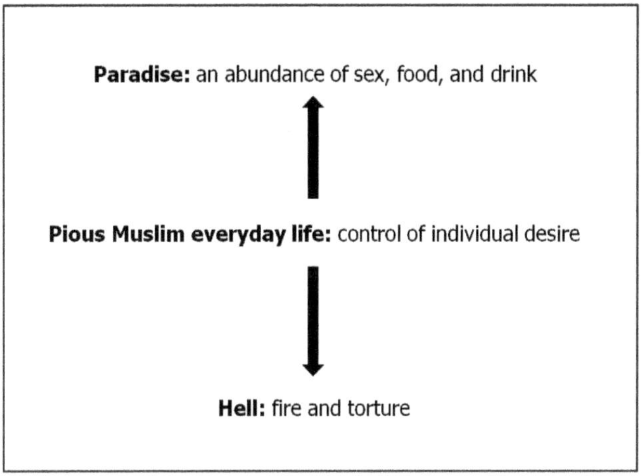

It is well known that Islamists have been arguing for the importance of Muslims (and non-Muslim others) to Islamise their conduct in order to construct a personal and social order that will lead them to the gates of Paradise. Muslims may differ, however, in their interpretations of exactly how Islamic dogma ought to be understood if one has the ambition to reach Paradise (Carlbom 2003, 2012). This is often expressed in terms of where to draw boundaries between *halal* and *haram* actions. For example, ideologically extreme Islamists generally express more strict boundaries for female behaviour than do mainstream Muslims (Carlbom 2012).

The importance for individual Muslims to follow Islam's straight path is well captured in Lena Gerholm's (2003) study of how men in Stockholm discipline their sexual desires by organising their minds and hearts according to Islamic ideas and ideals. The men in the study found themselves in a social situation where they had to cope with sexual feelings produced by Swedish women who are not, in comparison with pious Muslim women, 'oriented to helping men control their sexual desire' (ibid.: 409). Gerholm argues that the men used various Islamically informed strategies in order to avoid the frustration that came along with experiences of sexual desire. As an example, one of the men persuaded a Swedish woman to become his second wife in order to make their sexual union legal (ibid.: 408–409). To arrange a polygamous marriage was one way to control sexual desire and channel feelings into a morally accepted relationship, which would make it possible to arrive in Paradise on Judgment Day (ibid.: 408). This seems to be, as shown by Katherine Charsley and Anika Liversage (2013), a rather common strategy among Muslim men in Europe.

Most pious Muslims believe that Paradise is a fantastic place, which will bring all kinds of rewards for those who have followed the path of Islam. For example, on the webpage Islamguiden.se, Paradise is described in extraordinary terms as a land where true believers will not suffer from anything that made social life on earth troublesome. 'Thus', an anonymous writer asks on the webpage, 'for what reasons do we follow the laws of Allah?' The answer, according to the same writer, is to get access to this unknown place, characterised by bright lights, nice plants, exalted palaces, rivers, fruit, beautiful wives, an abundance of clothes, eternal and shining happiness, beautiful and high houses (ibid.).

Another quote from the webpage describes paradise as a place where Muslims will find 'bricks in gold and silver, mortar of savoury musk, small stones of pearls and sapphire, and earth of saffron', and 'whoever person entering this will be filled with joy and will never again feel unhappy' (ibid.). A pious Muslim man who has retired from paid work argued, during a conversation with me about religion and politics, that 'Paradise is our dream…we believe that real life starts in Paradise'. He described it as a 'place free of envy, with flowers, pure water, olives, figs and beautiful girls, extremely beautiful girls'. As the Swedish imam quoted above formulates it:

> Sexual desire is without doubt a powerful motivation for humans to live as healthily as possible. Besides that, sex is also one of the good things humans can experience and therefore it is also an enjoyable reward. In the context of all those verses and hadiths that talk about paradise, sexuality plays a minor but relevant role. Representations of Paradise [in the Koran] signify different dimensions of human enjoyment. The enjoyment of the eye by looking at nature, the enjoyment of the stomach by eating and drinking, and sexual enjoyment. However, the greatest enjoyment is the spiritual enjoyment of peace of mind, happiness and the presence of God. To watch God is traditionally seen as the highest reward and enjoyment in Paradise.

An important aspect of narratives of Islamic paradise is, according to Aziz al-Azmeh (1995), its sensual character in all senses of the word. However, it is especially so in terms of sexuality. Al-Azmeh describes men as particularly sexually potent:

> The sexual capacity of every man in Paradise is the equal to that of one hundred men of the world, capable of deflowering and copulating with one hundred virgins every day, an optimal potency which is a consummate maximum like the impeccable expression in terms of prophets that was encountered above – indeed, Solomon was credited with the libido of one hundred men while Muhammad, manifestly well provided, only had that of thirty to forty men (1995: 223).

The fantasy of extreme sexual potency for those men that are accepted by God into Paradise is also described by Abdelwahab Bouhdiba (2004: 76) in his famous book about Islam and sexuality. Indeed, his description of this potency emphasises that 'the penis of the Chosen One never slackens (see also al-Azmeh 1995: 225), the erection is eternal' and 'to each coitus corresponds a pleasure, a delicious sensation, so incredible in this vile world that if one experienced it one would faint' (ibid.: 76). Every climax, as Bouhdiba puts it, 'lasts for twenty-four years' (ibid.: 75). Consequently, no human woman would be likely to stand up to the sexual activity of this hyper-virile type of man.

Therefore, in Paradise, it is beings called *houris* that take care of the sexual satisfaction of the 'chosen one'. In Paradise every man will be married with the wives he married on earth and with 70 (or 72) *houris* which in most descriptions are characterised as super-feminine creatures with bodies made of saffron, musk, amber, and camphor and with hair of raw silk (ibid.: 75). *Houris* have the name of their husband written on their breasts and on each arm they wear ten gold bracelets (ibid.). Their eyes are beautiful and their breasts 'are the small breasts of pubescent girls in early adolescence, and which conform to the charms of Aisha which the Prophet so admired' (al-Azmeh 1995: 226). Of course, 'all the *houris* are in love with their husbands', as Bouhdiba points out (ibid.: 75). They are also described as creatures that can reconstruct their virginity over and over again. Hence, 'they are recursively virginal, in keeping with the spectacular consummateness of paradisical physiology' (al-Azmeh 1995: 225).

Thus, the Islamic paradise seems to be a profoundly androcentric place in the sense that it is made up only for male sexual pleasure. There is an awareness of this among Islamists active in Europe, something that can be seen in their public representations of paradise. For instance, on the webpage *Islam svarar* (Islam answers) an anonymous Muslim woman asks why the Koran does not mention anything about (sensual) rewards in Paradise for pious Muslim women. In the answer, it is emphasised that the message of the Koran is directed to both men and women. 'Allah turns', as it is argued in the answer, 'to both men and women… and all rules that concern men also concern women as long as there is no established evidence to the contrary, as for example when it is about Jihad (to fight for Islam), menstruation, parenthood, etcetera' (ibid.). Hence, 'all men and women will be treated as equals in terms of rewards…men and women who always thinks of God…God will forgive them their sins and reward them' (ibid.). As far as I know, however, there are no detailed descriptions available of exactly what kind of sexual pleasures women will enjoy in Paradise if they have lived a pious life on earth. One of my Muslim informants, a pious man who has worked as an Islamic counselor for many years, believes that 'all will be happy in Paradise' and that 'earthly wives will become queens over the houris'; a point also made by the islamologist Jonas Svensson (2010: 87) in a discussion about *fatwas* and Muslim women in Paradise.

The conceptions of Islamic paradise – especially the idea of 70 *houris* – are sometimes lifted up as a sensational aspect of Islam by Westerners, and used as an example of Islam's fixation with sexuality. Nerina Rustomji (2007: 90) argues that the idea of the *houris* is part of a discourse in the West that is used in order to represent Muslims as irrational. An imam and informant of mine seems implicitly to relate to this Western stereotype when he downplays the idea of sex in Paradise by saying that:

> to make the inference, from the fact that the Koran talks about sexual pleasure in Paradise, that it is only the idea of sex that motivates Muslim men to practice Islam, is a grave mistake. From such a logic it is possible to argue that they are more motivated by the image of beautiful trees than beautiful women, since the gardens are mentioned more times [in the Koran].

We can also see, however (even though Islamic narratives of paradise seem to have changed through history), that fantasies of Paradise are of importance for individual Muslims who dream of getting there after having practiced Islamic dogma in the best possible way. In fact, fantasies about Paradise and the awaiting *houris* seem to be an important motivational factor for activists that conduct terror in the name of Islam. For instance, the letter of instructions from Muhammad Atta to his fellow perpetrators on September 11, 2001, reminded of the *houris* in paradise:

> Do not seem confused or show signs of nervous tension. Be happy, optimistic, calm because you are hedding [sic] for a deed that God loves and will accept. It will be the day, God willing, you *spend with the women of Paradise*. Smile in the face of hardship young man/For you are hedding [sic] toward eternal Paradise (ibid.: 79, my emphasis).

A common argument, particularly from non-violent Islamic activists but also from Western scholars, is that Islamist political violence has got nothing to do with Islam. A better way to argue is to say that militant Islamists use well-established Islamic ideas for their own political purposes. Thus, politically radical activists interpret the use of violence in a different way than many other Muslims and Islamists who instead emphasise that *dawa* is the right method to use in order to discipline individual desire.

Summary

Basically, sexual fantasies inspired by pornography are understood as a moral problem for Islamic activists. They seem to have no problem with so-called passing sexual fantasies, but fear that pornography may become a mechanism that negatively influences a person's mind, breaks down the family and, in the long run, a whole society. From a religious perspective Islamic activists, just as

Christian fundamentalists, regard it as a sin to watch pictures where naked bodies have sex. Besides that, some of the activists also use ideas from psychological discourse when they warn of the dangers of pornography and sexual fantasies. The term 'addiction' summarises what this is all about. Indeed, the activists fear that pornography will produce the same problems for the brain as narcotic drugs, such as for example cocaine.

When it comes to fantasies about sex in Paradise, I have found no evidence that these have the status of sexual fantasies. The representation of Paradise as a place where sexual desire will be more than satisfied is a motivating factor for pious Muslims to live a morally righteous life on earth. If Muslims can control their sexual desire in a certain way (practice it within the boundaries of a heterosexual marriage) they redouble their chances that God will place them in the pornotopia of Paradise rather than in Hell on Judgment Day. In sum, paradoxically, a very lustful fantasy about unlimited sex is the motivating force behind the ambition to block out all sexual fantasies.

References

Ahrold, T.K., et.al (2011) 'The relationship among sexual attitudes, sexual fantasy, and religiosity'. *Archives of Sexual Behavior* 40: 619–630.

Al-Azmeh, A. (1995) 'Rhetoric for the senses: A consideration of Muslim Paradise narratives'. *Journal of Arabic Literature* 26: 215–231.

Almond, G.A., Appleby, R. S. & Siwan, E. (2003) *Strong Religion, The Rise of Fundamentalisms around the World*. Chicago: University of Chicago Press.

Berger, R.T., Searles, P.& Cottle, C.E. (1990) 'Ideological contours of the contemporary pornography debate: divisions and alliances'. *Frontiers: A Journal of Women Studies* 11(2–3): 30–38.

Bouhdiba, A. (2008 [1975]) *Sexuality in Islam*. New York: Routledge.

Borneman, J. (2011) 'Daydreaming, intimacy, and the intersubjective third in fieldwork encounters in Syria'. *American Ethnologist* 38(2): 234–248.

Carlbom, A. (2012) 'Islamisk sexualrådgivning – ett globalt fenomen'. In S.A. Månsson and L. Plantin (eds) *Sexualitetsstudier*. Malmö: Liber.

Carlbom, A. (2003) *The Imagined versus the Real Other*. PhD Dissertation. Lund: Department of Sociology.

Charsley, K. & Liversage, A. (2013) 'Transforming polygamy: migration, transnationalism and multiple marriages among Muslim minorities'. *Global Networks* 13: 60–78.

Clark, J. (2004) 'The conditions of Islamist moderation: unpacking cross-ideological cooperation in Jordan'. *International Journal of Middle East Studies* 38: 539–560.

Durkheim, E (2002 [1912]) *The Elementary Forms of Religious Life*. London: Blackwell Publishing.

Eickelman, D.F. & Piscatori, J. (1996) *Muslim Politics*. New Jersey: Princeton University Press.

Geertz, C. (2002 [1973]) 'Religion as a cultural system'. In M. Lambek (ed) *A Reader in the Anthropology of Religion*. London: Blackwell Publishing.

Gerholm, L. (2003) 'Overcoming temptation: on masculinity and sexuality among Muslims in Stockholm'. *Global Networks* 3: 401–416.

Ghilan, M. (2014) *How Watching Pornography Changes the Brain*. Downloaded from Islamguiden.se, April, 2014.

Hald, G.M. & Mulya, T.W. (2013) 'Pornography consumption and non-marital sexual behavior in a sample of young Indonesian university students'. *Culture, Health & Sexuality* 15(8): 981–996.

Haroun Sheik, A. (2010) *Sexual Issues in Modern Era and Its Solution in Islam*. New Delhi: Adam Publishers & Distributors.

Inglehart, R. & P. Norris, P. (2003) 'The true clash of civilizations'. *Foreign Policy* 135: 62–70.

Kotb, H. (2004) *Sexuality in Islam*. Doctoral diss., Maimonides University.

Malmström, M. (2009) *Just Like Couscous: Gender, Agency and the Politics of Female Circumcision in Cairo*. Doctoral diss., Gothenburg: School of Global Studies.

Ouis, P. (2009) 'The real clash of culture? Islamic sexual moralism in liberal Sweden'. *Socialvetenskaplig tidskrift* 3–4: 350–369.

Ramadan, T. (2002) 'Europeanization of Islam or Islamization of Europe'. In S.T. Hunter (ed) *Islam, Europe's Second Religion*. London: Praeger.

Rustomji, N. (2007) 'American visions of the Houri'. *The Muslim World* 97: 79–92.

Searl, J, (1996) *The Construction of Social Reality*. New York: Penguin Books.

Sisler, V. (2011) 'Cyber counselors'. *Information, Communication & Society* 14(8): 1136–1159.

Svensson, J. (2011) 'Kättja, kontroll och kontroverser: Muslimska perspektiv på sex'. *Sex, för guds skull*. Lund: Studentlitteratur.

Charlotta Carlström

Fantasies Becoming Practice: BDSM as Ritual

Introduction

> SM shows us how to turn even our "worst" fantasies into pleasures for both of us so we know that what is inside us is okay (Moser & Madeson 1996: 140).

BDSM, i.e. Bondage and Discipline, Dominance and Submission, and Sadism and Masochism (sadomasochism) is an acronym used to describe a variety of sexual behaviours including an implicit or explicit erotic power exchange. In this chapter, I intend to demonstrate that the role of fantasies is a fruitful starting point for an analysis of BDSM practices. The BDSM scene is built on fantasies, daydreams, thoughts and feelings and the practice stresses taboos, boundaries, prohibitions, and social norms. In interviews with people who define themselves as BDSM practitioners, the respondents highlight the impact of fantasies in their encounters.[1] They talk about fantasies that eroticise dominance and submission as a reason why they became involved in BDSM. I will initially provide a short background to BDSM, and continue with a discussion about how gender plays into BDSM practices. Furthermore, how can the relationship between fantasy and reality be described? How do taboo plays relate to power? Finally, I will discuss why people want to live out fantasies, in a BDSM context. What kind of purposes do the realisation and staging of these fantasies fulfil? The BDSM context enables a safe and secure place for staging and living out fantasies. I will suggest that, for many practitioners, living out fantasies is of central importance in life, comparable to spirituality and rituals in non-Western tribes and cultures.

Background

The literary depiction of sadomasochism has a long and broad history with literature found from both Eastern and Western civilizations. As far as scholarly

---

1 The chapter is based on empirical data derived from the author's ongoing research project. Ethnographic fieldwork was conducted in 2012–2013 within several BDSM communities in Sweden.

work, however, there is a shorter history (Westerfelhaus 2007). Psychoanalyst Richard von Krafft-Ebing coined the terms sadism and masochism in the late 1800s, in his famous book *Psychopathia Sexualis*. The term sadism is derived from Marquis de Sade, a French nobleman and writer whose books equate cruelty, pain, and violence with sexual pleasure. The term masochism is derived from the name of Leopold von Sacher-Masoch, whose novel *Venus in Furs* reflected his own experiences of pain, humiliation, and sexual pleasure. Sigmund Freud brought together the two concepts into the term *sadomasochism*. Freud noticed that a person could experience pleasure from both receiving and inflicting pain; sadism and masochism were therefore, in his opinion, two sides of the same coin (Weinberg & Kamel 1983).

From being dominated by clinical and therapeutic perspectives, research has increasingly been conducted with a sociological and psychological orientation in which BDSM is mainly seen as a sexual behaviour that is culturally produced and dependent on a social context (see for example Langdridge & Barker 2007; Plante 2006; Taylor & Ussher 2001; Weinberg 2006). Anthropologist Paul Gebhard (1969) stressed the importance of realising that pain, per se, is not attractive to BDSM practitioners, unless it occurs in an arranged situation. BDSM, he argued, is best known as a symbolic, interactive form of social behaviour where the setting reminds one of a planned ritual or theatrical production. After Gebhard, social scientists continued to study BDSM, and during the 1970s sociological research of BDSM as a ritualistic and social behaviour progressed. At the same time, there was a development of political BDSM gatherings and organised BDSM cultures, for instance SAMOIS, a lesbian-feminist BDSM organisation based in San Francisco (Westerfelhaus, 2005).

Many practitioners describe a sexual identity development marked by internal conflicts and a lack of confidence and feelings of shame in connection to their BDSM fantasies. In the introduction to the now legendary work *Coming to Power*, edited and published by SAMOIS, Davis (1982: 7) wrote: 'S/M fantasies and S/M sex between feminist lesbians have been one of the most avoided topics of discussion in the movement. We've allowed it to remain a scary skeleton hidden in the corner of our otherwise carefully cleaned-up closet. Few of us have been able to admit to anyone our interest in S/M or have been able to talk about the content of our fantasies. Some of us could not even admit those fantasies to ourselves.'

Despite the central impact of fantasies, imagination, and desire in BDSM, previous research has focused little on fantasies, and even less on fantasies in relation to gender, which I focus on in the next section.

Gender and fantasy

> BDSM is all about fantasies and expectations. It's the two key points, and pleasure of course. But imagination and expectation are absolutely necessary... (A switch woman)

BDSM practitioners adopt either dominant, submissive, or switch roles. There are different terms used to describe these roles. A dominant can for example define her- or himself as top, master, mistress, dom, owner, dominatrix, or sadist. The submissive can call her- or himself bottom, slave, sub, owned, or masochist. If a person is interested in both roles, she or he is called switch. For some practitioners the roles are limited to sexual role play, while others adopt the roles 24/7. It is important, however, to note that the submissive partner is never completely helpless or powerless. Before any interaction takes place, reflective negotiations are entered into in order to ensure an equally pleasurable exchange. Gender is not the most important factor organising S/M sexuality. Instead, role identity largely determines sexual fantasy content and the location of sexual pleasure (see for example Yost 2007; Beckmann 2009) or, as Califia, a co-founder to SAMOIS, (1995: 147) stresses: 'S&M roles are not related to gender or sexual orientation or race or class. My own needs dictate which role I will adopt.' Gosselin, Wilson, and Barrett (1991) found that female S/M practitioners were more active, both in terms of fantasy and activity, than the women of the control group. The female S/M practitioners fantasised more often about sadomasochistic themes, impersonal themes (e.g. using sex toys), and exploratory themes than did the control group. Zurbriggen and Yost (2004) examined sexual fantasies and desire among 162 heterosexual men and women. They found gender differences in fantasies of dominance and submission, with men fantasising more about dominance and women more about submission. They also found that men mentioned the sexual pleasure and sexual desire of their partners as well as their own, while the women tended to only mention their own pleasure and not the desire and pleasure of their partner.

One of the questions addressed by researchers, theorists, and practitioners is whether the dominant has control over the submissive, or if it is the submissive who, through the need to live out various fantasies, puts the dominant through his or her paces. A paradox in BDSM is the expectation on the person acting dominant to fulfil the fantasies of the submissive. Some people use the expression 'topping from the bottom' which indicates a person who exercises power in the relationship, despite being in the 'bottom' position. A self-labelled submissive woman says:

> He is very good at ferreting out my fantasies and ideas and translating them into his own and that's basically what I'm looking for. I don't want to order a scenario, I want to be dominated. I sure want my partners to take responsibility for my fantasies and

> what I want to experience as well… but especially… I want to serve them, that's what´s turning me on, not that they should serve me.

Another person who defines herself as submissive says:

> I think I have shared a lot of my fantasies, but he does not remember. As I said at some point, a little ironically, maybe I could write a script for you. And he said, yes it would be great… [laughs]. But for me it's like… it would be no tension or element of surprise if I write down exactly what he should do and say.

There is a tension between the elements of surprise and the pre-agreed upon elements to be included in the exercise. Though consent is described as central in the practice, several respondents stress that not knowing what will happen during a session involves tangible feelings of excitement. They also emphasise that another important part of the practice is to extend one's own limits. This is consistent with Scott's (1980) conclusion in her ethnographic study of female dominant and male submissive couples. She noted that it was the transgression itself that was erotic to many of her informants. Part of the erotic thrill lay in the taboo of men submitting to dominant women. Sexual fantasies, and in particular BDSM fantasies, were earlier viewed, by practitioners as well as theorists and clinics, with shame and also as a symptom of psychological disturbance and sexual dissatisfaction. Nordling (2009) remarked that it is often associated with feelings of shame and taboo for masochistic men to live out fantasies of dominance and submission and, as Weiss (2011: 177), notes: 'A submissive man risks his masculinity'. The fact that they carry a great sense of shame and have difficulties finding women who want to dominate them may be one reason why these men are found among sex buyers. Previous studies show that approximately twelve per cent of men buying sex have practised BDSM in the role of submissive with a prostitute (Milrod 2010; Stein 1974). Stein (ibid) could see a high incidence of guilt and shame of having masochistic fantasies among the submissive male sex buyers, and the escorts eased the anxiety by teaching customers about masochism and by saying that other men have the same desires. O'Connell Davidson (1998) points out that these 'domination clients' turn to prostitutes to embody sexual fantasies that centre upon tensions surrounding gender identity, risk, and control. She declares that the risk of discovery heightens their sexual pleasure (this is further discussed in Månsson's chapter).

BDSM – where your dreams come true?

> Like the infant who realizes that it is capable of influencing the surrounding world, the adult who manages to create reality from fantasy has taken the first step in exploring the complexity of sexual experience (Bronski 2004[1991]: 63).

BDSM gives its adherents the opportunity to live out their fantasies. Fantasies can be described as the inner theatre of the mind, and serve to function as an escape from reality. BDSM practice appears to fall within what Goffman (1974) calls the 'theatrical frame' in which practitioners interact within a particular frame, collaboratively setting specific limits to the scene. This means that the participants 'frame' their behaviour by the use of social definitions, which gives the behaviour a specific contextual meaning. Several of the informants mention childhood fantasies as a reason for why they became involved in BDSM. A woman who defines herself as a dominant sadist says:

> It has always been there, though I did not have words for it. I have denied it as well. But that kind of fantasies have been around since I was twelve years old.

A man defining himself as a dominant explains:

> I had quite explicit fantasies about my elementary school teacher... she was very foxy. She was newly graduated and with a determined manner... but it didn't scare me. I remember thinking, what if I could get control over her. I had quite explicit fantasies about how I rapped her with a ruler. I'm thinking... oh my god... say I was only eight or nine years old!

Common fantasies include for example boss/secretary, mistress or master/slave, employer/servant, teacher/pupil, owner/horse or dog, and parent/child. It can also be fantasies that allude to humiliation, violence, and abuse. The framing of the interaction enables the participants to enjoy the moment without feeling guilt. Fantasies are part of culture and not unique, private, or idiosyncratic. Instead, many of our fantasies are quite common. To some extent, we share the same existence, the same images and experiences (Weinberg, 2006). One respondent who defines herself as switch says:

> Staging fantasies, I think, is about finding the same feeling in the play as you have in your head. It's about building a framework with help of BDSM fantasies.

Cohen and Taylor (2002[1976]: 113) describe a free zone or a *free area* as 'a place where we can act out our fantasies.' Although free areas may take quite different forms, they have one thing in common: they offer options and can function as escape routes. They symbolise the tension between the known and the unknown, the secure and the insecure, the conventional and the innovative. They also harbour the expectation that something extraordinary will happen. The BDSM scene can function as a free zone, as it allows for an exploration of boundaries, taboos, and strong emotions. A submissive respondent reflects upon this:

> Certain emotions can be quite strong, emotions which I never would get to experience anywhere else. To become really, really scared or really, really angry or really... to be

> provoked into that kind of feelings in a safe and controlled situation… It will never be like the real thing, but to be there, in that feeling… it's not just something that turns me on or something that I enjoy doing. It's also very… very intense and very… it's scary as well, but… it's interesting to explore those things together with someone I trust and who gets to know me very well. So it's kind of relationship building, as well. But what I'm experiencing is… well, that it happens on different… like sometimes, playing out a rape scene… it happens on several levels. It is clear, it's not as it would have been if it had actually happened without consent, but part of me can still be so damn scared. So fucking scared.

Non-consensual acts are material for many sexual fantasies. It is important to distinguish true rapes from rape fantasies. True rape is non-consensual, while a rape play is a sexual game negotiated by the participants to gain reciprocal pleasure. Often, the scenario is scripted and discussed in advance. In a rape play the participants can stop, modify, or change the interaction. They have chosen their partner, the situation, and the time. In a real rape situation there is no such control. The respondents have some form of collateral arrangements to be sure that the participants are comfortable with what is happening. Since words such as 'stop', 'no' and 'it hurts' could have central parts in the play, the participants use safety words, often names of colours. While admitting that staging a fantasy never will be like the 'real thing', the informant above describes very strong emotions during a BDSM session. Living out a fantasy consists of various levels where disclosure to the other partner is crucial. The person describes feelings of fear and anger during the session, which occur although there is consent and the session can be stopped anytime. As described in the quote above, BDSM can be seen as a free zone and function as an alibi, allowing practitioners to explore and play with feelings and taboos in ways that would be difficult or impossible outside the free zone. However, in some situations, the consent and the communication around consent become complex and ambiguous, for example when it comes to challenging or transgressing boundaries, which is a central dimension of BDSM. Often it is the dominant trying to get the submissive to transgress his or her own limits. A woman defining herself as submissive says:

> He was into rape play and lending, at times he wanted to lend me to other men. It was a bit difficult for me. But it happened that we did it anyway. And it was also an expression of my… extreme submissiveness, I can see in retrospect. I did it even though I thought it was pretty tough.

Here the complexity of consent is clear. The woman describes how she accepted doing something that she had difficulty performing and sees it as an expression of her extreme submissiveness. It is also obvious that pride is an important factor.

Many of the submissive informants point out proudly that they never have had to use a stop word.

Playing with taboos

> My fantasies can be completely bizarre; sometimes I fantasise about having group sex with tiger avatars [laughter]… it's totally bizarre. That is nothing that I would like to play out, though.

This fantasy, told by a female switch, raises many questions. Is it preferable or even possible to act out all sorts of BDSM fantasies? Are there some fantasies that should remain just fantasies? And if so, where are the limits? I will briefly discuss the intersections between private and political, self-pleasure and social structures. Sexuality has a history of being encumbered with guilt, shame, fear, and anxiety, as well as taboos, both in words and in actions. Could it be, as Cohen and Tayler (2002[1976]: 97) suggest, that '[t]he taboos on the expression of fantasy – like the many other repressions and prohibitions of our civilization – are gigantic frauds, unnecessary mystifications'? Within BDSM, there are different forms of dominance plays, which allude to traditional power relations and hierarchies such as young and old, black and white, slave and master, animals and humans, etc. Taboo scenes in BDSM include race plays, enactments of childhood traumas, and age plays. The relationship between what was originally a trauma and a BDSM reproduction of the trauma in a play scene has occupied the debates about sexuality and power. Radical feminists have claimed that the power dynamics played out in BDSM are reproductions of overall patriarchal power structures (see for example MacKinnon 1989 and Dworkin 1981). According to Weiss (2011: 145), BDSM plays with real power to create distinct scenes and 'these scenes draw on socially meaningful, and powerful, historical relations of inequality, the same "regulatory ideals" that performatively produce subjects and, at the same time, reproduce social norms'. How can we understand that some individuals gain satisfaction from being positioned in the role of a racial subordinate and victim? When discussed with practitioners, it becomes clear that people do think about these issues. A male dominant says:

> The thing is, different sorts of fantasies can turn you on… slave/owner is primary, and the dependent positions. Erm… Vulnerability is appealing of course, as well as absolute power, but slave or Nazi symbolism is a bit dangerous. I think that's so… there's so many other connotations… vulnerability is something beautiful. But this is not… no… not that kind of stuff.

Like the respondent above, many practitioners' reflections could be described as a dichotomy between social responsibility and the allure of the taboo and forbidden. Kantrowitz (2004), writing from the perspective of being Jewish and a BDSM practitioner, discusses the swastika as an erotic symbol. He stresses that for many people the symbol carries the 'stigma of the forbidden' (p. 197), a taboo that makes it all the more attractive to those who perceive themselves as sexual outlaws. For himself, though, it represents: 'The ultimate horrors of anti-Semitism and homophobia, a reminder that had I been born […] in a different place […] I would have been one of those babies tossed into an already-crowded gas chamber (ibid.: 199). Further, he discusses the complex phenomenon of gay Jews taking part in Nazi fantasies and plays. He argues that the easy conclusion is that these people are victims of self-hatred, identifying with their oppressors in a silent statement of inferiority as Jews and gays. To fantasise about Nazis is equivalent to ignoring the sane limits of BDSM and to court destruction, according to Kantrowitz (ibid.). During my interviews, the respondents often expressed ambivalence about race and Nazi play and reflected on the dichotomy between morality/social responsibility and excitement/the allure of the forbidden. A female switch says:

> I can understand the arousal and excitement about using Nazi uniforms. They were designed by Hugo Boss and are very good-looking. I can understand that the power play makes people aroused, but there are other ways to make it, you do not have to do exactly 'that'.[2]

Likewise, a woman defining herself as submissive tells me:

> Yes, Nazi themes are something that I have encountered within the BDSM community… but to explore things like that… maybe you can liken it to exploring your own fears.

Lopez and Godard (2013) emphasise that for those involved in Nazi uniform role play, the favoured outcome is to be perceived as fearful and evil and a Nazi uniform facilitates this performance. In interviews, when discussing taboo play, the informants easily slip from one into another form of role play. Different taboo plays have many common denominators and power shift is the most primary. Fantasising and staging fantasies enable different forms of power relations to be explored. Another form of taboo play is age play. The roles in sexual age play are often the same as roles in everyday life. For example, role playing can include themes of teacher/student, daddy/daughter, mother/son, daddy/son,

---

2 According to Timm (1999), Hugo Boss did not actually design the SS uniforms but manufactured them. The Hugo Boss clothing factory in the 20th was not a fashion company. It was a manufacturing plant that produced uniforms for the German armed forces and the National Socialist institutions, including the SS, SA and Hitler Youth.

mother/daughter, and coach/player. One female informant describes the role play as follows:

> He can say things like… uh… "Now, you show how to serve your dad", and I am supposed to do things with my mouth or hands.
>
> [I ask]: Why daddy/daughter?
>
> Mm… uh… to me, it gives an extra taboo… It's very taboo and very emotive, I've thought a lot about this in psychological terms… somehow… well… I've been thinking about this… since we have learned in my education that children in general often have both love feelings and sexual feelings toward their parents, and that somehow… I don't know… some kind of exploration of such feelings. Now I am being very psychological which I don't know if I should be. But it's just something I've been thinking about a lot.

Sexual feelings and actions between parents and children are associated with strong taboos. The woman quoted above continues by saying that the father/daughter games have become a strong part of the relationship between her and her master, as the BDSM scene provides a safe place to explore these kinds of feelings. Consenting adult role playing explores, by drawing on meanings surrounding power and abuse, emotional states from childhood, which also happens to be pleasurable to the participants in a sexual context. In a study of BDSM services within prostitution (Carlström unpublished), age play often had a central role in the encounter with a sex seller. The extract below is a letter, written by a man defining himself as masochist, addressed to a sex seller providing BDSM services (ibid.). It is a description of a role play with a mother/son theme, which he wants to experience during the encounter:

> I come into the room: She cries and whimpers with pleasure: "Now you have been disobedient again. But I will teach you how to obey". She presses me down on the floor. She puts her foot on my neck and holds me firmly while she pulls down my pants. She says: "Now you will submit" and she starts whipping me. I scream and cry. She says: "Do you obey me"? Finally I whimper: "Yes, yes I promise". She says: "Now let's see if you have learned how to obey. Crawl over here and lick my feet". I obey and lick her foot. She laughs triumphantly and puts her foot on my neck and says: "Never forget that your place is under my foot".
>
> This is a role play to simulate how my mother subdued me. I hope it will relieve my feelings from when I was subdued and thereby let me become free from them.

The story is interesting in several ways. His willingness to meet with an escort can be seen in the light of the concept 'self-medication'. He wants to relieve the feelings he had when he was subdued by his mother and hopes to get rid of them by recreating the scenario at a symbolic level. In this way, he creates a new meaning of a previous abusive situation through BDSM play. Barker, et al. (2007: 197) discuss the 'healing narrative' of BDSM and stress that there is a narrative of BDSM as a safe place to explore issues that traditionally have been brought to therapy and counselling. If we return to Goffman's (1974) 'theatrical frame', we can see that practitioners give their behaviour a specific contextual and often symbolised meaning, which can transform an unpleasant activity into a pleasurable one. One female respondent who explores different sorts of role play, for example father-daughter play, tells me:

> One might say that taboo plays are a way to explore one's own fears, what is it that seems so dangerous, and is it really that dangerous? And what's in it that is so dangerous in that case?

This quote illustrates how BDSM may provide a subversive freedom in which some people gain control over a trauma by eroticising it. I suggest that living out fantasies and playing with taboos imply a complicated and complex chain of symbolism that affects overall perspectives on gender, ethnicity, oppression, and power. Weiss (2011) is critical of what she sees as a general notion among both practitioners and theorists, that BDSM is a cross-subversive culture which exists outside social relationships, norms, and hierarchies. Instead, she argues, to get an understanding of the complexity of BDSM we must explore how BDSM acts within larger social systems of power. A female BDSM practitioner reflects upon this:

> The problem is when you don't communicate. As in 24/7 relationships where the man is in power and the woman takes care of the household. They might say: playing a 1950s household turns us on, so it's okay. But there might be children who grow up in such households who don't understand that it's a sexual game between mum and dad and then… it becomes very difficult… and there are many people who don't take responsibility.

There are no fixed power positions in BDSM, but they must be agreed on. As the practice can interfere with and allows for a loosening of heteronormativity, I suggest that BDSM can be described as what Butler (2007[1990]) calls a subversive activity. Yet, BDSM is not practised in a vacuum, beyond structural inequalities of gender, class, race/ethnicity, and sexuality; individual performance can only exist and operate within these frameworks. Therefore, I agree with Weiss (2011) when she stresses that BDSM can produce a new radical and subversive sexual practice, but that simultaneously it can reproduce unequal social relations and hierarchies, as the practitioner reflects upon in the quote above. Further, BDSM activity differs from other sexual activities by being organised in an environment of shared rules, values, norms, and techniques to which initiated people have to relate.

Personal fantasies become collective rituals

Social gatherings in the BDSM scene are based on interaction, collective actions, rituals, tools with symbolic values, and clear boundaries against outsiders. The community offers to the individual a deeper meaning, a sense of security, and a sense of belonging. Several of the interviewed practitioners compared BDSM to a spiritual experience, and argued that participating in BDSM can serve the same purpose as religious rituals. During interviews, some practitioners discussed BDSM practice in relation to the Christian faith. Several have backgrounds in a Christian church and some are still active in the church. A submissive practitioner, who has left the church and the Christian faith, says:

> It's pretty funny how well it marries, BDSM and the Christian faith. And… well… I don't know… it attracts me a lot, to leave myself into someone else's hands, to worship, to have a God who knows better and who has the control and holds me in his hands… There are so many parallels to draw… to be submissive, as in my case, and the Christian faith… Practicing BDSM is something I do because it fulfils a purpose for me… To come to God and be loved for who I am, with all my faults and defects… It can be compared to BDSM, it is a sexuality that has been shameful for ages and then suddenly one comes to a context where… I can be exactly who I am and show all aspects of myself.

This informant draws several parallels between experiences of BDSM and spiritual experiences. The practice is based on emotional interaction; the person speaks about handing oneself over into someone else's hands, letting go of control where the emotions of the experience are central. BDSM is meaning-making, which becomes clear when the person says: 'It's something I do because it fulfils a purpose for me'. Finally, the quote above shows the importance of connectedness in a BDSM community, which can be compared to the community in a religious association. The sense of belonging plays a central role, both among BDSM practitioners and in Christian communities. Another aspect that BDSM, religion, and spirituality have in common is rituals. Rituals can be viewed as a form of realising individual fantasies and transforming them into collective emotional energy and myths. They can also function as ways to create collective feelings and experiences of ecstasy and euphoria (Westerfelhaus 2012). Westerfelhaus (ibid.) points out that Western psychiatry has often sought to describe S/M as a psychiatric disorder when better understanding would be gained by considering BDSM rituals and symbols as a sort of expansion of consciousness. The term 'peak experience' was formed by psychologist Abraham Maslow in his work *Religions, Values, and Peak Experiences* (1964) and aims to describe a transpersonal, ecstatic, and euphoric state. In interviews with practitioners, BDSM play is described in powerful terms, showing similarities to the description of a 'peak experience'. A submissive woman says:

> Yeah, it's an adrenaline rush and, at the same time, what can I say?… rushing hormones give pleasure and security and so forth, it gives you the most intense hormone cocktail which makes you very high.

The practitioners often characterised experiences of BDSM as possessing a mystical, spiritual, or religious essence. The sociologist Randall Collins (2005: 149) forms a theory of interactional rituals, based on Durkheim's religious theory. He raises the question: 'What determines which interactional rituals an individual will join rather than some other rituals and why some individuals develop more of a taste for ritual solidarity than other persons?' He argues that individuals who have taken part in successful interaction rituals develop a taste for more ritual solidarity and are motivated to repeat the practice. Successful interaction rituals give individuals both emotional energy and membership symbols. Myers (1983) notes that the individual and group dynamics of rites de passage, rituals, and initiatory practices in traditional non-Western cultures are strikingly similar to those of the BDSM community. For example, tattoos and piercings are common both in BDSM and in traditional non-Western cultures. A dominant man describes what he called a ceremony of love:

> We put on pretty rough nipple rings […] the symbolic act felt very important […] it symbolised her bond to me. There is some kind of ownership… an agreement, and a symbol of our relationship. There is a very strong act of love, I think, and it's also exciting since… it's the only time we have entered the public sphere in our BDSM roles. Since she was not allowed to talk… I told the piercer what to do, what should be used, what kind of rings, how they would be put on and so on.

On a symbolic level, this sort of ritual can be read as an intense bonding practice. Ganymede (2004[1991]), who labels himself a S/M practitioner, tantric mystic, and a shaman of ecstatic rites, describes how he, in his early adolescence 'longed for a manhood ritual, one like the native boys had, I felt so alone in the universe, completely out of harmony within my society' (p. 294). This, he claims, was one of the reasons why he became involved in BDSM. A female submissive describes a role play where she is acting a dog. The interaction is ritualistic and full of undertones of the socially forbidden:

> We practice dressage. He leads me around while he whips me […] Sometimes he puts in a tail plug, an anal plug with a dog tail.
>
> [I ask]: Is it the feeling of being an animal or the shift of power that is primary?

> Both. I think I find it easier to be here and now. To be in the moment, and everything else ceases to exist. It was awesome to experience this feeling… how happy I was. To really be in the moment: now it hurts… now it doesn't hurt and everything is beautiful and cozy… and now it hurts again… and not now… and so on. It was really cool.

She describes the BDSM play as a ritualistic moment, which enables the outer world to cease to exist, in which she is totally focused on the feelings and the interaction. Her description connotes to what Mains (2002[1984]) sees as a condition where the interaction steers the mind in a direction away from the ordinary, repressive everyday life and reality. Practitioners describe feelings of bonding, love, affection, and vulnerability after a play, and those feelings/emotions are characterised as very important for intimacy and closeness in a relationship. A man who defines himself as dominant says:

> After a punishment… all the women I've been with… it's almost like they come out of a trance, as they wake up after having fainted… very vulnerable. She wants me to hold her, and say that everything is fine and let her come back to reality. It is a completely different stage she comes to.

Likewise, a masochistic man describes strong emotions after a session. He depicts feelings of being touched and full of gratitude. He ponders the fact that he often starts to cry from joy, but at the same time he experiences feelings of shame and other less positive emotions. Sophia (2007: 271) reflects from the perspective of a practitioner: 'I think that the thrill of taking someone where they want to go and then bringing them back again safe and happy is too beautiful for words.' As described, BDSM sessions are associated with strong emotions and experiences. It has even been suggested that the letters S/M mean 'sex magic' rather than sadomasochism (Thompson 2004[1991]).

BDSM – both fantasy and reality

In this chapter, I have sought to explore BDSM fantasies and the process when fantasies become reality. Westerfelhaus (2007: 272) points out: 'BDSM as practiced in the West is both a product of and a challenge to the culture of which it is a part.' Fantasies and their staging play an important role in BDSM practice. Staging fantasies and playing with taboos form a complicated and complex chain of symbolism that embraces themes of gender, ethnicity, oppression, and power. Fantasising and staging fantasies enable different forms of power relations to be explored. The taboo plays have many common denominators, where power shift is the most primary. On the one hand, the process of staging and realising fantasies involves elements of thrill and excitement, and on the other hand it also involves concerns about one's own limits, and potential consequences if the fantasies are realised. Despite the fact that staging a fantasy is based on consent and can be stopped at any time, the session creates very strong emotions such as, for example, fear, gratitude, and anger. Even if staging a fantasy will never be like the 'real thing', the feelings are real. The fantasies and practice are multifaceted and built on several factors of which sexuality is just one. Participating in BDSM can serve the same purpose as a religious ritual, and several of the interviewed practitioners described BDSM as a spiritual experience. Living out fantasies has, for many practitioners, a central meaning in life. The BDSM community enables meaning and a sense of security and belonging for the individual.

References

Barker, M., Gupta, C. & Iantaffi, A. (2007) 'The power of play: the potentials and pitfalls in healing narratives of BDSM'. In D. Langdridge, & M. Barker (eds) *Safe, Sane and Consensual: Contemporary Perspectives on Sadomasochism.* New York, Palgrave MacMillan.

Beckmann, A. (2009) *The Social Construction of Sexuality and Perversion: Deconstructing Sadomasochism.* London and New York: Palgrave Macmillan.

Bronski, M. (2004[1991]) 'A dream is a wish your heart makes: notes on the materialization of sexual fantasy'. In M. Thompson (ed) *Leather Folk. Radical Sex, People, Politics, and Practice.* Los Angeles: Daedalus Publishing Company.

Butler, J. (2006) *Gender Trouble.* London: Routledge.

Califia, P. (1995) 'A secret side of lesbian sexuality'. In T. Weinberg & L. Kamel (eds) *S and M.: Studies in Sadomasochism.* Buffalo: Prometheus Books.

Carlström, C (unpublished) 'Eskortverksamhet med fokus på försäljning av BDSM-tjänster'. Master's thesis in Sexology, Malmö University, 2010.

Cohen, S. & Taylor, L. (2002[1976]) *Escape Attempts: The Theory and Practice of Resistance in Everyday Life.* London: Routledge.

Collins, R. (2005) *Interaction Ritual Chains.* Princeton: Princeton University Press.

Davis, K. (1982[1981]) 'Introduction: what we fear we try to keep contained'. In SAMOIS (Eds.) *Coming To Power. Writings and Graphics on Lesbian S/M.* Massachusetts: Alyson Publications.

Dworkin, A. (1981) *Pornography: Men Possessing Women.* New York: Perigee.

Ganymede (2004[1991]) 'Sacred passages and radical sex magic'. In M. Thompson (ed) *Leather Folk. Radical Sex, People, Politics, and Practice.* Los Angeles: Daedalus Publishing Company.

Gebhard, P. (1969) 'Fetishism and sadomasochism'. In J.H. Masserman (ed) *Dynamics of Deviant Sexuality*. New York: Grune and Stratton.

Goffman, R. (1974) *Frame Analysis*. Cambridge, Mass: Harvard University Press.

Gosselin, C.C., Wilson, G.D. & Barrett. P.T. (1991) *The personality and sexual preferences of sadomasochistic women*. London: Institute of Psychiatry.

Kantrowitz, A. (2004[1991]) 'Swastika toys'. In M. Thompson (ed) *Leather Folk: Radical Sex, People, Politics, and Practice*. Los Angeles: Daedalus Publishing Company.

Langdridge, D. & Barker, M. (2007) *Safe, Sane and Consensual: Contemporary Perspectives on Sado-Masochism*. New York: Palgrave MacMillan.

Lopez, D.A. & Godard, E. (2013) *Nazi Uniform Fetish and Role-Playing: a Subculture of Erotic Evil*. CSUN Scholar Works for Instruction and Research. Northridge Faculty Publications and Research.

MacKinnon, C. (1989) *Sexuality, Pornography, and Method: Pleasure under Patriarchy*. Chicago: University *of* Chicago Press.

Mains, G. (2002[1984]) *Urban Aboriginals: A Celebration of Leathersexuality*. Los Angeles: Daedalus Publishing Company.

Maslow, A. (1964) *Religions, Values, and Peak Experiences*. New York: The Penguin Group.

Milrod, C. (2010) *The Internet Hobbyist: Demographics and Sexual Behaviors of Male Clients of Internet Sexual Service Providers*. San Francisco: The Institute for Advanced Study of Human Sexuality.

Myers, J. (1983) 'Nonmainstream body modification: genital piercing, branding, burning, and cutting'. In T. Weinberg (ed) *S and M: Studies in Sadomasochism*. Buffalo: Prometheus Books.

Nordling, M. (2009) *Many Faces of Sadomasochistic Sex*. Åbo: Åbo Akademi.

Plante, R. (2006) 'Sexual spanking, the self, and the construction of deviance'. *Journal of Homosexuality* 50(2–3): 59–79.

O'Connell Davidson, J. (1998) *Prostitution, Power and Freedom*. New York: Routledge.

Scott, G.G. (1980) *Erotic Power: An Exploration of Dominance and Submission*. Secaucus, NJ: Citadel.

Sophia (2007) 'Who is in charge in a SM scene?' In D. Langdridge, & M. Barker (eds) *Safe, Sane and Consensual: Contemporary Perspectives on Sadomasochism*. New York: Palgrave MacMillan.

Stein, M. (1974) *Lovers, Friends, Slaves… The Nine Male Sexual Types. Their Psycho-Sexual Transactions with Call-Girls.* New York: Berkeley Publishing Corporation.

Taylor, G. & Ussher, J. (2001) 'Making sense of S&M: a discourse analytic account'. *Sexualities* 4(3): 293–314.

Thompson, M. (2004[1991]) *Leather Folk: Radical Sex, People, Politics, and Practice.* Los Angeles: Daedalus Publishing Company.

Timm, E. (1999) http://www.metzingen-zwangsarbeit.de/hugo_boss.pdfHugo Ferdinand Boss (1885–1948) und die Firma Hugo Bosshttp://www.metzingen-zwangsarbeit.de/hugo_boss.pdf. *Metzingen Zwangsarbeit* (in German).

Weinberg, T. (2006) 'Sadomasochism and the social sciences: A review of the sociological and social psychological literature'. *Journal of Homosexuality* 50(2): 17–40.

Weinberg, T & Kamel, L. (1983) *S and M: Studies in Sadomasochism.* Buffalo: Prometheus Books.

Weiss, M. (2011) *Techniques of Pleasure: BDSM and the Circuits of Sexuality.* Durham, North Carolina: Duke University Press.

Westerfelhaus, R.G. (2007) 'The spirituality of sex and the sexuality of the spirit: BDSM erotic play as soulwork and social critique'. In K.E. Lovaas & M.M. Jenkins (eds) *Sexuality & Communication in Everyday Life.* London: Sage Publications.

Zurbriggen, E.L. & Yost, M.R. (2004) 'Power, desire, and pleasure in sexual fantasies'. *Journal of Sex Research* 41(3): 288–300.

Yost, M. (2007) 'Sexual fantasies of S/M practitioners: the impact of gender and S/M role on fantasy content'. In D. Langdridge & M. Barker (eds) *Safe, Sane and Consensual: Contemporary Perspectives on Sadomasochism* New York, Palgrave MacMillan.

Ingrid Ryberg

Documenting Fantasy and Expanding Reality in Queer Pornography

> BDSM is a lot of like… using things that hurt you in real life and power dynamics that hurt you in real life and making them empowering and making them like good for you. Just because a lot of women are into rape role play or fantasies doesn't mean that actual rape is ever okay.
>
> Judy Minx, *Much More Pussy* (Emilie Jouvet 2010)

In this chapter, I discuss the relation between fantasy and reality in queer porn films where role playing and BDSM are represented.[1] Filmed in a documentary style and centered around interviews and mundane situations in the participants' lives, *Much More Pussy* (Emilie Jouvet 2010) and *Trans Entities: The Nasty Love of Papí and Wil* (Morty Diamond 2007), both perform an intriguing sliding between the political reality of the persons in the films and the fantasy scenarios that they enact in the explicit sex scenes. Both films are characterised by in-depth personal and political reflections about BDSM, such as the one from Judy Minx above, which provide a backdrop for the fantasy scenes and shape their meanings. In both films, sexual and political fantasies and realities are intertwined in a complex way. I highlight how this complex relation involves two interrelated debates regarding pornography and documentary and conflicting queer theoretical notions of sex as either 'redemptive' or 'anti-social'. I argue that the sliding between fantasy and reality in the two films is not only a matter of rendering the incoherence and potentially threatening nature of fantasy coherent or safe by framing it as a highly conscious and rational practice anchored in functional everyday life. Rather, I see these films as troubling the boundaries between fantasy and reality, and as opening up a zone of experimentation and change, where fantasy unsettles and leaves its mark on reality.

1 This chapter is an expanded and revised version of a talk given at the symposium 'Queer Vulnerabilities', Department of Media Studies, Stockholm University, 20 February, 2012, and draws on my doctoral thesis *Imagining Safe Space: The Politics of Queer, Feminist and Lesbian Pornography* (2012, Stockholm: Acta,). I would like to thank Mariah Larsson, Sara Johnsdotter, Anu Koivunen, Katariina Kyrölä, and Ulrika Dahl for valuable comments on previous versions of this text.

From Much More Pussy (2010).

Introduction to the films

Much More Pussy by French queer porn filmmaker Emilie Jouvet is the hardcore version of Jouvet's documentary *Too Much Pussy: Feminist Sluts in the Queer X Show* (2010). The Queer X Show gathered a group of American and European sex radical performance artists who toured around Europe in a mini-bus during the summer of 2009. Jouvet documented the performance as well as the social and sexual interactions that took place during the tour. Jouvet, as well as all the performers in The Queer X Show, are central figures in the recently emerged transnational queer porn film culture, where porn is used as an activist tool for sexual empowerment of groups marginalised by dominant notions of gender and sexuality. Her first porn film, *One Night Stand* (2006), was released the same year that a number of crucial events contributing to the establishment of the film culture took place, such as the launch of the annual Porn Film Festival in Berlin and The Feminist Porn Awards in Toronto. American trans activist Morty Diamond's *Trans Entities: The Nasty Love of Papí and Wil* is another example of this porn film culture. The film portrays the transgender couple Papí and Wil through talking-head interviews and documentary scenes from their life together – including their sex life. Diamond and the film's performers are, just like Jouvet's cast, central figures in contemporary queer porn, a notion that I in this chapter use as an umbrella term for a film culture in which I include films that are also labelled as trans porn, lesbian porn, and feminist porn.

Queer porn film culture draws on the legacy of sex radical activism that emerged in the USA in the 1980s, in opposition to anti-porn feminism's condemning of not just pornography, but also of lesbian butch/femme relationships and BDSM as patriarchal sexuality (cf. Vance 1992). Anti-porn feminism and its interrelation with cultural feminism's conceptualisation of women's sexuality as non-masculine, non-violent and non-penetrative (cf. Gerhard 2001: 153–173; Hallgren 2008: 275–420) clashed with lesbian sex practices involving dildos and role playing (cf. Hunter 2006: 21f). These different attitudes in regard to sexuality and pornography became more accentuated towards the end of the 1970s and resulted in the heated debates that came to be called the Sex Wars in the early 1980s (cf. Bronstein 2011: 397–407). The sex radical movement interrelated with queer activism as it emerged as a reaction to the AIDS crisis, homophobia, and assimilationist tendencies in the gay and lesbian movements. As Lisa Duggan and Nan D. Hunter contend in their personal account of the Sex Wars:

> During the porn wars, many lesbians who were alienated by lesbian-feminists' homogenizing, white, middle-class, anti-gay-male, antisex discourses, refused the category 'lesbian,' and adopted 'queer' as a mark of separation from such politics, a badge of principled dissidence (Duggan & Hunter 2006: 12).

Shaped in opposition to notions of female masculinity as patriarchal and to transphobia in lesbian culture, queer porn has not only celebrated the butch lesbian (cf. Butler 2004), but has also, especially in the current film culture, been inclusive of trans and genderqueer performers and directors (cf. Hill Meyer 2013; Lee 2013; Noble 2013).

From Trans Entities (2007).

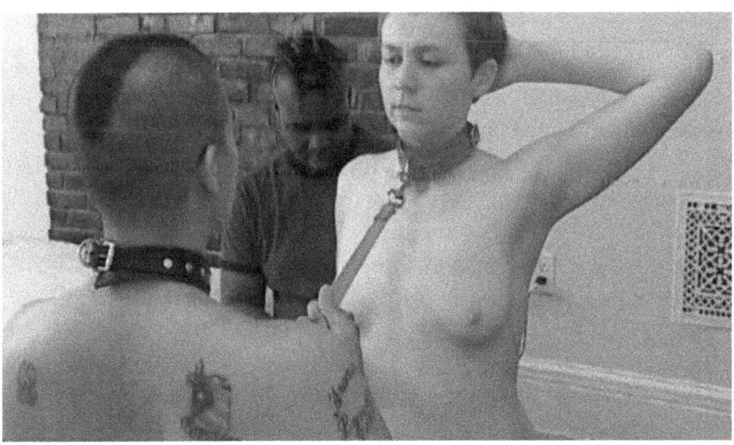

As examples of queer porn, *Trans Entities* and *Much More Pussy*, both represent bodies, sexualities and experiences that fall outside of dominant notions of gender and sexuality, and as such also pose a challenge to dominant pornographic representations. Queer porn is anchored in a political critique of how intersecting power structures shape personal and social realities, and explores and proposes new ways of expressing and representing sex. In representing queer sexualities, it also functions largely as a documentation and recognition of existing queer sexual cultures. Therefore, as pornography, it stretches beyond the so-called 'documentary impulse', (Hansen, et al. 1991: 211) that informs all pornography, as an assumed guarantee that viewers will become witnesses to real sexual activities. In the case of queer porn, this impulse entails more than the fact that 'people actually [have] sex' in front of the camera, as Richard Dyer (2004: 109) has put it. In this film culture, the documentary impulse also involves the political concern with making visible and validating queer bodies, lives, and sex cultures.

In *Much More Pussy* and *Trans Entities*' representations of BDSM and role play as integral parts of the participants' queer lives, sexuality is politicised. They draw attention to the ways in which sexual fantasy provides an arena for negotiating, reworking, and exploring power structures and personal and social histories and realities in empowering ways. In the following, I will address how the two films reactivate discussions about fantasy and reality, redemptive and anti-social positions and pornography and documentary. By troubling any clear-cut division between these notions, both films offer a zone of experimentation in which new worlds come into reach.

Validating queer reality

Much More Pussy and *Trans Entities* both represent sexual role play and BDSM in a documentary mode, where these practices are also discussed and analysed by the participants in the films. In addition to talking-head interviews and role play sessions in their private home, *Trans Entities* also contains documentary scenes of the couple in public, browsing through and commenting on clothes in a thrift store, walking down a city street at night, and kissing on the subway on their way back home. In the voice-over from the interview, which is also cross-edited with these scenes, they discuss their gender identities and how they came to define themselves as trans entities, a position they define as shifting, fluid, and in between male and female. *Much More Pussy* is not set in the participants' homes, but follows them on their tour, and documents situations such as discussions in the mini-bus, consciousness-raising and yoga sessions, hanging out at a beach, backstage preparations, performances on stage and sex scenes, that appear to be sometimes more spontaneous (happening between the participants in the show or with people they encounter on the road), sometimes planned and staged (such as a vampire role play session at a cemetery), and sometimes a combination of both (such as sex on top of a piano backstage). Hence, the footage stretches from mundane and familiar situations when the group hang out with each other in between shows, to the spectacular performances in the show (including fisting, needles, and peeing), with the sex scenes happening somewhere in between these poles. Both films portray the reality of their characters, and let them reflect over their positions and experiences in relation to dominant norms. BDSM and role play sessions are embedded in the films' documentary portrayal of the participants and their everyday realities.

As such, both films reactivate a long-running debate about the relation between fantasy and reality in sexual representations directed to other than straight cis male audiences.[2] For example, in her book *At Home with Pornography: Women, Sex, and Everyday Life*, about the home as a site for women's consumption of sexually explicit materials, Jane Juffer (1997: 136) discusses women's erotica in terms of a reconciliation of fantasy and reality. In opposition to Susan Sontag's (1967) celebration of literary pornography that refuses a reconciliation of fantasy and reality and therefore, according to Sontag, allows for complexity and the transcendence of personality, Juffer highlights the centrality of plot and everyday reality in women's literary and video erotica in the 1980s and 1990s. She sees these productions as taking off from 1970s feminist masturbation discourse where sexual pleasure and clitoral orgasms were inscribed into the routines of women's everyday lives, for instance in Betty Friedan's *The Feminine Mystique* (1963), Germaine Greer's *The Female Eunuch* (1970), Nancy Friday's *My Secret Garden* (1973), Erica Jong's *Fear of Flying* (1973) and Rita Mae Brown's *Rubyfruit Jungle* (1973). Hence, not only 1980s sex radicalism, but also early second wave feminism's politicisation of sexuality and promotion of women's sexual pleasure as a key to liberation, form an important historical backdrop for today's queer porn film culture (Ryberg 2012; 2014).

Juffer argues that the emphasis on everyday reality in pornographic texts addressed to women, in combination with the fact that these texts are also often being consumed in women's homes as part of their everyday reality, provide an important context and new conditions for women's access to porn and sexual

2 The term cis refers to gender identities where a person's legal gender, biological gender, and gender identity match each other.

agency. Similarly, Linda Williams (1999), in response to one male critic who finds that information about safe-sex techniques in women's pornography 'compromises the erotic status of the fantasy' (p. 263), contends that 'the mixture of safety with excitement [...] may be just what is needed *for* excitement' (p. 264), and for allowing women to explore 'a desire of their own', without fear of punishment or guilt. In both Juffer's and Williams's discussions then, the combination of reality and fantasy, and of safety and excitement, concerns the necessary conditions for women's exploration of sexuality.

The continued emphasis on documenting and recognising queer reality in queer porn proves that the question of the relation between fantasy and reality remains central in the contemporary proliferation of different forms of queer and feminist pornography at large. Queer porn functions largely as a form of activism that affirms, makes visible, and revalues not only queer sexuality and sex, but also queer lives, bodies, socialities and experiences that remain marginalised in dominant representations, as the scenes from *Much More Pussy* and *Trans Entities* described above also do. The importance of this function is also articulated in literature about lesbian porn. For instance, in 1997 Becki L. Ross found that:

> Erotic images validate our sexuality as one healthy, meaningful, and empowering part of our lives as lesbians (and gay men). Sexually explicit images produced by and for lesbians challenge the barrier of sexual fear, inhibition, ignorance, and shame by unapologetically foregrounding lesbian desire, and thus expanding the realm of knowable human sexual expression (Ross 2000: 300).

Chris Straayer comments on how expectations of verisimilitude and realism shaped the reception of lesbian pornography within the American lesbian community in the 1980s, in spite of the fact that 'pornography's generic otherworldliness encourages fantasy'. The audience 'looked for a visual representation of themselves' and prioritised 'reality-checking over fantasy experience' (Straayer 1996: 213ff; cf. Rhyne 2007: 45).

However, in contemporary queer porn film culture emphasis on notions of realism and authenticity also run parallel with aims at stretching the sexual imagination beyond everyday realities and constraints and calls for films that do not necessarily account for the subcultural context, circumstances, and politics of the production. One telling example of how notions of fantasy and realism are negotiated in this film culture is Swedish filmmaker Mia Engberg's two different porn projects, *Selma & Sofie* (2002) and *Dirty Diaries* (2009). *Selma & Sofie* is a short lesbian porn film, which featured a real-life couple. *Dirty Diaries* is a short film collection where twelve different filmmakers interpret the notion of feminist porn, using mobile phone cameras. In an interview during the production phase of *Dirty Diaries,* Mia Engberg reflected over a development that she felt had happened during the years since *Selma & Sofie* was released. In *Dirty Diaries,* the participants were more interested in expressing sexual fantasies than in documenting real people having sex.

> This thing with authenticity – yes it feels as if we have come a step further. Since *Selma & Sofie* felt as if it was the first film we made, it was important to get away from the artificiality. What characterizes sexist mainstream porn is that it is so artificial. There are no real breasts and no real nails, there are no real eyelashes, there are no real orgasms. So then it was natural to start with authenticity – that they would be in love for real, they would have sex for real. And *Selma & Sofie*, when you watch it today, it feels almost like a documentary, in a way like – yes we shoot when they have sex, they do not act and they are not performers who enact. But it is just real, just real body, real feelings. But now it feels more important to make… an artistic expression of, not sexuality, but of horniness or of the sexual fantasy – which is what I think porn is… Most of the films in *Dirty Diaries* move beyond the idea of authenticity (Engberg 2008-09-19, quoted in Ryberg 2012).

Much More Pussy and *Trans Entities* both maintain a documentary approach to the participants' everyday realities and experiences, and underscore the genuinely loving, caring, and friendly relationships between the participants. Nevertheless, I propose that in these films, Juffer's thesis about the reconciliation of fantasy and reality is both supported and unsettled. Instead of offering closure, the films open up a vulnerable zone of possibilities where reality is potentially remoulded. Despite, or perhaps because of, their documentary mode, I claim that these films are more about bringing fantasy into the realities they are documenting, than about bringing reality into fantasy.

BDSM as reparative criticism

This chapter's opening quote from Judy Minx is from a scene in *Much More Pussy* shot on the road in the mini-bus, between two gigs of The Queer X Show, where the women discuss their fantasies and desires. The French queer porn and performance artist and writer Wendy Delorme refers to an autobiographical book by the queer American writer Michelle Tea where she describes how she as a young feminist goes to consciousness-raising groups in order to get rid of her rape fantasies. She tries masturbating while thinking about being on a boat on the ocean and feeling the wind in her hair. As she gets close to orgasm, however, her fantasy gets twisted. She lands on an island and a group of men jump from a tree and rape her as she comes. Delorme says that similarly, for her, whenever she tries not to fantasise about 'something hardcore or degrading' it always 'jumps' at her at the last minute. 'At some point I had to make the conscious decision not to feel guilty about my fantasies. This is our duty also as feminists – not to guilt-trip ourselves and feel wrong about our desires', she argues.

In addition to reactivating the question about the relation between fantasy and reality, the scene invokes a queer theoretical debate where two conflicting conceptualisations of sex have been positioned against each other (cf. Halberstam 2008). On the one hand, a so-called anti-social position has been associated with gay male theorists such as Leo Bersani (1987), who celebrates the dysfunctional, self-shattering, and disintegrating aspects of sexuality. He argues against what he calls a '*redemptive reinvention of sex*' (p. 215, italics in original) in the writings of anti-porn feminists Catherine MacKinnon and Andrea Dworkin, as well as in the work of sex radical feminists Gayle Rubin and Pat Califia. In this discourse sex is imagined as 'less disturbing, less socially abrasive, less violent, more respectful of "personhood" than it has been in male-dominated phallocentric culture', Bersani (1987: 215) contends.

In response to Bersani's analysis, Ann Cvetkovich (2003) and Elizabeth Freeman (2010), two theorists that I draw from in this chapter, have theorised sex, including butch/femme practices and BDSM, in terms of reparative criticism and healing that nevertheless resist redemption and closure. In her discussion about butch/femme discourse, Cvetkovich (p. 62) highlights how powerlessness, receptivity, and loss of control are valued in accounts by femme lesbians, but how these qualities, instead of being romanticised, are struggled and strived for. She contends that there is a healing potential in lesbian writing about sex, for instance by Joan Nestle, Cherríe Moraga and Leslie Feinberg, where the traumatic dimension of sexuality is acknowledged and shared, not left behind or erased. '[F]emme accounts of receptivity avoid a redemptive reading of sex, insisting on the fear, pain, and difficulty that can block the way to and be conjured up by making oneself physically and emotionally vulnerable or receptive', Cvetkovich (p. 63) argues.

In her essay 'Turn the Beat Around' Elizabeth Freeman proposes a theory of BDSM as a sexual practice that manipulates time and calls temporal linearity into question. Her main example is Isaac Julien's film *The Attendant* from 1993. She reads Julien's representation of interracial sadomasochism between men as an examination of the traumatic histories of the transatlantic slave trade. She argues that in the film, race role play functions as a construction of new knowledge, using the body as instrument and therefore refusing traumatic historical moments the closure of pastness. She argues that 'S/M relentlessly physicalizes the encounter with history and thereby contributes to a reparative criticism that takes up the materials of a traumatic past and remixes them in the interests of new possibilities for being and knowing' (p. 144).

Freeman's analysis of interracial sadomasochism is invoked in *Trans Entities* in a sequence in which the film's couple, Papí and Wil, engage in sexual role play with a third, and unlike them, white, partner. In one interview sequence, the three of them together reflect over their polyamorous relationship and underscore the importance of actively dealing with race as a structure shaping dynamics between partners. Papí contends that they have previously avoided relationships with white partners, but that Chris, unlike many others, is politically conscious about race and that the three of them together are able to communicate about that. Together they engage in race play. They explain: 'We engage in race play that is very taboo… But there's honesty that lives here and there's struggle that lives here. We, you know, we wanna work through that.' Then the interview footage, in which Wil talks about how they dominate Chris and assign to Papí the role of assistant, gradually interweaves with documentary footage of the sexual role play scene, which includes Chris being leashed and flogged. One could argue that this scene is a precise illustration of a reconciliation of fantasy and reality, and hence belongs to the legacy of productions discussed by Juffer. The setting of the role play is the couple's domestic space and before it we even witness how the three partners literally integrate and schedule sex into the routines of their everyday lives, as all three of them bring out their calendars in order to book their dates. The emphasis on political reflection and explanation before and in voice-over during the first few minutes of the role play makes reality highly present in this enacted fantasy. Even if the session, after this introduction, is represented in length and without further comments from the participants, it is still firmly anchored in the reality of Papí and Wil's domestic life together, which continues to be documented in talking-head interviews also after this scene.

Trans Entities, if yet a film about a transgender couple, invokes both Juffer's and Williams' discussions about women's pornography's integration of fantasy and reality and safety and excitement respectively, not least in how questions of safe boundaries for sexual exploration are central in the film. One sequence documents how the couple negotiates the content and safe word for another role play session. Thus, while the film interweaves fantasy and reality, in the interviews the distinction between the two is also maintained. Similarly, in Judy Minx's statement in *Much More Pussy*, the distinction between fantasising about rape and actual rape is also stressed. Still, even if negotiations between fantasy and reality and safety and excitement are central in both films, unlike Juffer's and Williams' examples, these are not narrative but documentary films, and I want to think further about the realities they document and what the integration of fantasy implies in these cases.

A zone of experimentation

As discussed above, using documentary techniques in order to make visible and validate queer experiences is crucial in both my film examples, as they are based on the participants' own reflections and understandings of themselves in relation to dominant norms. The importance of political documentary and self-presentation in feminist filmmaking has been underscored by for instance Alexandra Juhasz (1999), in her discussion about her own AIDS activist videos. Addressing the legacy of the so-called realist debates in feminist film theory, Juhasz argues against a contention that talking-head interviews and other documentary techniques equal assuming naïve, stable, or fixed ideas about reality and identity. Instead she points out that political documentaries applying such techniques often revolve precisely around the politicised construction of identity and of a particular vision of reality. She writes that:

> Because so much of feminist and other 'identity' video movements are specifically about constructing our own identities in a society that has usually done this for minorities, much of the 'realist' footage in minority-produced productions ends up recording people reflexively discussing the meaning, reinterpretation, and importance of their own identity (Juhasz 1999: 208).

I find this argument especially useful for bringing out how *Much More Pussy* and *Trans Entities*, rather than reconciling fantasy with reality, challenge the very depiction of and reconstruct reality. In both films the emphasis on gender performance and sexual role play destabilises fixed notions of reality and identity. At the centre of both films are the constructions and reconstructions of roles and identities through their focus on costumes, props, play and performance – in *Much More Pussy*, both on and off stage, and in *Trans Entities* the domestic space as such turns into a stage for various enactments. I propose that fantasy in these films, rather than being reconciled with reality, is a means of unsettling and therefore potentially expanding reality and everyday lives.

From this perspective, the clip from *Trans Entities* discussed above is not only a matter of overlap and interweaving of fantasy and reality, but also of how fantasy floats into and reshapes reality and the domestic setting of the couple's everyday life. The fantasy scenario turns the reality of the domestic space on its head. To borrow from Sara Ahmed (2006: 170), domestic space is queered and becomes slantwise. The contrast between the conventional format of the talking-head interviews and their sudden and unapologetic juxtaposition with the role play could be said to produce a queer moment, which, as Ahmed puts it, can be moments of disorientation, but also exciting and joyful. Queer moments, according to Ahmed, are vital moments where new objects may come into reach and where it may be possible to extend into space in a new shape. Freeman (2010: 161) theorises BDSM precisely as a question of expansion and elongation, both in temporal and in spatial terms. In her reading of *The Attendant*, BDSM involves a meeting up with time and history that is not one's own, as well as an extension of the body and its erotic zones. I find that such an expansion of both temporal and spatial boundaries is precisely what takes place through the combination of documentary and BDSM in *Trans Entities* and in *Much More Pussy*, for instance in one extended backstage sequence documenting a rough sex scene that almost all the women in the show engage in together. The sex scene functions almost as a farewell ritual to one of the women who will leave the tour and travel back to the U.S.A. In the scene the women enact a violent gang-bang scenario, but the intensity of the scene comes just as much from the fact that they are in the process of saying goodbye and from the trust and love they share between themselves in the group after touring together. The hard sexual role play blends into the political and social reality of these women's care for each other. This sliding is less about reconciliation than about enacting or creating a vulnerable zone of experimentation and potentiality. It is a scene in which the force of queer sociality and political fantasy is channelled into the violence of the role play. For a moment – a queer moment – sexual and political fantasies and realities merge and new worlds come into reach.

In sum, I argue that in the two films, the combination of documentary and BDSM is not so much a question of a reconciliation of fantasy and reality or a redemptive rendition of violent sexuality. The 'healing' or 'reparative' element here should not be seen as a matter of getting rid of or over past traumas. In their very integration and remixing of fantasy scenarios into documentary filmmaking, these films are more about future possibilities and the creation of new ways of being and knowing. In these films, fantasy leaves its mark on reality and reality is vulnerable and receptive.

References

Ahmed, S. (2006) *Queer Phenomenology: Orientations, Objects, Others*. Durham & London: Duke University Press.

Bersani, L. (1987) 'Is the rectum a grave?' *AIDS: Cultural Analysis/Cultural Activism* 43: 197–222.

Bronstein, C. (2011) *Battling Pornography: The American Feminist Anti-Pornography Movement, 1976–1986*. Cambridge: Cambridge University Press.

Butler, H. (2004) 'What do you call a lesbian with long fingers? The development of lesbian and dyke pornography'. In Linda Williams (ed) *Porn Studies*. Durham & London: Duke University Press.

Cvetkovich, A. (2003) *An Archive of Feelings: Trauma, Sexuality and Lesbian Public Cultures*. Durham & London: Duke University Press.

Diamond, M. *Trans Entities: The Nasty Love of Papí and Wil* (2007).

Duggan, L. & Hunter, N.D. (2006) *Sex Wars: Sexual Dissent and Political Culture.* New York & London: Routledge.

Engberg, M. *Selma & Sofie* (2002).

Engberg, M. *Dirty Diaries: Twelve Shorts of Feminist Porn* (2009).

Freeman, E. (2010) *Time Binds: Queer Temporalities, Queer Histories.* Durham & London: Duke University Press.

Gerhard, J. (2001) *Desiring Revolution: Second-wave Feminism and the Rewriting of American Sexual Thought, 1920 to 1982.* New York: Columbia University Press.

Halberstam, J. (2008) 'The anti-social turn in queer studies'. *Graduate Journal of Social Science* 5(2): 140–156.

Hallgren, H. (2008) *När lesbiska blev kvinnor – När kvinnor blev lesbiska. Lesbiskfeministiska kvinnors diskursproduktion rörande kön, sexualitet, kropp och identitet under 1970- och 1980-talen i Sverige.* Göteborg: Kabusa böcker.

Hansen, C., Needham, C. & Nichols, B. (1991) 'Pornography, ethnography, and the discourse of power'. In B. Nichols (ed) *Representing Reality.* Bloomington & Indianapolis: Indiana University Press.

Jouvet, E. *Too Much Pussy: Feminist Sluts in the Queer X Show* (2010).

Jouvet, E. *Much More Pussy* (2010).

Juffer, J. (1998) *At Home with Pornography: Women, Sex, and Everyday Life.* New York & London: New York University Press.

Juhasz, A. (1999) 'They said we were trying to show reality – All I want to show is my video: the politics of the realist feminist documentary'. In J.M. Gaines & M. Renov (eds) *Collecting Visible Evidence.* Minneapolis & London: University of Minnesota Press.

Hill-Meyer, T. (2013) 'Where the trans women aren't: the slow introduction of trans women in feminist and queer porn'. In T. Taormino, et al. (eds) *The Feminist Porn Book.* New York: The Feminist Press.

Hunter, N. D. (2006) 'Contextualising the sexuality debates: a chronology 1966–2005'. In L. Duggan & N.D. Hunter (eds) *Sex Wars: Sexual Dissent and Political Culture.* New York & London: Routledge.

Lee, J. (2013) 'Uncategorized: genderqueer identity and performance in independent and mainstream porn'. In T. Taormino, et al. (eds) *The Feminist Porn Book.* New York: The Feminist Press.

Noble, B. (2013) 'Knowing Dick: penetration and the pleasures of feminist porn's trans men.' In T. Taormino, et al. (eds) *The Feminist Porn Book*. New York: The Feminist Press.

Rhyne, R. (2007) 'Hard-core shopping: educating consumption in SIR video production's lesbian porn'. *The Velvet Light Trap* 59: 42–50.

Ross, B.L. (2000) '"It's merely designed for sexual arousal": interrogating the indefensibility of lesbian smut [1997].' In D. Cornell (ed) *Feminism and Pornography*. Oxford: Oxford University Press.

Ryberg, I. (2012) *Imagining Safe Space: The Politics of Queer, Feminist and Lesbian Pornography*. Stockholm: Acta.

Ryberg, I. (2014) 'Affirmation and critique: political and aesthetic legacies of queer, feminist and lesbian pornography'. In E. Biasin, et al. (eds) *Porn After Porn: Contemporary Alternative Pornographies*. Milan-Udine: Mimesis International.

Sontag, S. (1967) 'The pornographic imagination'. In *Styles of Radical Will*. New York: Farrar, Straus and Giroux.

Straayer, C. (1996) *Deviant Eyes, Deviant Bodies: Sexual Re-orientation in Film and Video*. New York: Columbia University Press.

Vance, C. S. (ed, 1992) 'More danger, more pleasure: a decade after the Barnard sexuality conference.' In C.S. Vance (ed) *Pleasure and Danger: Exploring Female Sexuality*. London: Pandora Press.

Mariah Larsson

Fantasies Becoming Illegal: The Manga Case, Child Porn Law, and the Regulation of the Sexual Mind

In the fall of 2009, a search was made of the home of a translator of so-called Manga comics in Uppsala.[1] The translator was involved in an embittered custody case, and a report to the police had instigated the search, which led to the confiscation of his computers. On these computers, images were found that could be described as child pornography (Westrin 2013). These images were Manga images – images from a particular Japanese comics tradition and consequently drawn and/or painted. In a long trial process – from March 2010 to June 2012 – the translator was found guilty in the District Court, guilty again in the Court of Appeals, and upon the last appeal to the Supreme Court, he was acquitted. Of the fifty-one images that had in the District Court been deemed child pornographic, twelve were dismissed in the Court of Appeals, and all the rest except one in the Supreme Court. Possession of that one single image that was deemed child pornographic was, however, by the court regarded as defensible, considering that the translator worked with Manga material (Supreme Court case no B 990-11).

During this process, the translator lost his job – the consequences of which are clearly highlighted by the fact that his first penalty was set at eighty 'day fines' which was calculated as 24,800 SEK ('day fines' are based on the convicted person's income). In the Court of Appeals half a year later, the number of 'day fines' was retained, but the sum had decreased to less than a quarter of the original fine (District Court case no B 6344-01: 1; Court of Appeals case no B 6389-10: 1).

The case became quite controversial and was debated in Swedish media and on the Internet (e.g., Edenborg 2010; Leijonhufvud 2010; Liljestrand 2010; Juridikbloggen 2011). In spite of the fact that the case was about child pornography, several people and organisations rose to the translator's defence. A Swedish journalist and Member of Parliament, in an attempt to protest the law,

1 I would like to thank Lotta Wendel, who kindly read through this chapter and gave valuable comments.

reported herself for child porn crime for possession of one drawn image (not Manga, however). The court dismissed the case since they did not find that the image was child porn (Thurfjell 2013).

The translator's work and his professional knowledge of Japanese culture was cited as a defence, most likely because child pornography is not only a sensitive matter but a highly inflammatory one and even, seemingly, contagious. As British cultural studies scholar Stephen Maddison observes: 'As a fetish it [child porn] achieves power through its oxomoronic status: to see it, to know its existence is to be guilty; one can only remain free from its taint by being ignorant of its existence and vociferous in its denunciation. Only the Other knows it, and to see it is to become Other' (Maddison 2010: 32).

Since they are not available for viewing, it is very hard to say something about the images in themselves. However, the judicial reasoning provokes a suspicion that it is not the images in themselves that are criminal but the circumstances surrounding their possession. By this, I mean that the Swedish journalist and Member of Parliament loudly publicised her own actions and motivations, and it was very apparent that she did so in order to protest a law she found problematic. The translator's possession of the one image deemed, by the Supreme Court, to be child pornographic, was considered 'defensible' in relation to his work. In a previous case, a man had been convicted for possession of drawn Japanese images on his computer that were regarded as child porn (Court of Appeal case no B 3868-08). This man's conviction, on the other hand, might have had to do with the fact that the trial against him also contained sexual harassment. Thus, the circumstances surrounding the possession seem to be of consequence for how the images are understood.

Nevertheless, there are several issues in the Manga case that are very disturbing – besides the highly personal and individual consequences for the persons involved – and that make further discussion imperative. These do not have so much to do with the particular images in this case – actually not even with child pornography – but are rather significant on a more abstract level. They have to do with society's relation to images; with what and whom the law is supposed to protect; and how laws, regardless of the atrociousness of the crimes they want to prevent, may or may not tangle with our minds. In this chapter, I will argue two things: First, considering how the Swedish law on child pornography is written, the acquittal of the translator is actually problematic – not because he was guilty, but because the law is construed out of a conception of images that ascribes a metaphysical quality to them which, in reality, makes even quite abstract images of children in sexual situations illegal. Or at least should, had the law been carried out and enforced consistently.

Second, by construing the law in this manner, Swedish lawmakers have made a point of attempting to regulate thinking. This is not an unusual thing – many laws are normative, that is, they are made to shape our attitudes towards things. For instance, when corporal punishment of children was forbidden in 1978 – in schools and by parents alike – the idea was to not only stop corporal punishment but to make the idea of hitting your child unthinkable. Another such example is the sex purchase law from 1999, which, although its effects on actual prostitution are debated (e.g. Dodillet 2009; Westerstrand 2014), also had the intention to shift focus from the seller of sex to the buyer, and to make the thought of buying sex taboo or unthinkable (cf. Kulick 2005). It seems that the law has had at least some of that intended effect, since the original resistance to it has been replaced with a more wide-spread support, even though it is still surrounded by controversy (see e.g., Westerstrand 2014).

In that regard, lawmakers have been very successful since child pornography is considered one of the lowest crimes and a clear indication of the possessor's innate monstrosity. This is clear not only from general attitudes and spontaneous comments on the Internet and in dinner conversations,[2] but also from the way child pornography is used in popular fiction where it functions as definitive proof of the criminal's evil mind. In Stieg Larsson's successful *Millennium* series (2005–2007), one of the worst villains, the psychiatrist Peter Telleborian, not only misuses his doctor's authority and mistreats Lisbeth Salander, he also has large amounts of child porn on his computer, thereby becoming 'Other', as Maddison so aptly put it in the quote above: 'Only the Other knows it, and to see it is to become Other'.

Then again, whether it is the lawmakers who were successful or whether the laws on child pornography have been passed because this attitude was already prevailing is hard to know. Arguments have been raised whether society's reaction to child pornography might be what sometimes has been termed a 'moral panic' (Ost 2001: 446). Regardless, an unintended consequence of what has for the past decades been an increasing awareness of and restrictions regarding sexual crimes against children, has been that we have, in a sense, come to regard children as objects of desire – not, obviously, our own desire, but the paedophile's. Thus, the paedophilic gaze has become incorporated into the general public's mind (Ost 2001: 458–459). Again, I want to underline that by this I do

2 See for instance the discussion on the flashback forum about Hans Nestius, *I last och lust: sexuella bilder förr och nu* (Stockholm: Prisma, 1982) which contained – as an argument against pornography – child pornographic images. https://www.flashback.org/t2057395.

not mean that grown-ups in general have become more attracted to children, but that the fear of the paedophile has made us see what might possibly be paedophilic. In past years, children have not only become under more surveillance than before, but also have become sexualised with relation to nudity. We cover our children not because we find their bodies sexual, but because we fear that someone else might.

The sexualisation of children can be illustrated by how children have been represented in mainstream media. In the 1960s and 1970s, children could be depicted in the nude, or in short skirts and dresses. The Swedish films and television series about Pippi Longstocking (1969; two in 1970), for example, showed Pippi in a short dress, with the garters for her iconic mismatching stockings peeping out underneath. Her friend, Annika, was shown sliding down the stair banister with her skirt being pulled up and her underwear showing. These images were not regarded as child pornographic in any way at the time. In 2001, the artist Palle Torsson made a video, titled *The Pippi Examples*, with twenty-seven scenes from the Pippi films and television shows. The scenes were presented in slow-motion, without sound, and depicted images such as the ones described above. The reaction from the public, from Astrid Lindgren (the author of the original novels), and from the film production company SF, was so strong that Torsson had to withdraw the video from the exhibition and ultimately destroy all five copies. SF claimed that the artist had infringed on their copyright, which was why Torsson was forced to destroy the copies. However, it is quite clear that SF reacted so strongly because of the nature of the images. Images and movement that had, previously, been void of sexual meaning became, for several reasons, highly controversial. One reason that the scenes were reinscribed with meaning was the fact that the images were taken out of context, and by showing them in slow-motion they became eroticised. Another likely reason was that the artist in question was a (grown) man, and, as a carrier of the 'male gaze' (Mulvey 1975) thus susceptible to accusations of sexual objectification. A third reason had to do, simply, with the changing times: what was regarded as representations of childishly acceptable behaviour and manner of dress in the early 1970s was not so in 2001 (see Widegren 2004).

Background

Pornography was legalised in Sweden in 1971. After 1971, the production of child pornography was illegal but the possession and distribution of it was not. As pornography was debated during the 1970s, one of the recurring issues that were regarded as highly problematic was the existence of child porn. In 1979, it became illegal to sell and distribute and in 1998 it became illegal to possess. The law does not explicitly say anything about photographic images versus drawn, painted, or computer-generated images (CGI), but there is an understanding that if a crime against a child has been committed in order to produce it, the image is supposed to be deemed as a gross rather than a regular or a slight offense (Penal Code, Ch. 16, sec.10). By child is meant someone who is younger than eighteen or has not completed puberty. By pornographic is meant that it is provoking and intends to influence the observer sexually, unless such an image is intended to be used for scientific or artistic purposes. However, any image that shows a child acting sexually is always pornographic.

Child porn has been understood in different ways. It is part of a pathology – people who are turned on by children, so called paedophiles, are considered the consumers, and thus, the discussion has been raised whether child porn could encourage sexual abuse of children or if it provides an outlet for paedophiles, actually preventing crimes because they would not need to turn to real children for their sexual urge (Kutchinsky 1972; 1999). As the Swedish law is written today, the preventative measure – that is, to stop paedophiles from being inspired by child porn to commit sexual acts against children – does not seem to be the foremost motive. Rather, the underlying rationale for the law is that actual children are hurt, that child porn can be used to persuade and coerce children into participating in sexual activity, and that it is degrading to children (see e.g. Prop 1978/79: 179; Prop 1997/98: 43: 65).

There are several problematic issues that have to do with the changes in the law and our perception of child porn. For instance, films that were perfectly legal in one context – such as Danish porn films with performers above the age of consent (fifteen) but under eighteen made during the 1970s – are now illegal. Recently, a book that was published in the early 1980s, arguing against pornography and for erotic images, was put away in Swedish libraries when it became known that there were child pornographic images (to illustrate the bad side of porn) in it (Nestius 1982; Svensson 2014). Since child porn today is often spread via networks over the Internet, images are reproduced and circulated to a much wider extent than before. This also means that there is an accumulation of images, adding newer material to older, of which some is from the 1970s (Andersson 2005).

According to Per Ole Träskman, professor of Law, criminalisation should only and always pertain to actions that are harmful and reprehensible and only when there is no other option to stave off certain behaviour. 'Only actions that typically are the most harmful and the most reprehensible shall be criminalised' (Träskman 1998: 556, my translation). Träskman seems to regard the changes in laws against child porn and the purchase of sexual services as a result of a feminist critique of sexual politics. Although radical feminist thought had gained some measure of influence during the 1990s in Sweden, it is my contention that this is not enough to explain the view on child pornography that has been pervasive not only in Sweden but the European Union, USA, as well as the United Nations since around the 1980s. Rather, paedophilia is a sexual variation that, although rare, has been and has become considered even more monstrous at least throughout the 20th century and into to the 21st. Sexual abuse of children has received increased attention since the late 1970s, and child porn has become an unforgivable crime, since it is regarded as an expression of a deplorable desire, as images that may be made through sexually abusing children but also that tickle that deplorable desire, and as exploitation of vulnerable minors. With the advent of the digital revolution, the fear – both real and imagined – of transnational networks of paedophiles has also increased (see Maddison 2010).

Theoretical framework

In order to tease out the problematics of the non-photographic child porn image, I will turn to C.S. Peirce's semiotics as they have been deployed within film theory (Wollen 1998). Although not very recent (Peirce described his theory of signs in the 19th century and his ideas were brought into film theory in the 1960s), it provides a very fundamental way of understanding signs – what they represent and how they represent. Non-photographic images have a particular relation to the reality they purport to represent since, in contrast to still or moving photographic images with live models, actors, or performers, there is not necessarily a living person in front of the camera to become registered by the film within. In addition, a drawing can be more or less surrealist, abstract, or fantasy-based. A drawing or a computer generated image can contain anthropomorphised animals, things, or fantasy-creatures – like in many Disney or Pixar films where toys, animals, or monsters are animated with human-like characteristics. Such an image – still or moving – can, in addition, be more or less realistic, in the sense that we appreciate the way the animated, non-human characters move and behave as in line with a realistic logic of how the world works, although the talking, moving toys or monsters are not, per se, realistic. This adds several layers to how the Manga images in the present case can be understood and interpreted, something which is quite obvious in the somewhat awkward manner the court speaks about these images. I will explain this more further on.

For the purposes of this chapter, Peirce's classification of signs into icons, indices, and symbols is highly relevant. Furthermore, Peirce claimed that all signs are included in a three-way system – the sign itself, the object that the sign refers to, and the interpretant, that is the understanding of the sign (which should refer back to the object itself but does not necessarily). The interpretant is the most ambiguous part of this triad, but simply put, someone has to see the sign and make the connection (although that connection may be to something other than the object the sign refers to).

The terms icon, index, and symbol describe how the sign (in this case the image) refers to an object. An iconic sign refers to its object by looking like it, for instance as a portrait does or a picture. An indexical sign is the trace left of something, like a footprint in the sand refers to a foot. The third kind of sign, the symbol, is understood through a norm or a code, like a stylised image of a heart refers to love. These norms or codes are often conventional but can also be created from the circumstances of the sign.

Because of the innate photo-chemical technology of photography and cinematography – that is the photographic process that registers images onto film, cinema has been discussed within film theory as a sign language that is simultaneously iconic and indexical. It can also be symbolic. These discussions do not refer to animated film, however, which is more purely iconic but can also be symbolic. Animated films are not indexical because what has been registered by the camera is the drawings – the index in this case would pertain to the process of making the film itself, rather than to the object portrayed.

When discussing child porn, it is the indexicality of the image that brings the strongest response. In order to create a photograph or a film clip of a child in a sexual situation, you have to put that child in that situation, thus abusing, humiliating, and/or traumatising the child. There has to be a 'profilmic' moment, at the very least the staging of a situation that captured by the camera looks sexual. Thus, the image becomes evidence of a crime committed. The fact that someone uses the image for purposes of sexual arousal is regarded as an even further crime, especially the notion that such an image will create a demand for other images of the same kind. However, with a non-photographic image, the indexicality is not there. Even a drawing of one or several models is not a trace of the motif but a rendering of it. Drawings have several indexical signs, but they refer to the pens or pencils used to draw, the ink or lead that has left marks on the paper. Rather, it is the iconicity (the likeness) and the symbolism (its transferred or figurative meaning) that would bring a response to the observer. Thus, the interpretant becomes quite significant in the process of discussing child porn in the form of drawn, painted, or computer generated images.

A criminalisation of the mind?

Träskman discussed the law prohibiting possession of child porn in an article published around the time the law was changed (1998). He claims there are three problems involved in the implementation of the law. Two are definitional and deal with how to define pornography and how to define child. The border between childhood and adulthood has been set at eighteen years, or when puberty has not been completed. The age limit of eighteen is reasonable, considering that it is the UN's definition of a child – a person under eighteen – but it nevertheless conflicts with the Swedish age of sexual consent, which is fifteen. This means that between the ages of fifteen and eighteen, a person can legally be involved in all manners of sexual activities as long as he or she is not being photographed. In addition, the definition stipulates that puberty has to be completed, which is also difficult to determine from pictures (Träskman 1998). Women with small breasts may be discriminated against as they can be deemed as not having completed puberty (cf. the 'A-cup ban' in Australia, in Ozimek 2010). The third problem, according to Träskman, is whether the law actually protects the ones it is supposed to protect, i.e. the children. Träskman argues that there are already laws in place that prohibit the production of child porn and sexual abuse of children, which should be enough.

Träskman does not go into the actual character of the depiction, except to seem to take for granted that it is photographic images – still or moving – that are the topic. Hence, the reference to actual crimes committed at the moment of photographing. Because of the photograph's indexical nature, the crime is photochemically registered by the camera film (or photodigitally) and thus evidence of a sexual abuse. However, drawn images, or, for that matter, images generated by computer (so-called CGI), do not (necessarily) have a 'pro-filmic' moment – of course, in regular film production some CGI:s are created through motion capture of live actors (as in *The Lord of the Rings* [2001–2003]; *King Kong* [2005]; or *Avatar* [2009]), and, again of course, a painter or drawer might use real-life models in order to create life-like paintings or drawings. For instance, when *Snow White and the Seven Dwarfs* (1937) was made by Walt Disney in the 1930s, footage of dancing actors functioned as instruction on how to draw dancing cartoon characters.

Nevertheless, a painter or a drawer may also just as well draw upon images conjured up in his or her mind, using their experience and knowledge to create more or less realist images. One could then say, although this is stretching the meaning of indexicality a bit, that the drawn, fantasised image is a trace or an evidence of a person's thoughts. This is how the prohibition of drawn, painted, or computer generated child pornographic images can be considered a regulation of sexual fantasies. A society cannot forbid what people think about, but it can make attempts at directing thoughts onto certain paths and it can definitely create taboos surrounding certain ideas of the imagination.

The point of criminalising drawn images as well as photographic ones, is that child porn is considered degrading to children in general (e.g., Prop 1978/79: 179; Prop 1997/98: 43, p. 65). All kinds of child porn, accordingly, degrade the very idea of the Child. Children are, in our society, not meant to be thought of as sexual – at least not by adults. As Ost observes: 'The breadth of the chasm between innocence and depravity serves to justify the legal prohibition upon any activity which draws the innocent child and the corrupt possessor of child pornography together, even if the child's presence is in the form of a visual representation only' (2001: 457).

There is a higher, almost metaphysical conception of the image implicit in this – a bit similar to the prohibition of images of God within certain religions – in which the image and what it depicts can degrade, debase, humiliate or blaspheme. However, when the law is interpreted in this way, drawn images without models would actually be even more 'pornographic' than any images with a real-life motif that has been captured, because what the drawer or painter has captured is not one actual child but the abstract idea of a child. Consequently, it would be logical to prohibit and punish the possession of such images because there are endemic qualities to them that pertain to all children.

One of the acquitted images in the Manga case (in Sweden 2010–2012).

The Manga case

In the Manga case, as mentioned previously, fifty-one images were deemed child porn in the first instance, and thirty-nine in the second. In the final instance, only one was deemed to be child pornographic. The description in the decision states:

> The drawings at hand represent fantasy figures. However, it is clear that it is a question of depictions of human beings, and in that sense it can without doubt be said that they are images of humans. From this point of departure, the images depict children whose puberty is not completed. The children are wholly or partially naked and represented in such a way that must be considered as appealing to the sexual drive. In most of the images the genitals are visible and in some images sexual acts are performed. The drawings should be considered pornographic (Supreme Court B 990-11: 4, my translation).

Although this certainly sounds as if the images should be deemed child porn and therefore criminal, the court argued that the law should be interpreted cautiously so that not all nude images of children would be punishable by law: 'A reasonable conclusion is that an equivalent caution should be observed regarding drawn images and other depictions that do not bear reference to real children' (Supreme Court B 990-11: 5, my translation). The thirty-ninth image, however, was deemed as different from the others because 'the child in the picture has features that stand out as real. Also in other ways, the picture must be considered true to real life'. (p. 4, my translation) Further on in the decision, it states that 'Even if the present thirty-eight pictures can appear offensive, the risk for identification and thereby also the risk for degradation of children in general should be considerably much less regarding such images than regarding realistic images with a sexual content. Regarding these images it appears as if self-evident that it does not present a real assault.' (p. 9, my translation) In addition, the risk that children would be shown these images in order to instruct them for a sexual situation, was not deemed realistic (p. 9).

Weighing this against the freedom of expression and information, the court thus found that these thirty-eight images could not be deemed criminal. However, the court expressed itself very carefully: 'That it at all exists pornographic drawing that might bring up the thought of children is hardly such a degradation of children in general that it motivates the relatively far-reaching encroachment of freedom of expression and information that would be implied if such unrealistic drawings without exception were criminalised' (p. 9, my translation) As blogger and professor of Law, Mårten Schultz, interpreted the decision, it did not resolve the issue of drawn images of children in sexual situations, but left it to a case-by-case judgement (Schultz 2012).

In this case, there were three variables to consider, which could be disputed as open to interpretation. Standard in child porn cases are the variables of pornography – can this be defined as pornography or not – and the variable of age – whether this is a depiction of a child in the meaning of the law, that is, the person is under the age of eighteen and has not completed puberty. Pornography seems to be defined by the somewhat old-fashioned expression 'appeals to the sexual drive' (*vädjar till könsdriften*), whereas child is defined through observation and a certain set of norms derived from the Tanner scale that is based in physical appearances of the genitals (male), the breasts (woman), and pubic hair (both genders) (described in District Court B 6344-09). The reason the second court instance acquitted twelve images was that it was not without a doubt that they depicted children. The third variable, which was particular to this case – and for other cases concerning Manga images – is whether the depiction is fantasy or not. In the Court of Appeals, the images are described thus: 'All images on trial depict human beings. Some of the depicted characters have catlike ears and tails whereas others lack nose or mouth. Even if a few of the images do not in all detail stand out as realistic, there is no doubt that they represent humans' (Court of Appeal B 6389-10, my translation). This interpretation, however, was disputed by the Supreme Court, where all except one image were deemed so close to fantasy that they could not be said to realistically depict children.

Interestingly, the only variable that seems to have been unambiguous to the judges were whether the images were pornographic, whether they appealed to the sexual drive. Pornography is notoriously both hard to define and easy to recognize, as the famous quote 'I know it when I see it' by Justice Potter Stewart bears witness to (cf. Williams 1999). However, images once deemed pornographic may lose their ability to arouse sexually over time (such as old stag films), or become, by virtue of historic tradition, regarded as art (like Japanese *shunga* prints), and images that in one context are completely non-sexual can in another context be regarded as controversially eroticised (such as the Pippi Examples; cf. Lehman 2006). In encyclopaedias, pornography is often defined as 'printed or visual material containing the explicit description or display of sexual organs or activity, intended to stimulate sexual excitement' (Oxford online dictionary). Thus, intention, a slippery element of any definition, takes a central role in what may be regarded as pornography. Very likely, the images in this case were produced with an intention of sexual arousal in the viewer. Considering, however, the context of Japanese culture vis-a-vis the Western – in this case Swedish – context, intentions may be difficult to narrow down.

The Manga case was complicated by the fact that although Manga has been popular among young people in the Western world since the 1990s, it is a Japanese cultural form that is not completely understood by the courts. The Court of Appeals explained it through a reference to the Swedish national encyclopaedia, *Nationalencyklopedin*, which bears evidence to the amount of research actually done in relation to the case. The description of the phenomenon of Manga was 'Japanese comics for children and young people, but also for grownups. These comics span all kinds of topics, also eroticism, and have their roots in older Japanese culture. The style of drawing is simplified and stylised. Typical of the characters depicted is that their facial features are simple, often incomplete, and the eyes are large'. (See further e.g., *Nationalencyklopedin*) (Court of Appeal B 6389-10, my translation)

Added to this could be that Japanese art forms rarely focus on realism. Art is seen as a form of presentation, not representation, which means that animated films and drawings are at least as significant as photographs and live-action films. This is why it took a long time before the documentary form gained any influence and why the Japanese audience was not as outraged at fake newsreels as were other audiences (Richie 2005). The artist must be present in the artwork, by arranging and organising whatever is the motif. Therefore, what can be regarded as stylised or artificial in a Western context is considered normal in a Japanese context. Several Manga productions – whether comics or films – are not at all intended for a young audience, but tell quite serious and adult stories. For a Western audience not attuned to Manga, the juxtaposition of stories of war, violence, and misery in stylised, simplified drawings that emphasize *kawaii*, or cuteness (e.g., large eyes, small noses, pink hair) can be quite jarring.

Even further added to this, Japanese culture has long tradition of erotic imagery. So called *shunga* – erotic images often made through wood block printing – have existed for more than a thousand years, and often depict sexuality in ways that might seem strange to Western eyes. Extremely enlarged male genitals, contorted bodies in strange positions, various non-human creatures, tentacles, and robots form the visuals of a sexually imaginative landscape. If realism is important in Western pornography (see Williams, 1999; Larsson 2008), the presentation, the artificiality of the image seems to provide a vital part of the experience of watching such images in a Japanese context. To understand and correctly interpret such images demands a certain knowledge and awareness of Japanese culture – the interpretant, so to speak, needs to have a context in which to place them. Within Manga, the genre of Hentai – erotic Manga pictures – is major, and divided into several subgenres, among them the Lolicon or the Lolita erotic Manga.

However, it might be argued that in a Western context, images that are understood in one way in Japan find a new and somewhat different, although related, meaning. Therefore, the unfamiliarity of this culture might not be a problem for the Western interpretant, because when Manga reaches Western culture it is understood mainly through the genre conventions that are communicated intrinsically through the comics and films themselves rather than by the entire cultural context of their origin (extrinsically). The Manga case nonetheless illustrates that although pornography frequently is defined through intention, context may be an important variable as well, since context shapes the interpretant's frame of understanding – and thus his or her connection of a sign with its meaning.

Concluding discussion

The three variables at hand in this case point to the C. S. Peirce's notion of the triadic nature of the sign: the sign itself, the object that the sign refers to, and the interpretant, the understanding of the sign. If each of the images is considered a sign, what kinds of objects the signs referred to were thus quite dependent on the understanding of the signs. Were they human children in sexual situations? Or were they non-human, fantasy figures, non-realistic, referring not to children in any actual sense but some made-up characters that had been anthropomorphised? Or were they human beings made fantasy-like? That three different courts could make different interpretations of what these signs actually were referring to, indicates that there was vagueness in the interpretant.

This vagueness has to do with both the potential knowledge of and familiarity with the type of images at hand, and the context in which they were made. That the intention of the images was pornographic seems to have unambiguous to all the courts. However, how to understand the signs apart from this intention was quite a different matter.

I would assert that these images actually might have referred more to an abstract idea of a child (or, even, the Child) than to actual children. Focusing on the cute, the soft, the innocent, the vulnerable is to focus on the aspects of childhood that we deem important to protect (cf. Kalha 2011). As Ost points out, studies have shown that actual child abusers do not only use child pornographic images but Walt Disney images, children's clothing catalogues, and advertisements with babies – anything that emphasises the very qualities we associate with childhood and wish to protect (Ost 2001: 457). One rationale of the law – to prohibit child pornography because it is degrading to all children – might thus be operative in this case. I am not saying this in order to claim that the Manga translator should have been convicted, but rather to show the absurdity of this arguing. Raising the idea of the Child to such an implicit and symbolic level would render any kinds of combinations of "cute" and pornography highly problematic.

Considering the crimes most often committed when child pornography is produced, criminalising is beyond a doubt reasonable. However, the issues raised in this chapter demonstrate several highly problematic dimensions of going so far as to treat drawn, painted, or computer generated images in a similar manner as photographs or live-action films. This pertains to both how the law is written and to how that writing relates to the encounter between image and interpretant, the observer of the image – be that interpretant a judge, a paedophile, an artist, an art historian, an expert on for instance (in this case) Manga, or simply a general audience. First, claiming that such images are degrading to children in general implies an abstracted and idealised notion of the Child, making the boundaries between what should or should not be understood as a child in an image ambiguous, especially in cases where the images are not realistic. Second, since the child or children in such a drawn, painted, or computer generated image – unless a model has been used – are fictitious, they should be regarded as constructed out of the creator's imagination. Accordingly, regulating such images becomes a way of attempting to regulate the mind. In addition – and third – the understanding of such an image, the connecting of that image to both children and pornography – is highly dependent on the interpretant, the person observing that image. Thus, the interpretation of the image may very well be influenced by the fantasies the observer has.

References

Andersson, M. (2005) *Porr: en bästsäljande historia*. Stockholm: Prisma.

Court of Appeal (Hovrätten), case no B3868-08, September 4, 2008.

Edenborg, C.-M. (2010) 'Gräv ner era serietidningar!' *Aftonbladet*, July 21. http://www.aftonbladet.se/kultur/article12398244.ab.

Juridikbloggen (2011) Mangadomen. January 28. http://juridikbloggen.wordpress.com/2011/01/28/mangadomen/

Kalha, H. (2011) 'What the hell is the figure of the child? Figuring out figurality in, around, and beyond Lee Edelman'. *Lamdba Nordica* 2–3: 17–46.

Larsson, M. (2008) 'Det förbjudnas cinéma vérité: amatörpornografi på Internet'. In E. Hedling, E. & M. Jönsson (eds) *Välfärdsbilder: svensk film utanför biografen*. Stockholm: Kungliga biblioteket.

Leijonhufvud, M. (2010) 'Det ska inte vara straffbart att avbilda fiktiva barn'. *Dagens Nyheter*, August 4. http://www.dn.se/debatt/det-ska-inte-vara-straffbart-att-avbilda-fiktiva-barn/.

Liljestrand, J. (2010) 'Barnporrlagen tillämpas på ett kulturfientligt sätt. Här behövs en öppen och saklig debatt.' *Dagens Nyheter*. August 3. http://www.dn.se/kultur-noje/kulturdebatt/jens-liljestrand-barnporrlagen-tillampas-pa-ett-kulturfientligt-satt-har-behovs-en-oppen-och-sakli/.

Maddison, S. (2010) 'Online obscenity and myths of freedom: dangerous images, child porn, and neoliberalism'. In F. Attwood (ed) *porn.com: Making Sense of Online Pornography*. Basingstoke: Palgrave Macmillan.

Mulvey, L. (1975) 'Visual pleasure and narrative cinema'. *Screen* 16(3): 6–18.

Nestius, H. (1982) *I last och lust: sexuella bilder förr och nu*. Stockholm: Prisma.

Ost, S. (2002) 'Children at risk: legal and societal perceptions of the potential threat that the possession of child pornography poses to society'. *Journal of Law and Society* 29(3): 436–460.

Oxford online dictionary, http://www.oxforddictionaries.com/definition/english/pornography.

Ozimek, J.F. (2010) 'Aussie censor balks at bijou boobs: Gets confused about other female bits also.' *The Register*, 28 January. http://www.theregister.co.uk/2010/01/28/australian_censors/.

Penal Code, Ch. 16, sec.10 https://lagen.nu/1962:700#A2.

Prop 1978/79:179: Om ändring i Tryckfrihetsförordningen m.m.

Prop 1997/98:43: Tryckfrihetsförordningens och yttrandefrihetsgrundlagens tillämpningsområden - barnpornografifrågan m.m.

Richie, D. (2005) *A Hundred Years of Japanese Film: A Concise History, With a Selective Guide to DVDs and Videos*. Tokyo: Kodansha.

Schultz, M. (2012) 'Bild 39. Och några andra svårigheter med Mangadomen'. *Juridikbloggen*, June 15. https://juridikbloggen.wordpress.com/2012/06/15/friande-dom-i-mangamalet/.

Supreme Court (Högsta domstolen), case no B 990-11, June 15, 2012.

Svensson, M. (2014) 'Lust och last i biblioteket'. *Smålandsposten*, March 11. http://www.smp.se/ledare/lust-och-last-i-biblioteket%284194543%29.gm.

Thurfjell, K. (2013) 'Abrahamsson frias från barnporr'. In *Svenska Dagbladet*, April 9. http://www.svd.se/nyheter/inrikes/maria-abrahamsson-frias-fran-barnporrinnehav_8066892.svd.

Träskman, P.O. (1998). 'Går det att tygla lustan? Om straffbar pornografi, pedofili och prostitution'. *Tidskrift utgiven av juridiska föreningen i Finland* 134(3–4): 352–372.

Westerstrand, J. (2014) 'Sexköpslagen – motstånd över tid och former'. *Retfærd* 145(2): 4–36.

Westrin, S. (2013) 'I skuggan av teckning 39'. *Svenska Dagbladet*, July 9. http://www.svd.se/kultur/ett-ar-efter-mangadomen-har-seriesverige-mentala-handklovar_8247466.svd.

Widegren, K. (2004) 'Sexualiserade bilder av flickor. Pippi Examples och den manliga blicken'. *Kvinnovetenskaplig tidskrift* 4: 9–27.

Williams, L. (1999) *Hard Core: Power, Pleasure, and the "Frenzy of the Visible"*. Berkeley: Univ. of California Press.

Wollen, P. (1998) *Signs and Meaning in the Cinema*. London: BFI Publ.

Sven-Axel Månsson

Johns' Fantasies of 'the Prostitute'

> I did have some fantasy about the type of people that would be involved – they would be mysterious, not run-of-the-mill people on the street. She was going to be very overbearing about it ... I thought she would be very mysterious, hardly any talk, just walk in and take over the situation. I thought that she would have something, for sure, like a dildo strapped to her... or gloves, a whip.... I had envisioned all kinds of neat stuff like she'd turn out the lights and we'd only have one tiny candle and she would take over, maybe incense, or she'd get us all wild with some exotic oil (Holzman & Pines 1982: 104).

Until rather recently the phenomenon of men buying sex and the fantasies attached to it has been overlooked in research. The focus of interest has been on the sellers, primarily women, and not on the buyers. Alfred C. Kinsey's determined idea about this was that the extent of public attention which the subject receives is all out of proportion to its significance in the lives of most males. Or in his own words: 'For an activity which contributes no more than this does to the sexual outlet of the male population, it is amazing that it should have been given such widespread consideration' (Kinsey 1948: 605). Certainly, he says, 'the older accounts would make it appear that prostitution was much more important in the life of the male who lived at any time between the dawn of history and World War 1 than we have evidence of its having been since then' (ibid.: 606).[1] On the other hand, states Kinsey, prostitution continues to exist, and one may well ask why men buy sex. I agree with him on this, and the fact

1 In his pioneering research on North American men's sexual behaviour, Alfred Kinsey stated that the majority (69 per cent) of all grown (white) men had had experiences of paid sexual encounters. This was probably an exaggeration. Furthermore he qualified the high number by emphasising that the proportion of men with repeated or regular contacts in commercial sex was relatively low. More recent research in the United States and Europe provides a somewhat different picture. Only 16 per cent of men in the United States have ever visited a prostitute, according to a nationwide survey conducted in 1992 (Michael, et al. 1994: 63). A similar study in Sweden showed that about every eighth man over eighteen years of age (approximately 13 per cent) had at some point in their life paid for sex (Månsson 2000: 236). A questionnaire survey among a representative sample of Norwegians aged 18–49 years showed that 13 per cent of the men had bought sex at least once (Traeen, et al. 2005: 2). The corresponding figure from a Danish study is 14 per cent (Lautrup 2005: 50). The results from Sweden also confirm Kinsey's observation that buying sex on a more regular basis is done by a minority; i.e.

that relatively few men seek sex from prostitutes does not mean that many more do not fantasise about it.

The studies that do exist in the field (for example Monto 2002, Legardinier & Bouamama 2004, Månsson 2005, Bernstein 2007, Sanders 2008a, Milrod & Monto 2012, Gerheim 2012) suggest that there are multiple reasons for men engaging with women who sell sex, both with respect to what *pushes* the buyers to do so (emotional needs, unsatisfactory sex 'at home', loneliness, etc.) and what *pulls* them to it (horniness, curiosity, excitement, etc.). In actual fact, there seems to be no sharp dividing line between the pushes and the pulls; unsatisfactory sex at home could lead to ideas and fantasies of the kind of sex that one misses out on, and so on. In this article I am not primarily concerned with the individual variation of fantasies about the prostitute and what she can deliver, but rather what these fantasies represent on a social and cultural level, i.e. their social meaning and significance. It is my contention that men's images and fantasies of the prostitute in heterosexual commercial sex reflect dominant themes of sexual culture and gender relations in society. Some of these themes seem to be relatively stable over time with roots far back in history, while others can be conceived as results of changing social and economic conditions, sexual cultures, and relations between men and women in present day Western society. In this respect, I will primarily focus on what pulls men to the prostitute. I rely on my own observations and writings in the field for more than thirty years (Månsson 1984, 1988, 2000, 2001, 2005), but also in part on the writings and research of others.

Forbidden fruit

To some men, the fantasies attached to 'the prostitute' are sexually exciting in a distinct and very immediate way, as can be seen from the introductory quote from Holzman and Pines. This can probably be ascribed to the contradictory character of the sex trade, as being both attractive and repulsive; repulsive because it is often looked upon as 'bad' and forbidding. At the same time, forbidden or secret impulses attached to sexual fantasies often add to sexual arousal in a number of ways. Sometimes, it seems that sex buyers handle these contradictory feelings by projecting the image of 'dirty whore' onto the woman who makes herself publicly available. Or, as O'Connell Davidson puts it in her seminal book *Prostitution, Power and Freedom* (1998) in a chapter titled 'Fucking dirty whores':

---

approximately one fifth of them had done it ten times or more, while approximately 60 per cent had done it three times or less (Månsson 2000: 238).

'Such men eroticize both the idea of the prostitute's public availability and her instrumental, impersonal approach to sex' (p. 140).

However, this kind of projection often occurs *after* the sexual contact is terminated, argue Holzman & Pines (1982: 109). From the first moment, when the intent to pay for sex is conceived, a fantasy is created, and most of the buyer's energy is directed into structuring the situation and encounter in harmony with this fantasy, whatever the content of this may be. Distractions from this fantasy (the looks of the prostitute, how she behaves, what she says, how she says it, etc.) are dismissed and/or worked into it. However, soon after the sexual contact has terminated, when the excitement is over, the client's focus broadens, and his awareness of other aspects of the situation and the character of the woman increases. By labelling her as a whore, she becomes for the buyer the embodiment of low morals, someone who has allowed herself to be used by numerous other men. Furthermore, from the point of view of the buyer, this labelling serves as a form of liberation from guilt, marking him off from the prostitute; he – not she – appears as the socially respectable and morally innocent. She exposed herself, and made herself available. Consequently, she is the one to blame, not he, etc. (Holzman & Pines 1982, Månsson 1984, O'Connell Davidson, 1998).

In this process there seems to be a more or less gradual movement, a sliding away from sexual fantasies which functions as an attraction in relation to women who sell sexual services to fantasies which function as some sort of justification in relation to the possible guilt and shame involved in the act of buying sex. In some cases these fantasies blend into one another, when the idea that 'she really likes it' is arousing, added to by her coming across as skilled and experienced (such as in the introductory quote). O'Connell Davidson (1998) discusses this in terms of 'the contradictions of clienting'. The woman's deliberate professionalism, as conceived by the buyer, automatically functions as a justification for the act of buying. Both parties are seen as equally strong and the exchange of money for sex thus a highly justifiable transaction.

Space and place

As the introductory quote also implies, access and situational circumstances seem to be important factors in triggering men's attraction to women in prostitution. The whole idea of 'the prostitute' as a 'public woman' has been and still is a strong element in men's fantasies, even if the space of prostitution has been thoroughly transformed over the last decades (Monto 2000). The commercial sex milieu itself seems to evoke curiosity and excitement. In the red light districts or other places where sex trade occurs, the environment functions as an 'invitation' to sex. This is underscored by the pornographic script and framework, for example the sex clubs and porn stores, which border 'the strolls' or 'beats' in the red light districts of big cities, or the pornographic content of advertisements on the web sites of the Internet. In no other places are women so openly exposed sexually. Or as the Netherlands Board of Tourism and Convention puts it when identifying the red light district of Amsterdam as a key place to visit, where 'women of all nationalities, parade their wares in red-fringed window parlours, many ready to offer more than a schoolboy peep-show in a private cabin' (quote in Hubbard & Whowell 2008: 1745).

Although prostitution has long existed in a variety of forms and expressions in public life, it has taken on new modalities over the last few decades as the sex industry itself has diversified and become more accessible. Hubbard and Whowell (2008) offer a thorough analysis of the changes in the 'geographies of sex work,' noting important continuities as well as major shifts in the location of prostitution. They argue that spending on sexual services has reached new levels and become more or less mainstream, normalised, or even gentrified ('adult entertainment'), imbued with new-found respectability, as a growing sector in consumer-based societies in the post-industrial world (ibid.: 1745; cf. Bernstein 2007, Månsson & Söderlind 2013). Moreover, they propose that such a diversification and normalisation of the sex industry problematises any clear distinction between prostitution, adult entertainment, and pornography, given that all of them provide sexual gratification for payment in some form or other. Furthermore, such a diversification stresses that the stigmatising term 'prostitute' may be unduly restrictive when considering the diverse and various ways in which sex is bought and sold in contemporary public space. According to North American sociologist Bernstein (2007), the new technologies of the post-industrial society have helped to remove 'shame' from selling sexual services. The idea is that the prostitution stigma, intimately tied to the street, has been lifted. The public woman is not so public anymore. A new space has emerged, a new space for a new subject, a subject that is like 'anyone else'. Bernstein speaks of the relocation of prostitution from the outdoor public space to indoor private spaces as a 'privatization of public women'. Hulusjö (2013), in her study of prostitution in Sweden, shows how some women actively position themselves against 'the street prostitute', equating her with 'the whore', someone worn down, an outsider, *the other*.

It is interesting to reflect on the impact of these changes, how the practices and meanings of prostitution have shifted in relation to the spaces it occupies. Shame and stigma being 'taken away', one could argue that some of the excitement disappears in relation to the element of darkness and danger, of 'forbidden fruit'. As we pointed out above, however, even if most encounters between seller and buyers today take place indoors, Hulusjö argues (2013) that most of the imagery around prostitution is still tightly connected to the public woman of the street: women leaning into cars, standing on street corners, etc. She says: 'The placement of "prostitutes" in space clearly does much to inform conceptions and constructions of the status of women involved in prostitution' (2013: 209).

This process of normalisation (which I will discuss later on in this chapter) does not change the fact that the state and laws in most countries continue to have a regulating influence on the forms, expressions, and locations of commercial sexuality, i.e. on the moral geography of prostitution, to use a term from Hubbard and Whowell (2008). This includes countries where the buying (but not the selling) of sexual services are forbidden, such as Sweden and Norway, but also countries with a licensing system such as the Netherlands and Germany, where there still are restrictions which ban the selling of sexual services in many neighbourhoods. Thus various expressions of the legal framing of prostitution in public space clearly demonstrate that sexual services are not regarded as part of a 'normal' service economy. And partly as an effect of these restrictions and regulations, men's buying of sexual services still remains relatively covert or hidden away from their normal spaces and functions in everyday life.

One aspect of this is that, without venturing out of one's own private space to expose oneself, the buyer can *anonymously* explore online spaces of prostitution (Scarmuzzino 2014). Interestingly, Hulusjö (2013) finds in her study of prostitution experience in Sweden a similar pattern among the women she interviewed. Some women state that they probably would not have entered into prostitution if it had not been possible to familiarise oneself with it beforehand in privacy. The online spaces, forums, and sex-dating sites offer possibilities for approaching prostitution and exploring the *modus operandi* of negotiations and transactions without the risk of exposing oneself and without having to enter into the 'real' prostitution space. The review function of the forums sends a clear message as to what the buyers expect and are willing to pay for. And even though the women interviewed by Hulusjö resisted the idea of themselves as commodified body objects, they also spoke of conforming to culturally prescribed norms of feminine sexuality as a tactic to attract the potential buyers (2013: 258).

Somewhat paradoxically, it seems that the more accessible and normalised prostitution becomes in the era of the Internet, the more anonymous and hidden the sex buyers' behaviour. Gradually, research is starting to explore the ways in which changes in the moral geography of prostitution have contributed to the consumer experience by eventually heightening or lowering specific desires and fantasies. Below, I will discuss some of these research findings.

Curiosity and sexual variation

Interestingly enough, only few of the men (approximately one in ten) I have interviewed explicitly discuss their sexual needs as the reason why they visit women in prostitution (Månsson & Linders 1984). The same phenomenon was pointed out by Charles Winick in his classical study of North American sex buyers (1962): the men remarkably seldom mention their sexual urges in connection with buying sex. Winick offers the following interpretation to this apparently noteworthy observation.

> It seems possible that the emotional meanings and overtones in visiting a prostitute are much more salient for the man than the desire for a sexual experience. Another way of expressing this is that the desire for sexual experience manifests itself and is translated into different ways of looking at the prostitute and himself, as the interviewees voice it (Winnick 1962: 231).

This interpretation is based on constantly recurring statements from interviewees who say 'the prostitute gives me what I want' and 'I get something different out of the visit', statements that are not accompanied by any closer precision or exactitude. This makes Winick draw the conclusion that the 'prostitute' as well as the visit itself has an important symbolic meaning for the men, suggesting that the actual content of the experience is sometimes of less importance than the meaning that it – and the 'prostitute' – has in the man's fantasy. This is, however, not the same as saying that the men have no sexual needs when they visit prostitutes, argues Winick. It only means that they often do not spontaneously talk about their own sexuality when they discuss why they buy sex. They talk about other things, through which this need is expressed. Thus, they frequently talk about 'curiosity', 'excitement' or 'variation'. And the statements that deal with curiosity seem to reflect a desire in the men to be able to have a sexual experience which only in exceptional cases can be acquired in encounters with non-prostitute women. Not entirely unexpected, curiosity is a strongly driving motive behind the first visit to a prostitute. This curiosity can involve different elements in commercial sex: the 'prostitute' or 'whore', the setting in which she is found, and the type of sexual activity she is expected to offer (Månsson & Linders 1984).

Another kind of sex

In this respect, men's fantasies around prostitution often involve encountering a sexually advanced and experienced woman, who is willing to perform the kind of sex that they cannot have with their steady partners. A typical saying is: 'My wife does not want to try anything new'. Consequently, the desire for sexual variation can imply that the man has special sexual fantasies which he dares not, or cannot, express in the relationship with his steady partner. It may be that he feels ashamed of asking, or of 'forcing something on someone' he 'loves and respects', as one of my interviewees put it. A key issue here seems to be the idea that one's partner does not enjoy sex, which ultimately gives one the right to seek out prostitutes. In this way, one is actually doing one's partner a favour:

> Well, you should know, I'm actually married… married to a wonderful, fine, little human being, sweet and lovely in every way, but her sexual need is not as strong as mine. And I don't want to force her into something that she doesn't fancy. In fact, I think that it would be dead wrong. That's why I don't do it. Instead, I sneak away, so to say, and find someone who can help me out of this dilemma. And I feel no remorse, neither with regard to my family, nor to the prostitute (Månsson & Linders 1984: 126).

In Holzman and Pine's study, some of the men expressed excitement over the element of risk that they envisage prevailing over such encounters (p. 104). Furthermore, for some men, this excitement seems to be based on the fantasy of the 'professional' woman, someone with exceptional sexual skills and powers, willing to provide special services. At the same time, there is also research showing that most clients do not request exotic or kinky sex; instead they tend to buy regular intercourse or masturbation (Lautrup 2005). This observation is substantiated by Milrod and Monto (2012) who interviewed close to 600 men who solicit women who sell sex through an internet website. When asked what sexual activities they most often participated in with a prostitute, the men selected penile-vaginal intercourse. This preference for the most culturally conventional sex act can also be contrasted with their relatively infrequent preference for anal sex. Milrod and Monto found that only 1.6 per cent reported this as the activity most often engaged in with a prostitute (p. 806).

However, it all seems to depend on who you ask. Interviews with women in prostitution sometimes suggest that men's demands seem to be inspired by what they see displayed in pornography (Månsson 1981). It is also interesting to note that some men openly demand a different and more passive sexual role for themselves in their contacts with prostitutes, compared to how they behave in their ordinary relationships. In a study conducted by American sexologist Martha Stein (1974) on the clients of call-girls, it appeared that the act most requested was the woman performing oral sex on the man. Many 'johns', especially the older ones, expressed displeasure with their wives' unwillingness to perform this particular act. The second most requested act was the woman sitting on top of the man.[2]

---

2 A position also preferred by many of the women – for security reasons; this way they can more easily control the movements and actions of the buyer.

According to Stein, about half of the men assumed a passive role and left it to the prostitute to lead the encounter and take all the initiative. It thus appears as though, in certain situations, men prefer to abandon their socially constructed power position (the majority of the men in Stein's study were from the upper echelon of society) and assume a role that allows them to relinquish control and ignore demands concerning sexual performance. In one of our own studies a man told us about his 'passive' experiences with women in prostitution:

> I think that more than half of those who seek out prostitutes are given a hand-job, which is what they really desire. Because then they get the right kind of contact with the woman. Only then does he get to look her in the eyes. Only then is he allowed to feel her hand around his pole, and only then will he see her breasts and other parts of her body. The sexual contact with a woman does not necessarily imply having intercourse. It can also be that she masturbates for you. It won't break you; you won't lose your pride (Månsson & Linders 1984: 107).

Julia O'Connell Davidson (1998) discusses men's eroticising of the prostitute as a sexually powerful woman. Her focus is a bit different from Stein's in that it primarily deals with men who pay prostitutes for sexual domination. After having interviewed a variety of 'johns', whose preference it is to be hurt or humiliated, dressed as a slave, etc., she concludes that in their fantasy they 'want to construct the prostitute as an immensely powerful, "phallic" woman, for it is her (illusory) power to debase them as masculine and sexual beings which they find erotic' (1998: 148). O'Connell Davidson underlines the fact that these men are not interested in having sex with any 'dirty whore'; and they do not like 'cheap' places but prefer 'classier' set-ups. And they emphasise that they never use street 'hookers', because they strongly associate these women with 'powerlessness and vulnerability' (ibid.).

What is displayed here is a power game that is both complex and contradictory, argues O'Connell Davidson. The man does not surrender to the woman in any real way. On the contrary, he uses his power to construct a situation where the traditional sexual roles are reversed. Thus the woman's power connected to her dominant position in the sexual act is only situational and so is the man's willingness to release his control. Ultimately the woman's value is attached to the fact that 'the prostitute *is* a prostitute'. In fact, one may argue, writes the author, that the client dehumanises her and refuses to recognise her as anything more than her body and her sexual agency (p. 150).

It is likely, though, that this view would be contested by the men themselves, at least those who define the relationship as personal and emotional, for example in connection with the so-called *girlfriend experience* (GFE), i.e. the idea that the relationship is something more than a commercial transaction, meaning that there are authentic emotions and real intimacy involved and that the experience of sexual pleasure is mutual.

The girlfriend experience

In his round up and overview of some recent books on prostitution and sex work, U.K. sociologist Ken Plummer (2010) argues that over the last fifty years there has been a major widening and speeding up of the worlds of prostitution and sex work due to globalisation, mediaisation, digitalisation and the spread of neo-liberal markets of postmodern capitalism. Among other things, this shift has caused a reworking of the boundaries between intimacy and commerce 'in new and challenging ways' (Plummer 2010: 398).

Plummer refers to U.S. sociologist Elizabeth Bernstein who claims that the meaning of commercial sexuality has begun to shift towards what she calls a 'bounded authenticity'. Sex in prostitution is no longer just about buying and receiving a quick bodily release, she argues. It is more and more developing into a complex relationship linked to intimacies. Bernstein claims that there is no longer a simple cash nexus and market relation, but increasingly one where many women in commercial sex are paid to provide erotic acts premised upon the promise of an 'authentic' interpersonal liaison. Bernstein is not alone in claiming these changes. Sociologist Teela Sanders (2008b) parallels Bernstein in suggesting that sex work and prostitution should no longer be seen as about sex alone, but about new forms of the search for intimacies.

In her work Sanders explores the relationship between intimacy and sexual commerce. She asks herself 'whether the sexual script amongst male clients in the commercial sexual relationship differs significantly from that of heterosexual men seeking conventional relationships' (2008b: 401). The answer according to her is no. Based on evidence taken largely from interviews with twenty-eight men who describe themselves as 'regular' visitors to the same sex worker(s), Sanders argues that there are striking similarities in the acting out of sexual scripts (the role of communication, courtship rituals, sexual familiarity, the desire for mutual satisfaction, and the development of friendship and emotional connections), and in the process of sexual engagement and emotional desires between men and women in conventional and commercial sexual relationships (ibid.).

In other words, what men in her study seem to be looking for in commercial sexuality is the regular and ordinary, not the irregular and extraordinary. In that respect, Sanders' interviewees clearly differ from the man in the introductory quote from Holzman and Pines (*I did have some fantasy about the type of people that would be involved – they would be mysterious, not run-of-the-mill people on the street*).

This is not what the regulars in Sander's study are looking for and fantasising about. Furthermore, for them, the sex act itself is not the main objective of engaging women who sell sex but just a component of interpersonal intimacy charged by the desire for mutual satisfaction, as Sanders puts it. The desire for mutuality is intrinsically functional in men's individual sexual stories, she argues, tied closely to issues of self-esteem, sexual performance, and body image. Some, maybe most, men do realise that 'faking pleasure' on the woman's part is just part of the service. 'Some of them are very good actresses…', as one of Sander's interviewees puts it. Still many men convince themselves – fantasise – that the experience is mutual (p. 408).

Like most other contemporary researchers in the field (for example Earle & Sharp 2007, Holt, et al. 2007) Bernstein and Sanders attribute this development to the internet and to the significant amount of time spent in front of computers and on wireless mobile devices viewing and downloading sexual images (as 'food' for fantasies), viewing porn, and locating sex partners. One of the most ambitious empirical studies of the behaviours and preferences of male customers of 'internet sexual service providers' (another term for prostitutes), is Milrod's and Monto's 'The Hobbyist and the Girlfriend Experience' (2012). The target population of this extensive questionnaire study is a sample of close to 600 adult American men who are paying members of the Erotic Review, a review website on the internet. The results show a strong preference among the men for a GFE. When asked directly about the most attractive characteristics in an 'internet sexual service provider', more than 80 per cent of the responding men check the alternative *Happy and cheerful personality* and more than two-thirds check *They act like girlfriends, not like prostitutes*. Conversely, Milrod and Monto conclude, 'providers' who rush sessions and act emotionally cold are turn-offs to the respondents. The challenging performances thus required from the women means that they must not only sell various sex acts but also persuade the buyer that they are personally interested in him, 'even amid the obvious contradiction of payment' (p. 806).

I think that it is important to point out that 'the girlfriend experience' is not a new phenomenon in prostitution. The traditional Japanese geisha system comes to mind. Traditional Japan embraced sexual delights and men were not constrained to be faithful to their wives. The ideal wife was a modest mother and manager of the home; in Confucian custom love had secondary importance. For sexual enjoyment and romantic attachment, men did not go to their wives, but to courtesans. The wording 'the girlfriend experience' might be recent, but the phenomenon is old, so to speak. Furthermore, the idea of intimacy as a commodity has been and still is prevalent and central in much of sex tourism and in the fantasies and mythologies surrounding sexual interaction between the first world's male tourist and the third world's native woman. In Cohen's seminal work (1996) *Thai tourism – Hill tribes, Islands and Open-Ended Prostitution* the tourists' own definition of their relationships with the Thai women emphasises the reciprocal and intimate aspect. This comes close to what Cohen defines as 'open-ended prostitution', i.e. a relationship that starts with an exchange of money for sexual services but later, during the men's stay in the country, develops 'into a more protracted, diffused and personalized relationship, involving both emotional and economic interest' (1996: 275). Another example of this is to be found in Gunther's study of sex tourists, in which men who have bought sex in another country reject the label 'prostitution' (Gunther 1998: 71). Instead, the men's own definitions of their relationships with the women emphasise the reciprocal and intimate aspects. Eventually, they admit that there was an exchange of money for sexual services at some point, but they argue that this took place within a personalised and emotional relationship. Such relationships presuppose a tacit understanding where *both parties* contribute to a 'romantic' staging of the relationship, which tones down the visibility of the economic aspects of the transaction (cf. Bang Fossum 2001).

It is my contention that prostitutes' *claims* nowadays to provide a 'girlfriend experience' is what is new, even if there is evidence that women involved in commercial sex have traded in capacities other than the sex itself throughout much of history. Of course, the claims-making in itself is tightly connected to the revolutionary changes of *impression management* (Goffman 1959) that the internet has provided the sex industry: a new platform for marketing the merchandise and for empowering the 'providers' to frame and present their services according to their own script. This often includes distancing oneself from stigmatising preconceptions and ideas of the 'prostitute' (doing respectable femininity), and shifting the focus from the economic transaction to the desire of mutual satisfaction.

The fantasy of the kind-hearted comforter

> Many of the men that you meet are in a relationship in which the sex isn't working and they are starved for touch and comments and praise for their bodies and all these things. ... Some are just into the sex and it's very straightforward but my experience tells me that there are many who are looking for something else. They want what they don't have otherwise and *sometimes it's some special kind of sex but sometimes it's just to be seen and held and that whole thing.* [...] I think that a man's experience of this moment will be based on different things and it's not only about whether the sex was one hundred percent, it's mostly about whether he feels like he got what he was missing (Interview with Sonja, in Hulusjö 2013: 242, my emphasis).

Not too distant from the fantasy of the girlfriend experience lies what has been called the image of the *kind-hearted comforter* (an expression coined by O'Connell Davison 1998: 152). Oftentimes, GFE is not only about sex but also about emotional needs. The idea of the kind-hearted comforter refers to some men's self-experienced difficulties in approaching women, in particular women as sex-partners. Primarily, we are talking about men who consider themselves as having great difficulties in making contact with women due to looks, physical and mental handicaps and age, i.e. factors that may push them towards prostitutes. An expression like 'there are no other women for me' does not necessarily mean that those who say it in reality have no opportunities for making contact with women. It rather refers to men's own views of what they imagine is available to them on the non-commercial sex market. A man in his forties recounts his attempts to establish contact with women:

> I have tried…ever since I was 16–17 years of age. First in my own circle of friends, and later on at dances. But in my circles it was a sign of honour not to try *it* with the girls, or to sexually take advantage of them. Instead, one was supposed to protect them. Later, at dances, it was like a wall of bricks that appeared between me and the girl, if I tried to get close to her. However, I don't think that this was the only reason. I just couldn't dance, not even one step. The girls I tried to approach were girls that danced and they surely noticed my inability. I also drank too much, so it wasn't at all strange that they didn't accept my invitations (Månsson 1988: 31).

The most important criterion in commercial sex is the man's ability to pay, not his social abilities or sexual attractiveness. To some men, this obviously comes as a relief, a relatively simple economic transaction, and the problems are gone, at least temporarily.

O'Connell Davidson harshly criticises what she calls the discourse about prostitution as a form of sexual therapy or healing. She argues that presenting the prostitute as a kind-hearted comforter permits the buyer to tell himself that it is not simply lust but rather his loneliness that makes him seek out prostitutes. 'But behind such narratives', she says, 'there are generally sexual scripts which have as much to do with vengeance and control as those enacted by any other client' (1998: 152). As the buyer sees it, in his inner world of illusions, it is the duty of the prostitute to make him feel potent and to support his sense of being in control. The buyer simply transfers his urge for potency on to her. This is one of the keys to his vulnerability, but sometimes also to his potential dangerousness. Transferring the fantasy to become potent (and sexually released) on to the prostitute, also means that he projects his possible sexual impotence on to her.

Interviews with prostitutes show an awareness of how to act if the buyer has problems with impotence or erectile dysfunction (Borg, et al. 1981; Hedin &

Månsson 1998). Among other things, it entails taking an understanding and supportive position, a position that will not offend the buyer or cause his anger. As the saying sometimes goes among women in prostitution: 'a man who fails to get an erection can become a dangerous man' (Hedin & Månsson 1998: 106). Simultaneously, in this situation, lies also the power of the woman who possesses the opportunity to reject him and thereby to shut him out, not only from the sexual act, but also, in a deeper sense, from experiencing himself as potent and feeling alive. Of course, this can be a dangerous position of power to be in, because the man cannot always realise or admit to himself that the impotence lies with him. In such situations there is a fine line between sexual inadequacy and violence. The buyer may seek revenge, because in his fantasy she refuses him his right to potency. Shutting him out and thus denying him the 'ultimate proof' of his masculinity may end in her being violated (Borg, et al., 1981, Månsson 1988).

Fantasies of another kind of woman

I started this exposé of what men are looking for in prostitution by discussing men's fantasies about another kind of sex, sex that one can only get from 'whores', and how these fantasies have their roots far back in history. However, to refer back to Winick's classical study (1962), it is clear that the visit to a 'prostitute' and the sex that comes with it, is of less importance than the meaning it has in the men's fantasy, as a symbolic proof of masculinity or manhood. As it turns out, some men are not primarily looking for another kind of sex but rather for another kind of woman. And this seems to have its roots, not so much in history as in changing gender relations in contemporary society. For some men the extension of equal rights to women is sometimes experienced as a loss, rather than a gain. As sociologist and gender researcher Michael Kimmel puts it: 'As women advance in real life, they are pushed back in men's fantasies' (Kimmel 2005: 125). Some men react strongly to this development, showing strong regressive and anti-feminist attitudes. And it is probably fair to argue that this also pulls some men into seeking compensation in prostitution.

Sex tourism is an arena where this power game is played out (Truong 1990, Skrobanek, et al. 1997, Bishop & Robinson 1998). This becomes clear just by looking at the marketing of women in the sex tourist 'paradises' around the world, in which sexual-racist and ethnic stereotypes play a big role (Bishop & Robinson 1998). Asian women are portrayed as loving and submissive, African women as wild, and Latin American women as free and easy. It is not difficult to visualise how these stereotypes can give rise to men's talk and fantasies about 'another kind of woman' as a compensation for the reduction of masculine and sexual power in their own everyday relationships.

O'Connell Davidson, who has studied sex tourism, writes: 'The sex tourists… are certainly not alone in their disquiet, but they are distinguished by the fact that they attach such an immediate *erotic* significance to this sense of loss' (O'Connell Davidson 2001: 13). These men project their images of a 'true' femininity on to the women they encounter on their trips abroad. The women are regarded by the men as being close to a 'state of nature', implying that the women themselves have recognised the essential differences between men and women, and that they have accepted their 'natural born' roles as comforters of men's sexual needs.

It is my contention that men's search for and fantasies about 'another kind of woman' signify both change and continuity from a historical point of view. Continuity in relation to the image of the woman in prostitution whose 'natural' obligation is, and has always been, to take care of men's sexual needs; change in relation to how these needs express themselves in a time when women's structural position in Western society is undergoing radical changes that some men cannot handle, not least because these changes pose new challenges in sexual relationships between men and women.

In this perspective, it is interesting to note that some Scandinavian buyers are eager to emphasise that they buy sex only from independent, grown-up women who can vouch for themselves; they would never buy sex from a woman if they felt that she sold herself against her free will (Lautrup 2005: 15). In a comparative study between Thai, Indian, Italian, and Scandinavian sex buyers, interview data show that when the prostitutes were ranked according to attractiveness, migrant prostitutes perceived as having been forced into prostitution and trafficked were deemed less attractive than local women whom the interviewees imagined as having entered sex work voluntarily, thus enjoying better conditions (Anderson & O'Connell Davidson 2003: 22). In reality, it is of course difficult, not to say impossible, for the sex buyer to penetrate or see behind the surface. What he encounters is in most cases a masquerade of 'shameless' advertisements and smiling faces, faces that confirm his idea that she likes what she is doing and that it is not against her free will.

Nevertheless, it is interesting to see how the moral dilemma that some men say that they experience in relation to buying sex sometimes is brought out into the open, for example on web sites where men trade information and review women they have met at home or abroad. Some members write lengthy, sexually explicit, and quite detailed stories reporting on their visits to a certain prostitute or to a red light district. These stories sometimes have a definite pornographic quality to them, and they all more or less seem to support the idea that one of the sexual attractions of prostitution is to talk, fantasise, and brag about it. Interwoven with these stories, discussions about the women's conditions in prostitution and the men's responsibility, as buyers, vis-à-vis these women sometimes appear. The discussants often argue that they do what they do because they 'need sex', and they buy it from grown-up, mature women, who sell it voluntarily (Scaramuzzino 2014).

But not only grown and mature, also happy and cheerful, if we remember the most attractive characteristic of the sexual service provider in Milrod's and Monto's study (2007 op. cit.), or as in Sanders' study, where the men did not want the women to be vulnerable or at risk, drug addicted or coerced by pimps. Rather they wanted the image of the woman in prostitution be that of an independent entrepreneur who has choice and control (Sanders 2008b, p. 411). Nobody wants to see someone who is down and out. On the contrary, the buyers prefer a woman who enjoys her work and takes pleasure in what she is doing; someone with whom paid sex can take the shape of mutual sexual intimacy, the girlfriend experience. 'If you don't maintain that illusion they won't book you again', as one of the women in Hulusjö's study concludes (2013: 244).

Concluding comments

Following this analysis, it is clear that buying sex is a phenomenon which carries meaning at many levels. It has both individual and social dimensions, and in order to understand it completely one must comprehend the complex interplay between these dimensions. On the individual level, it seems to concern the satisfaction of different sexual demands, wishes, and fantasies and/or the solution to problems that men say that they have in their relations with non-prostitute women. In many cases there seems to be a certain degree of ambivalence in the sense that the buying of sex is viewed by the men as an anonymous market-like relationship with no moral obligations, at the same time as there seems to be a wish for affection, intimacy, and reciprocity.

I started this chapter by arguing that men's images and fantasies of 'the prostitute' reflect dominant themes of sex and gender in society, some of them relatively stable over time, others objects of change. So, what we have is both continuity and change. On the one hand, men's images and fantasies about the woman in prostitution seem to be continuous with respect to what she can deliver, without moral obligations, i.e. just plain sex. On the other hand, what comes out clearly from interviews with buyers over time, mine and others', is that seeking out women in prostitution is not only about the desire for a sexual experience.

Already in the 1960's, Winick suggested that the symbolic and emotional meanings and overtones are much more salient for the buyer than the desire for the sex itself, which translates into different ways of looking at the prostitute and himself. The fantasy of mutual intimacy, the girlfriend experience, is a typical example of this, which in its contemporary form can be described as a phenomenon at the intersection between men's fantasies and desires about 'something else', something intimate, beyond the commodified character of the sexual encounter, and women's desire to distance themselves from the whore stigma by introducing themselves as 'escorts', insisting on being encountered as 'sex professionals'. As Hulusjö points out, these 'gender performances', i.e. ways of being 'escort' or 'client', are being continuously negotiated, not least online, in different forums where buyers and sellers interact (Hulusjö 2013: 233, also Scaramuzzino 2014).

One aspect of these negotiations is that some buyers are particularly concerned with distancing themselves from the image of unscrupulous and remorseless exploiters. As mentioned above, some are eager to emphasise that they only buy independent, grown-up women who can vouch for themselves; they would never buy sex from a woman if they felt that she sold herself against her free will. Furthermore, they stress their adaptation to a new behavioral sex buyer's code that underlines the responsible, considerate, and humane side of their actions. In fact, they tend to view themselves as modern, gender-equal men, something that justifies and fuels their fantasy of a non-exploitative, mutual sexual contract between seller and buyer. It is not an exaggeration to say that this self-image goes against the official view of prostitution, especially in Sweden, where the buying of sexual services is criminalised (since 1999).

The fact is that sex buyers are a rather small group of all men in society. The significance of buying sex from prostitutes in the lives of most men seems to be declining, if we are to believe the incidence figures from most Western countries. This does not mean, however, that the significance that men attach to the image of the prostitute is less important now than it ever was before. And this is where research is lacking. What we know so far is mainly based on interviews with men who have the actual experience of buying sex, on occasion or more or less regularly. We know next to nothing about why most men do not buy sex, how they reason, if and how they still fantasise about it, and what those fantasies imply in their sexual life. As we know, a person may not wish to enact a sexual fantasy in real life, and since the fantasy process is entirely imaginary, it is not limited to acceptable or practical fantasies. These mechanisms would be interesting and important to investigate further.

References

Anderson, B. & O'Connell Davidson, J. (2003) *The Demand Side of Trafficking? A Multi Country Study.* Stockholm: Foreign Ministry.

Bernstein, E. (2007) *Temporarily Yours: Intimacy, Authenticity, and the Commerce of Sex.* Chicago: University of Chicago Press.

Bang Fossum, M. (2001) '"– men sådan er min kæreste ikke…" Om mandlige turisters forhold til prostituerede kvinder i et thailandsk feriemål'. *Kvinder, Køn & Forskning* 3(1): 62–87.

Bishop, R. & Robinson, L. (1998) *Night Market: Sexual Cultures and the Thai Economic Miracle.* London: Routledge.

Borg, A., Elwien, F., Fruhling, M., Grönwall, L., Liljeström, R., Månsson, S.-A., Nelin, A., Olsson, H. & Sjöberg, T. (1981) *Prostitution. Beskrivning, analys, förslag till åtgärder.* Stockholm: Publica, Liber.

Cohen, E. (1996) *Thai Tourism – Hill tribes, Islands and Open-Ended Prostitution.* London: White Lotus Press.

Earle, S. & Sharp, K. (2007) *Sex in Cyberspace: Men Who Pay for Sex.* Aldershot, UK: Ashgate.

Gerheim, U. (2012) *Die Produktion des Freiers. Macht im Feld der Prostitution. Eine soziologische Studie.* Bielefeld: Transcript.

Goffman, E. (1959) *The Presentation of Self in Everyday Life.* Harmondsworth: Penguin.

Gunther, A. (1998) 'Sex tourism without sex tourists'. In M. Opperman (ed) *Sex Tourism and Prostitution: Aspects of Leisure, Recreation and Work.* New York: Cognizant Communications.

Hedin, U-C. & Månsson, S.-A. (1998) *Vägen ut! Om kvinnors uppbrott ur prostitutionen.* Stockholm: Carlssons.

Holt, T. J., Blevins, K. R. & Kuhns, J.B. (2008) 'Examining the displacement practices of johns with on-line data'. *Journal of Criminal Justice* 36: 522–528.

Holzman, H. & Pines, S. (1982) 'Buying sex: the phenomenology of being a john'. *Deviant Behaviour* 4(1): 89–116.

Hubbard, P. (1998) 'Red-light districts and toleration zones: Geographies of female street prostitution in England and Wales'. *Area* 29(2): 29–40.

Hubbard, P. & Whowell, M. (2008) 'Revisiting the red light district: still neglected, immoral and marginal?' *Geoforum* 39: 1743–1755.

Hulusjö, A. (2013) *The Multiplicities of Prostitution Experience: Narratives about power and resistance*. Malmö: Malmö University, Health and Society. Doctoral Dissertations 2013: 5.

Kimmel, M. (2005) *The Gender of Desire: Essays on Male Sexuality*. New York: State University of New York Press.

Lautrup, C. (2005) *"Det skal ikke bare vaere en krop mod krop-oplevelse...": En sociologisk undersögelse om prostitutionskunder.* Copenhagen: VFC Socialt Udsatte.

Legardinier, C. & Bouamama, S. (2006) *Les Clients de la prostitution: l'enquète.* Paris: Presses de la Renaissance.

Michael, R.T., Gagnon, J.H., Laumann, E.O. & Kolata, G. (1994) *Sex in America: A Definitive Survey.* Boston: Little, Brown and Company.

Milrod, C. & M. Monto (2012) 'The hobbyist and the girlfriend experience: behaviors and preferences of the male customers of Internet sexual service providers'. *Deviant Behavior* 33: 792–810.

Monto, M. (2000) 'Why men seek out prostitutes'. In R. Weitzer (ed) *Sex for Sale. Prostitution, Pornography and the Sex Industry*. New York: Routledge.

Månsson, S.-A. (1981) *Könshandelns främjare och profitörer. Om förhållandet mellan hallick och prostituerad*. Karlshamn: Doxa.

Månsson, S.-A. (1988) *The Man in Sexual Commerce*. Lund: Lund University, School of Social Work, Report 1988: 2.

Månsson, S.-A. (2000) 'Commercial Sexuality'. In B. Lewin (ed) *Sex in Sweden. On the Swedish Sexual Life*. Stockholm: The National Institute of Public Health.

Månsson, S.-A. (2001) 'Men's practices in prostitution: The case of Sweden'. In B. Pease & K. Pringle (eds) *A Man's World? Changing Men's Practices in a Globalized World*. London: Zed Books.

Månsson, S.-A. (2005) 'Men's practices in prostitution and their implications for social work'. In S-A. Månsson & C. Proveyer Cervantes (eds) *Social Work in Cuba and Sweden*. Göteborg: Göteborg University, Department of Social Work/Havana: University of Havana, Department of Sociology.

Månsson, S-A. & Linders, A. (1984) *Sexualitet utan ansikte. Könsköparna*, Stockholm: Carlssons.

Månsson, S-A. & Söderlind, P. (2013) 'Technology and pornography: the sex industry on the internet'. In K. Daneback & S-A. Månsson (eds) *Sexuality and the Internet. A Collection of Papers 2003–2013*. Malmö: Malmö University.

O'Connell Davidson, J. (1998) *Prostitution, Power and Freedom*. Cambridge: Polity Press.

O'Connell Davidson, J. (2001) 'The sex tourist, the expatriate, his ex-wife and her "Other": the politics of loss, difference and desire'. *Sexualities* (4)1: 5–24.

Plummer, K. (2010) 'A round up of some recent books on prostitution and sex work, review article'. *Sexualities* 13(3): 394–400.

Sanders, T. (2008a) *Paying for Pleasure: Men who Buy Sex*. Cullompton: Willan Publishing.

Sanders, T. (2008b) 'Male sexual scripts: intimacy, sexuality and pleasure in the purchase of commercial sex'. *Sociology* 42(3): 400–417.

Scaramuzzino, G. (2014) *Sexförsäljares och sexköpares kollektiva handlande på internet: En svensk "fuckförening"?* Doctoral diss. Växjö: Växjö University, Department of Social Work.

Skrobanek, S., Boonpakdi, N. & Janthankeero, C. (1997) *The Traffic in Women*. London: Zed Books.

Stein, M.L. (1974) *Lovers, Friends, Slaves… The 9 Male Sexual Types. Their Psycho-Sexual Transactions with Call Girls*. New York: Berkeley Pub. Co and P.T. Putnam & Sons.

Traen, B., Eek-Jensen, L. & Stigum, H. (2005) 'Sex customers in Norway 2002'. *Electronic Journal of Human Sexuality* 8(26): 80–87.

Truong, T.D. (1990) *Sex, Money and Morality: Prostitution and tourism in South-east Asia*. London: Zed Books.

Winick, C. (1962) 'Prostitutes' clients' perception of the prostitute and of themselves'. *International Journal of Social Psychiatry* 8(4): 73–95.

Daniel D. Hutto

Just Faking It? Pretend Theory Meets Sexual Fantasising

reality, however utopian, is something from
which people feel the need of taking pretty frequent holidays
— Aldous Huxley, *Brave New World*

The great pretenders

Kendall Walton (1990) proposed an influential, general theory of how we psychologically respond to fictions. According to Walton's theory, those psychological engagements are of a special variety because they always, only occur within contexts of pretence. Thus by Walton's lights, our enjoyment of works of representational art share a fundamental feature with children's games – the artworks serve as props in more sophisticated, adult games of make-believe. In playing such games we adopt attitudes of make-believe, not that of genuine belief. Our framing epistemic attitude in fictive contexts is, at best, only belief-like. Walton delivers a similar verdict with respect to other psychological attitudes, including our seeming emotional responses. For him, when engaging with fictions we only ever pretend to experience fear, lust, or anger. When playing games of make-believe – consuming fictional films and novels – we do not really experience the appropriate emotions demanded of us by the works, rather we only ever adopt phenomenologically similar, emotion-like states of mind – states which Walton dubs quasi-emotions.

The upshot is that Walton's theory – known as pretend theory – incorporates a quite general vision of psychology of participating in and with fictions. It makes strong claims about the sorts of attitudes that come into play in such games. Importantly, although pretend theory accepts that we can be viscerally moved by fictions – physiologically and phenomenologically – it holds that those ways of being moved are at best akin to, but do not constitute, the having of relevant beliefs and emotions. Technically, in fictive contexts we only ever experience quasi-emotions that are interestingly similar to the emotions they allow us to pretend to be experiencing. Quasi-emotions and real emotions are easily confused precisely because the former are phenomenologically charged states of mind with felt features that mimic features of the emotions that particular fictions seemingly ask us to experience. Unsurprisingly, this makes it hard to distinguish these two types of attitudes from one another.

After reviewing some arguments for and against pretend theory, and then getting clear about the wider stakes of the debate, this paper turns to the task of putting pressure on the plausibility of pretend theory's claim about the less than *bona fide* nature of the affective and emotional aspects of our psychological participation with fictions. It does so by looking closely at the features of one kind of sexual fantasy – one that appears to provoke a range of emotions – women's rape fantasies. Consideration of that case highlights reasons why we may want to move away from pretend theory and to rethink how it is that real and relevant emotions can be and are experienced in response to fictions.

Why believe in Pretend Theory?

What motivates pretend theory? Walton focuses on selective cases that illustrate, convincingly, that the ways adults engage with fictions strongly resemble the ways in which young children also do so. He asks us, for example, to imagine a cinema-going person, Charles, enjoying a horror film. Charles is 'quaking with quasi-fear as the green slime bore down on him from the screen. We know he is not really in danger. He knows this too, and he is not really afraid … His condition needs attention nevertheless. What is the nature of his experience?' (Walton 1990: 241).

By way of rhetorical reply, Walton reveals the very heart of pretend theory, telling us: 'It is not true but fictional that he fears the slime' (p. 242). The logic seems compelling. On the face of it, if Charles were truly afraid his reactions should be quite different. He would not remain in his seat and would find no pleasure in his encounter with the filmic green slime. So whatever Charles is experiencing it cannot be real fear – it must be something at best only akin to fear. Charles is in a state of mind connected to his excitement but which lacks the full gamut of motivational and behavioural consequences that come with really being afraid. Because he is going along with a game of make-believe Charles only experiences quasi-fear, not real fear, according to pretend theory.

A major virtue of pretend theory is that it offers a way of getting around the so-called 'paradox of fiction' that Radford (1975) famously identified: its three conflicting premises are reconstructed below.

P1. It is only rational to be emotionally moved by that which we believe exists.
P2. We do not believe in the existence of that which is purely fictional.
P3. We are emotionally moved by that which is purely fictional.

On a weak reading of the paradox that assumes that we can and do experience genuine emotions when engaging with fictions it seems we have little choice but to say that such emotional responses are irrational, however natural and irresistible they may be for us. Following this line of thought, genuine emotional engagement with fictions is relegated, quite generally, to being no more rational than the sorts of emotional responses invoked by neurotic phobias. Being terrified of a spider that we know to be perfectly harmless is not rational. For someone afflicted with such a phobia aberrant emotional reactions may be hard or impossible to avoid. Understanding their condition, we can excuse the person's behaviour. Even so, knowing better and failing to bring their behaviour in line with what they know is irrational. By the same token, if we assume that fictions evoke real emotional responses in us then, on Radford's analysis, it seems we must also regard emotional responding to be 'irrational, incoherent, and inconsistent' (Radford 1975: 75).

On the strongest reading, the situation is even worse. For it follows that it just is not irrational to have such emotional responses to fiction, it is simply not possible to have them at all. Thus in places Radford presents the problem in the form of a conditional, in purely logical terms: 'It would seem that I can *only be moved* by someone's plight *if I believe* that something terrible has happened to him. *If I do not believe* that he has not and is not suffering or whatever, *I cannot grieve or be moved* to tears' (Radford 1975: 68, my emphases). The required existential belief is precisely what is missing when we engage with fictions. Explicating the standardly assumed constitutive link between having certain beliefs and having certain related emotions, Sainsbury (2010) highlights the deeper philosophical problem raised by Radford's paradox.

> At least some emotions require corresponding beliefs. For example, we can only fear something if we believe it to be dangerous. Moreover the corresponding belief plays a role in determining what emotion that the state of arousal actually constitutes; its fear rather than excitement or curiosity because of its link with danger, rather than a link to other beliefs. In reading fiction we have genuine emotions of fear, sadness, anger and so on. We do not have the corresponding beliefs (for example Charles does not believe the green slime in the horror movie is dangerous, for he knows in reality there is no such thing) (Sainsbury 2010: 15, my emphases).

In denying that we truly experience the relevant emotions, Walton's analysis offers a convenient way around the implications of both of these readings of the implications of Radford's paradox since it denies the third premise that comprises the paradox. Lovers of fiction are thus absolved of the charge of being irrational or having to explain how it is even possible to respond emotionally to the merely fictive plights or situations of merely imagined persons for the simple reason that they do not really experience emotions in such cases. They never have the emotions in question, but only ever pretend to have those emotions, for the sake of enjoying the fiction. It is all part of the game.

This has another advantage. For if our encounters with fictions did stir real emotions, there could be cases where the emotions we experience while engaging with a fiction might come into conflict with – and, crucially – even contradict other emotions that are directed at the very same intentional objects. Friend (2003) provides an analysis precisely along these lines – one that aims to show how, if genuine, her real feelings of loathing for the actual Jim Garrison would contradict her feelings of admiration for the main protagonist of Oliver Stone's film *JFK*, also Jim Garrison, as played by Kevin Costner. The logical conflict arises so long as it is accepted that '*JFK* makes it fictionally the case of the real Jim Garrison that he was a noble, self-sacrificing individual pursuing the truth' (Friend 2003). The problem is that Garrison was, in reality, none of these things. Indeed, Friend believes he was an obsessive individual who willingly abused the powers of his office in an attempt to convict an innocent man.

Friend argues that if we insist, contra Walton, that engagements with fiction engender real emotions, then we run into the problem that it is possible for there to be cases like this – cases in which the emotions inspired through fictions and emotions based on our beliefs and knowledge will directly contradict one another. Yet since it is not clear that harbouring contradictory emotions is even possible, it would be best if our theory of fictive engagement did not allow it to be so. This problematic result is avoided, if we accept, along with Walton, that quasi-emotions are not real emotions and that they remain forever compartmentalised and restricted to pretend contexts. On that view the problematic, contradictory emotional states of mind Friend describes can notarise. Pretend theory therefore usefully avoids that problem and explains how the proper organisation of our minds is possible. More than that, it also explains why, when it comes to practical reasoning, 'only certain emotional responses take priority over others in our cognitive organization' (Friend 2003: 49). The rule there is that real emotions, based on beliefs always trump quasi-emotions sponsored by acts of make-believe.[1]

Real emotional responding to fictions

Despite its apparent philosophical and explanatory virtues, Pretend Theory is not universally loved. Indeed, it has a goodly number of prominent detractors

1 Friend makes this second point by enlisting another example of potential conflict between belief-based and fiction-inspired emotions. She writes: "Suppose you believe Nelson Mandela to be a great man and you admire him. Now, if I made up a story in which Mandela tortured kittens, and you knew this story to be pure fantasy, it would be inexplicable for you to change your feelings towards him" (Friend 2003: 44).

(Carroll 1990, Currie 2010, Goldie 2012). A fair few philosophers and literary theorists are unhappy with the idea that we do not experience real emotions but only quasi-emotions in response to fictions. This strikes some as deeply counter-intuitive. Focusing on the horror genre, Noël Carroll (1990) speaks for the dissatisfied in observing that:

> The key objection to Walton's theory, of course, is that *it relegates our emotional responses to fiction to the realm of make believe*. Purportedly, when we recoil with apparent emotion to *The Exorcist*, we are only pretending to be horrified. But I, at least, recall being genuinely horrified by the film. I don't think I was pretending; and the degree to which I was shaken by the film was visibly apparent to the person with whom I saw the film. Walton's theory is a clever solution to the logical problem that art-horror raises. However it does not seem to square with the phenomenology of art-horror. That is, Walton's theory appears to throw out the phenomenology of the state for sake of logic (Carroll 1990: 74, my emphasis).

Carroll's assurance that there are crucial differences in felt phenomenology – differences that enable him to detect that what he experiences as real, and not merely quasi-, emotions when engaging with certain fictions – will not cut much ice with fans of pretend theory. Even when accompanied by the strongest avowals and based on the most careful acts of introspection there seems no way to distinguish real from quasi-emotions on these grounds alone. This is because, presumably, being in a quasi-emotional horrified state feels much the same as responding with genuine horror or fear.[2] Hence, even 'from the inside' the two might be easily confused.

Yet, apparently, these states of mind can be distinguished by other means. Fans of pretend theory will insist that there is superb evidence for believing that quasi-fear is what we experience when engaging with fictions in make-believe contexts. For if true emotions – true horror, say – were evoked by engaging with fictions then we should expect the person's outward reactions to be different to what they are when such people are (or believe they are) responding in fictional contexts. We should expect different responses to those they exhibit when they are, so to speak, conspiring and cooperating with the pretence. If Carroll was really terrified by *The Exorcist* – for instance – then we should expect him to respond differently than he did. He would have a need to respond in ways that go beyond the mere exhibiting of *some* of the characteristic physiological, behavioural and phenomenological responses that are associated with (and, even in some ways alike to) to being afraid. That one has a racing pulse, squirms, is unable to look at

2 According to Friend, "the phenomenology […] is exactly the same" (Friend 2003: 41).

the screen and so forth, falls short of what we expect from a truly terrified person. Someone who is truly afraid will seek help, attempt to flee the cinema, and so on. In other words, such a person would begin to take other, more drastic and characteristic fear-driven measures in reply to the perceived threat.

So, on the flipside of Carroll's phenomenologically inspired objection there is an easy reply available to proponents of Pretend Theory. It is that if we look closely at the details of the relevant cases we will find non-phenomenological differences – in the surrounding behaviour – that clearly distinguish them. Pretend theory is on its strongest ground in emphasising the disanalogies in the behavioural patterns initiated by merely pretend or quasi-emotions as opposed to real emotions. Walton is careful to highlight precisely such differences. He tells us:

> In many ways Charles is like a child, Timmy, playing a game of make-believe with his father. The father pretends to be a ferocious monster who cunningly stalks him, and, at the crucial moment, lunges "viciously" at him. Timmy flees screaming to the next room. The scream is more or less involuntary, and so is the flight. But Timmy has a delighted grin on his face even as he runs, and he unhesitatingly comes back for more. He is perfectly aware that his father is only playing, that the whole thing is a game, and that only fictionally is there a vicious monster after him. He is not really afraid. But it is fictional that he is afraid (Walton 1990: 242).

Like Timmy, Charles 'does not scream or run or betray his fear in any other especially overt way' (p. 244). And, also like Timmy, Charles can not be truly afraid of the green slime because he is also – in a crucially telling sense – enjoying his predicament. At first blush, this seems both a fair and pivotal point. The advocate of Pretend Theory wonders why and how, if true emotions are in play in both cases, it is possible that consumers of fictions manage to find any modicum of enjoyment in films, stories and imagined scenarios that truly evoke fear and horror in us.

Despite this, it would be unsafe to conclude on this basis alone that Pretend Theory must carry the day. There are clear cases in which we plausibly experience real emotions both when the characteristic behaviours are absent and even when we have no motivations to act in such ways. For example, when we reflect on actual and hence non-fictive past happenings, we might feel embarrassment, shame or pride concerning our behaviour but we will neither act or be motivated to intervene on such distant occurrences (see Goldie 2003: 56, Goldie 2012). It seems we cry over spilt milk even when we can do nothing, any longer, to prevent such spillage. There seems little reason to doubt that we can become genuinely emotional when reflecting on our past doings even though we do not expect those emotions to be connected to actions (or, even, motivations for action) that would exhibit anything like the full set of overt behaviours – running from the room, hiding one's face – that would normally arise in cases of in-the-moment shame or embarrassment.

In sum, experiencing shame when thinking about what one did in the past might elicit no current overt responses – or at least, nothing above and beyond the having of certain characteristic physiological reactions and phenomenological feelings. Yet despite this, in ordinary parlance, we are perfectly happy to count such a shame-tinted remembering as bringing full-fledged, *bona fide* emotions into play. If so then it is at least possible that Charles and Timmy can feel real fear, even though the full and characteristic suite of motivations and dispositions to act out of fear are not in evidence when we are operating in pretend contexts.[3]

Friends of Pretend Theory seem to be on stronger ground when they argue that we cannot be experiencing the actual emotions that are demanded of us by any given fiction – hence, that we must be only pretending to have such emotions – because having such emotions conflicts with other sorts of emotions to which such engagement gives rise. Thus Timmy and Charles cannot really be afraid or horrified because they are, on some level, enjoying, or even enthralled by, their predicaments. But, here too, there is a ready line of reply available to those sceptical about Pretend Theory. For even if the behaviour of Timmy and Charles reveals that they cannot rightly be said to be *only* afraid or horrified this does not preclude the possibility that they might be in complex states of mind that involve some degree of fear or horror, albeit mixed up with some degree of pleasure. It hardly follows from the fact Charles and Timmy are occupying states of mind that are complex and multi-faceted (and hence not easily classified given their heterogeneous character) that they do not involve genuine emotions. What justifies ruling out, a priori, the possibility that we can 'enjoy fear' (Gaut 2003: 18)?

Finally, although Walton may be right that both Timmy and Charles are perfectly aware that they are engaging with fictions it seems quite a stretch to suppose on this basis that they are only pretending when it comes to adopting certain emotions. Carroll is surely right to observe that in engaging with fictions we do not seem aware of our pretending vis-à-vis our seeming emotive reactions. This is not simply to stress the obvious fact that we sometimes get absorbed or carried away, and apparently forget that what we are reading or watching is fictional when engaging with fictions. Of course, some maintain that this is a requirement if we are to be properly moved at all by a fiction. It seems that for a fiction to grip

3 This shows that 'there is reason to deny that if an emotion is detached from its normal inputs and outputs, it is only a simulated emotion. Emotions can be detached from beliefs … or not motivate actions … while being perfectly genuine' (Gaut 2003: 22). In sum, 'the absence of motivated action does not prove that I do not pity' (Gaut 2003: 21).

us we must be convinced by it to such an extent that we lose sight of – or at least fail to focus on – its fictional status. But the point being made here is different and more specific. We might be wholly aware that we are engaging with a fiction yet still our apparent emotional reactions to it will be elicited by the work and not projected on the work by us. If so, we are not engaged in any game of pretending when it comes to our responses to a fiction; indeed, such responses are not even under voluntary control. As Carroll notes, if this sort of thing were a matter of pretending, 'I could elect to remain unmoved by *The Exorcist*; I could refuse to make believe I was horrified. But I don't think that was really an option for those, like myself, who were overwhelmingly struck by it' (Carroll 1990: 74). Amplifying the point, he stresses that 'the fact that whether I am art-horrified or not seems to be beyond my control, makes the notion that it is a matter of my game of make believe dubious' (ibid.). The conclusion is that this is 'a real problem in Walton's theory' (ibid.).

A radically enactive take on sexual fantasising with real emotions

Focusing on the ways in which we engage with sexual fantasies, the remainder of this paper develops, amplifies, and strengthens the initial case against Pretend Theory presented in the previous section. The motivation for this strategy is simple. Pretend Theory looks less and less attractive when we give detailed attention to the way we engage with certain kinds of fictions in special contexts – those that bring to light some similarities but also significant differences from the way we engage with fictions when playing children's games, watching films in the cinema, or reading literary narratives (these being the stock examples favoured by advocates of Pretend Theory).

Why attend to sexual fantasies *per se*? An immediate advantage of doing so is that, on the one hand, there are obvious parallels in the ways we engage in sexual fantasising and the ways we engage with other sorts of fictions. For example, there are similarities in the use of scripts and paraphernalia in children's make-believe games and the kinds of sexual fantasising that involve special props and role play. On the other hand, sexual fantasising is also, at the same time, a quite serious, adult pursuit – it typically has a particular point and purpose, aiming for specific outcomes.

In the remainder of this section I consider some facts about sexual fantasising that put pressure on the credibility of Pretend Theory, starting with general observations and then considering the characteristic features of a specific kind of sexual fantasising.

Sexual arousal as a basic emotion

Most people engage in sexual fantasising because they find it sexually arousing. This is hard to deny. Consider Wollheim's (1984) description of the effects of the 'familiar phenomenon of the erotic daydream':

> Let us suppose that I centrally imagine myself engaged in some sexual activity with a strange figure, or a close friend. As I do so, I centrally imagine myself becoming excited over what occurs between us … And as I centrally imagine myself becoming excited, so I become excited (Wollheim 1984: 81-2).

Certainly, in such cases people are sexually aroused, not quasi-sexually-aroused (what would be the point?). Backing this up, it has been empirically established that the very same physiological responses had during orgasm can be induced by imagery used in fantasising and genital self-stimulation (Stock & Geer 1982; Whipple, et al. 1992).

So what? Defenders of Pretend Theory need not doubt this. It might turn out, for all that has been noted so far, that genuine sexual arousal and associated emotional responses, such as, say, lust, fear and anger, are logically quite distinct phenomena.

Consider that in discussing Wollheim's remarks about erotic daydreams, Goldie (2012) conceptually distinguishes the having of feelings of arousal from the having of emotions (ironically for us, he does so while in the same breath taking issue with Pretend Theory). Thus Goldie writes: 'So Wollheim holds … that we can have real feelings of arousal as a result of what we imagine … And I agree that the same holds for emotion' (Goldie 2012: 82). This underscores the fact that there is logical space for holding that being sexually aroused and having feelings of arousal might not qualify or suffice for having an emotion: sexual arousal may involve real feelings, but having real feelings is not the same as, and may fall short of, being in any kind of emotional state.

Many philosophers are inclined to accept this verdict on the grounds that only certain states of mind count as real emotions. Which kinds? Answer: States of mind that are bound up with contentful states of mind in normatively appropriate ways. So understood, having an emotion requires being in a state of mind that is connected in the right way to a host of other attitudes – beliefs, desires, and the like: the propositional attitudes of folk psychology. The reason for insisting on this requirement is that these other contentful states are thought to play *defining and individuating roles* in determining (a) if an emotion is in play, and also (b) which emotion is in play. To give this idea a name, call it the folk network view of emotions. Gaut (2003) explains how it informs cognitive-evaluative theory and standard views about the intentionality of emotional states of mind.

> An emotion … has an intentional object: I am afraid of something. I pity someone. According to the dominant (and I would argue correct) cognitive-evaluative theory of the emotions, an emotion not only has an intentional object, but also *essentially* incorporates an evaluation of that object. So to be afraid of something essentially involves evaluating that thing as dangerous; to pity someone *essentially* involves construing her as suffering, [and so on] (Gaut 2003: 16, my emphases).

On this reading of cognitive-evaluative theory, having an emotion necessarily requires having a range of other propositional attitudes – most importantly beliefs and desires with the right kinds of content. This is why merely having certain feelings does not suffice for having an emotion. Consider a case in which you feel insulted by a perceived slight. That feeling only suffices for your being emotionally upset as long as you believe that you have been insulted. If that same feeling were to persist after you discover and come to believe I did not insult you it would make no sense. The feeling would not connect with the rest of your contentful attitudes in the right way, hence it would not count as an emotion at all. The contentful attitudes in the folk network are taken to exist within the rational space of reasons, thus emotional states of mind must have appropriate kinds of contents – they must be contentful evaluations, construals or judgements – so they can stand in normatively constrained relations to other contentful attitudes. Notably, it is this assumption about the emotions that breathes life into the Paradox of Fiction, making it seem impossible for us to have real emotions in response to fictions if we lack the relevant beliefs.

That emotions must be normatively constrained by a constellation of other attitudes comes out most clearly and strongly when the kind of evaluations of which Gaut speaks are understood as involving contentful judgments. Thus 'The feelings that we experience when we are ashamed and when we feel guilty, for instance, might well be identical, and what individuates them is *the content* of the respective evaluative thoughts' (Gaut 2003: 17, my emphasis). On the further assumption that such evaluations are judgement-based it is clear why merely having certain feelings (feelings of sexual arousal included) does not suffice for the having of emotions. According to the folk network view of emotions, it is not possible to individuate an emotion by 'a unique feeling associated with it' (Gaut 2003: 17).

Prima facie, and quite independently, some empirical literature seems to lend further support to the idea that sexual arousal and its associated emotions must be logically distinct. It can seem that this must be the case because the emotions and states of sexual arousal have the potential to causally interact with one another (implying their distinctness). Thus:

> In order to understand the complex way in which *emotions and sexual arousal interact*, it is first necessary to realize that emotions are comprised of multiple dimensions. These include a positivity-negativity dimension, a level of physiological arousal, and a cognitive recognition and labelling process (i.e. interpreting the situation as fear, anger, joy, or whatever, depending on the situation). Each of these dimensions has the *potential to affect sexual arousal differently* (McAnulty & Burnett 2006: 55–56, my emphases).

There is a wealth of evidence that sexual arousal and emotions do causally interact. Emotions that involve a general state of arousal (anger, anxiety) are likely to increase sexual arousal. Also, 'extreme emotional arousal has strong potential to interfere with basic genital response' (McAnulty & Burnett 2006: 56). This makes it possible for a '*complex interplay* between the arousal strength of the stimulus, the specific emotional state that is elicited (anger, fear, frustration, excitement, enjoyment, etc.) and the degree to which the feeling is tied to sexual performance and self- or partner-evaluation within the sexual situation' (McAnulty & Burnett 2006: 57, my emphasis).

All of this looks like good news for Pretend Theory. For as long as it is accepted that sexual arousal and emotional responding are logically distinct, Pretend Theory can easily handle the fact that most sexual fantasising is sexually arousing. It can do so precisely because Pretend Theory already assumes that engaging with fictions is exciting and that we have real physiological responses and real phenomenologically charged feelings in our engagement with fictions. In this light, fans of Pretend Theory can argue that sexual arousal, though genuinely arousing, is not any kind of genuine emotional response. This is consistent with maintaining that when sexual arousal occurs in sexual fantasising it only occurs in the presence of quasi-emotions.

There is, however, a problem with this apparently very tidy line of reply: it arbitrarily forecloses an important possibility for understanding sexual arousal. For despite the popularity of the folk network view of the emotions, it is a live question whether or not sexual arousal ought to show up on the list of basic emotions. Basic emotions, according to Elkman's (1999) theory, each have a distinctive 'affect program' – they exhibit script-like patterns of physiological and behavioural responses.[4] Griffiths (2013) explicates Elkman's main idea on basic emotions, underscoring the fact that according to this view:

4 Affect programs have script-like structures with the following standard steps: 'Step 1: paradigmatic recognitional element involved in X; Step 2: paradigmatic outward expression of X; Step 3: paradigmatic bodily changes and feeling of those changes; Step 4: paradigmatic motivational response involved in X; Step 5: paradigmatic action out of X' (Goldie 2000: 94).

> basic emotions are homologues—categories defined by shared evolutionary origins. The basic emotion of fear, for example, exists in many mammalian species and it is the same thing in each just as the femur or the hypothalamus is the same thing—it has a shared evolutionary origin in the common ancestor of those species (Griffiths 2013: 2).

Why take the idea of basic emotions, understood along Elkman's lines, seriously? Griffiths (2013) hits the nail on the head: 'the view that emotions are judgments creates a dilemma. Commonly accepted statements of the content of emotional judgments involve sophisticated social and normative concepts' (p. 2). This mundane fact is apparently at odds with another hard to deny fact: that many sentient beings – those apparently quite capable of emotion, including infants and animals, for example – lack the sorts of concepts that are allegedly needed for having certain standard types of emotions. Indeed, it seems such beings are quite capable of emotion even though, according to some accounts, they lack any concepts or even the capacity to form any contentful judgements at all (Hutto & Myin 2013). As Griffiths (2013) observes, none of this sits well:

> with the plausible claim that adult human anger has something deeply in common with anger in frustrated infants, or the anger of a dominant monkey towards a subordinate. Either these agents possess the [relevant] concepts ... or they are not angry in the true sense of the word. This problem is made worse by evidence that emotions in adult humans can be produced by low-level processes that seem equally implausible locales for such concepts (Griffiths 2013: 2).[5]

We can either (A) deny that such beings – including ourselves in many cases – are capable of having emotions, strictly speaking; or (B) accept that such beings – including us in many cases – are capable of real emotion even when the appropriate links to conceptually informed contentful attitudes are absent. Which way should we go? Here it is instructive to consider Goldie's (2000) proposal about how to understand affect programs – namely, those basic episodes of emotional experience and response that are at once 'complex, coordinated and automated' (Griffiths 1997: 105). Goldie stresses that such basic modes of response should not be confused with culturally informed emotions proper (for him the latter can only be understood under the auspices of the folk network view of emotions).

---

5 Importantly, this way of understanding basic emotions breaks faith with the sort of functionalism that is rife in today's philosophy of mind. As Griffiths (2013) observes: 'This approach to categorization is very different from classification by shared function, which would place in the category of fear any psychological mechanism designed to detect and respond to danger. Biologists call such categories analogies' (p. 2).

Even so, Goldie (2000) admits that affect programs provide 'a good characterization of some short-term episodes of emotional experience involved in the recognition-response tie, which could be a suitable object of study for evolutionary science' (Goldie 2000: 105). And, taking this a step further, he insists that despite the importance of distinguishing these 'episodes of emotional experience' from 'emotions proper', it must be admitted that the former necessarily involve what he calls 'feeling towards'. Crucially, Goldie understands the latter as 'an intentional element which is neither belief nor desire, and which is, in many respects more fundamental to emotional experience than either of these … To reflect the fact that this intentional element is both intentional and involves feelings, I will call it feeling towards' (Goldie 2000: 19). A capacity for 'feeling towards' is thus a central feature even of what he classifies as basic episodes of emotional experience.

How exactly should we understand this rudimentary kind of intentionality – this feeling towards –that is exhibited by such basic forms of emotional response? Hutto (2012) makes the case that this is best achieved by abandoning representational theories of mind and adopting a Radically Enactivist framework. Doing so involves thinking of basic emotional responses as target-directed instead of as inherently content involving. Another feature of the radically enactive approach is that it requires conceiving of emotional attitudes as embodied attitudes of whole creatures – thus the intentionality of such attitudes is not merely a feature of some functionally specified and semantically individuated mental state internal to emotional beings.[6]

6 The way the intentionality of basic emotions is understood by Radical Enactivism and the way it is understood by DeLancey, under the auspices of affect program broadly agree (see Delancey 2001: 89–98). Summarizing DeLancey's view Griffiths writes: 'Basic emotions can be intentionally directed at a state of affairs, so that their content is a proposition. For example, I may be afraid that this dingo will bite me. But *the very same emotion may be intentionally directed at* what DeLancey calls *a "concretum"*, meaning an object as such, rather than as an element in a proposition. For example, I may be afraid of this dingo. This is where affect-program theory comes in. Because emotions are intrinsically action-directing, an emotion whose content is a concretum can nevertheless explain action. I flee the dingo because I am afraid of it. In order to flee I do not need a proposition about the dingo, such as that it is dangerous, or that it will bite me, combined with a desire to avoid danger, or not to be bitten. *I just need to be afraid, and for the target of my fear to be the dingo*. What we have in common with other animals, DeLancey argues, is *the ability to have emotions that are intentionally directed at a concretum*. What distinguishes us is *the ability to have emotions intentionally directed at propositions*. This ability introduces a far greater flexibility into our emotional responses' (Griffiths 2013: 2–3, my emphases). The main points of agreement are that Radical

Essentially, in this view, basic emotions possess the same sort of core structure as emotions proper – the sort of structure that cognitive-evaluative theory assigns to them. However, important differences remain. As just mentioned, the intentionality of basic emotions is neither based in nor entails having propositional attitudes. Moreover, and just as importantly, the evaluative aspect of basic emotions – on this view – should not be understood as rooted in contentful and conceptually grounded judgements. Rather the so-called 'evaluations' of basic emotions are best understood as natural responses. When fearful a creature responds to and treats some X *as if* it were dangerous – e.g., by approaching with caution, avoiding it where possible, and so on. What explains this? The fact that both we and many other creatures are, thanks to our evolutionary histories, naturally set up to be set off by certain types of things and situations as opposed to others. Since our embodied evaluations are not contentful judgements of any kind, rational or otherwise, these basic emotional modes of response are not to be understood as always already tied up with some kind of norm-bound content

---

Enactivism holds that basic minds, including emotional attitudes, exhibit a kind of Ur-intentionality – in adopting such attitudes a creature is directed at or towards particular worldly objects or states of affairs (Hutto 2013, Hutto & Satne, in press). Yet it denies such basic attitudes are content-involving. However, Radical Enactivism also assumes that it is possible, at least for beings that have been socio-culturally scaffolded in the right kind of ways, to adopt the same basic type of emotional attitude, directed at a particular state of affairs, but doing so in a way that is content involving. So, for example, I may respond with fear to the situation of being confronted by a dingo – without forming any contentful attitudes at all. In another case I might respond with fear but in such a way that is bound up with a range of contentful attitudes – specific thoughts, beliefs, hopes and so on. According to Radical Enactivism, what is common in the two cases is the emotional attitude of fear, which is directed at the particular state of affairs (the dingo facing off against me), usually with attention focused on specific aspects of it (the dingo's snarling, its barred teeth and glaring eyes). In cases of non-basic emotional responding one will also form contentful thoughts about the given states of affairs. This is where Radical Enactivism differs slightly from Delancy's account, as rendered above. This is because Radical Enactivism breaks faith with a familiar tenet, one taken as axiomatic by many in analytic philosophy of mind. It is widely assumed that adopting a psychological attitude toward a state of affairs entails adopting an attitude towards a proposition (see, e.g., Fodor & Pylyshyn 2015: 6–7). Radical Enactivism denies this. Why? Because it is sensitive to the fact that, "Propositions are very different from states of affairs. In particular, propositions are true or false, while states of affairs are not the sort of things that can be either true or false. On many standard ways of thinking about propositions and states of affairs, states of affairs are the things that make propositions true or false" (Bermúdez 2011: 404).

or linked, in the first instance, to a constellation of other propositional attitudes that exist in the space of reasons. Yet such embodied, emotional responding still counts – for all that – as *bona fide*, if basic, emoting.

Radical Enactivism's two-tiered framework of basic and scaffolded minds, allows us to recognise both our most fundamental ways of emotional responding and those bound up with other properly propositional attitudes as genuine emotions.[7] This allows us, following Griffiths (2013), to properly acknowledge what we share – emotionally speaking – with other animals – namely, a tendency toward script-like responding to certain worldly triggers, while at the same time noting what distinguishes us from them too, again emotionally speaking – namely, a further capacity for having those same emotions but bound up with content-laden attitudes. In this multi-faceted framework, we are not faced with a simple either/or choice when it comes to thinking about emotions.[8]

Yet what of the second worry, raised above, that sexual arousal cannot be an emotion because it causally interacts with emotions? This is easily dealt with if the above distinction between forms of emotions is permitted. For it is possible that the interactions in question can be understood as interactions between different kinds of emotions, basic and non-basic. And this might help to explain and make better sense of other findings, according to which: 'multivariate statistical procedures typically identify those two concepts [sexual arousal and emotion] as *being part of the same dimension*, at least in sexually functional men and women. Such findings imply that *sexual arousal may itself represent a type of emotional state*' (McAnulty & Burnett 2006: 57, my emphases).[9]

---

7 In developing this idea we could follow another lead supplied by Griffiths. He notes, 'Jason A. Clark [...] has argued that basic emotions and more cognitively sophisticated forms of the same emotion may be homologous to one another (Clark 2010a, 2010b)' (Griffiths 2013: 3). Expanding on this, he emphasizes, 'Clark's innovation is to propose that simple and complex emotions in the same species may be homologous. The same evolved developmental patterns are used twice, just as the developmental patterns that produce skeletal elements are used twice in our arms and legs (serial homology). Clark proposes that a form of shame similar to that in other primates and a more cognitively sophisticated form unique to humans are both found in humans' (Griffiths 2013: 4).

8 Medina (2013) gives the correct diagnosis of the source of the apparent problem here. He takes it that the so-called Paradox of Fiction and its so-called solution, Pretend Theory, both get their life from the mistaken assumption that 'all cases of emotional experiences have to fit one mold' (p. 330).

9 More than this, 'The prototype for sexual arousal overlapped considerably with the emotional prototypes for "joy", "warm feeling" and "merry"' (McAnulty & Burnett 2006: 58).

With all of this in hand, we can also return to another fundamental issue. Giving attention to the way we respond to and make use of sexually arousing fantasies in our lives puts some pressure on Pretend Theory's mainstay – its behavioural disanalogy arguments. This is because the ways that we engage with sexual fantasies are markedly different from the ways we engage with other sorts of fictions in other familiar contexts. In particular, the ways and contexts in which we engage in sexual fantasising can be quite different from the ways and contexts in which we engage with other fictions of the kind that Walton makes his primary focus: namely, children's games of make believe and the consumption of films and literary writings. The important difference with the way we engage in sexual fantasising is that the latter often enables, sometimes enhancing, the completion of the entire, set of characteristic behaviours and acts associated with sexual activity. In good cases, sexual fantasising often does the heavy lifting in seeing that sexual encounters are brought to full completion satisfactorily. It is no accident that sexual fantasising is strongly correlated with high sexual satisfaction (Leitenberg & Henning 1995; Person, et al. 1992).

To drive home the point by means of a literary example, recall Huxley's *Brave New World*, we can compare this to an imagined case in which arousal – understood as mere physiological responding that is equivalent to but not identical with emotional responding – is produced under controlled conditions: fully contained and corralled.

> 'Men and women must have their adrenals stimulated from time to time.' … It's one of the conditions of perfect health. That's why we've made the V.P.S. treatments compulsory.' … 'V.P.S.?' … Violent Passion Surrogate. Regularly once a month. We flood the whole system with adrenin. It's the complete physiological equivalent of fear and rage. All the tonic effects of murdering Desdemona and being murdered by Othello, without any of the inconvenience.'

Yet unlike the occupants of *Brave New World*, for us, the outcome of at least a good deal of sexually arousing fantasising is, to make use of Huxley's turn of phrase, full of 'inconvenience'. For the fact is that women who sexually fantasise regularly also show higher rates of orgasm during masturbation and intercourse (Leitenberg & Henning, 1995, Sue 1979). It seems safe to assume that is also true for men.

So it seems there will be many cases in which sexual fantasy plays the role of helping to bring about predictable behavioural outcomes – they play a part in completing and bringing sexual acts to, so to speak, their natural conclusions. This shows that sexual fantasising is importantly unlike the case of Charles, the chair-bound cinema-goer, who fails to behave in all the ways frightened people tend to in the immediate presence of real threats. At least in many cases of sexual fantasising the behavioural disanology argument that supports Pretend Theory fails.

Taken together these considerations surely put Pretend Theory on the back foot. There is no obvious way to defend it without arbitrarily and unjustifiably foreclosing on the live and debatable possibility that sexual arousal may be a genuine emotion.

Full emotional spectrums and fantastical manners

We can further amp up the worries about the plausibility of Pretend Theory by giving attention to the ways in which we respond to specific kinds of sexual fantasising. For the truth is that our responses to sexual fantasies are not always psychologically straightforward. Some types of sexual fantasies inspire what looks, on the face of it, to be a complex mix of conflicting and competing affective attitudes. Women's rape fantasies, which have recently received fresh empirical attention, are shining examples of this fact (Bivona, et al. 2012).

Although women's rape fantasies come in different varieties, they are defined – as a class – using the legal criteria of rape and sexual assault, as acts of imagining about scenarios involving 'the use of physical force, threat of force, or incapacitation to coerce a woman's self-character in a fantasy into sexual activity against her will' (Bivona & Critelli 2009: 33).

That women should ever fantasise or become aroused by imagining scenarios involving their own rape is regarded by some as deeply perplexing (Bivona & Critelli, for example, deem it an 'enigma'). How could fantasising about so traumatic and repugnant an event *ever* sexually arouse? Without supplying anything like a full answer, puzzlement is reduced, somewhat, by the observation that 'rape fantasies are not all that popular, that the fantasies are not very realistic, and that women can control their fantasies but they cannot control actual rape' (Bivona & Critelli 2009: 33).[10]

Analysing the details of women's sexual fantasy logs, Bivona and Critelli (2009) aim to shed light on the content of women's rape fantasies and the character of

10 Elaborating on this, Critelli and Bivona (2008) make clear that for the purpose of their studies, 'the term "rape fantasy" will follow legal definitions of rape and sexual assault (Corpus Juris Secundum, 2002). This term will refer to women's fantasies that involve the use of physical force, threat of force, or incapacitation through, for example, sleep or intoxication, to coerce a woman into sexual activity against her will, that is, against the will of the character she identifies with in the fantasy' (p. 58).

their psychological responses to such fantasies.[11] Using a three-point scale these researchers conducted a systematic empirical investigation, going beyond mere anecdote, to investigate the fantasisers' self-rated levels of arousal and aversion during their fantasising, at the beginning, middle, and end of it. They also collected data on the levels of aggression involved in such fantasies. Their major finding is that 'rape fantasies exist on an erotic-aversive continuum' (Bivona & Critelli 2009: 35). In the authors' own words:

> Rape fantasies were […] categorized as aversive, erotic, or erotic–aversive based on responses to the following two self-report items: the fantasizer's highest level of sexual arousal in response to the fantasy […] and the level of aversiveness of the fantasy […] Sexual arousal and averseness showed a strong negative correlation (r._.70, p<.001), supporting the use of an erotic–aversive continuum (Bivona & Critelli 2009: 39).

> A continuum between exclusively aversive and exclusively erotic was formed by subtracting aversive scores from erotic scores […] the results of the continuum: 9% of the fantasies were exclusively aversive, 45% were exclusively erotic, and 46% had both erotic and aversive elements (Bivona & Critelli 2009: 39).

These results are consistent with previous findings which suggest that, while still technically satisfying the definition of rape fantasies provided above, often the imagined scenarios are typically softened, eroticised and romanticised.[12] Most often fantasies at the erotic end of the spectrum take the form of portrayals of forced sexual acts involving attractive individuals or even loved partners.[13] Rarely do such fantasies take the form of realistic depictions of brutal, unwanted

---

11 They conducted a study examining the character of rape fantasies of 355 female undergraduates 'using a fantasy checklist that reflected the legal definition of rape and a sexual fantasy log that included systematic prompts and self-ratings' (Bivona & Critelli 2009: 33).

12 To fully understand this sub-class of sexual fantasy it would be necessary to learn much more about the specific contents and modes of presentation of the rape fantasies in question: these can vary significantly, and getting clear about the details of particular fantasies would require answering many questions. While not exhaustive, an indicative list would include: 'What type of force is typically used? How much resistance is offered? Is the non-consent real or token? Does non-consent change over the course of the interaction? What is the perpetrator's primary motive? […] how typical is it that the perpetrator is faceless or the woman incapacitated? How often is the man concerned with enhancing the woman's pleasure? How often is the perpetrator selfish and uncaring?' (Bivona & Critelli 2009: 33).

13 Erotic literature in which the rape of the female protagonist is a familiar theme often presents storylines in this general mode (Thurston 1987).

stranger rape, and the more that they resemble the latter the less likely they are to sexually arouse.

Importantly, for our assessment of Pretend Theory is the fact that 'the women themselves reported these as rape fantasies that involved both fear and sexual arousal' (Bivona & Critelli 2009: 34). The degree of fear in relation to the degree of sexual arousal is in one trivial sense determined by the particular content of the fantasy, of course, but what does the real work is the manner or way that such content is imagined, portrayed or narrated. What really matters is the specific details of its depiction (see Cobley 2014: 9–11 for a wonderfully revealing and hair-raising discussion of this very point, which makes powerful use of an example from Stephen King's 1992 book *Gerald's Game*).[14] A combination of these factors, with the manner and detail of the portrayal carrying the greatest weight, ultimately decides exactly where the responses of individual women lie on the erotic–aversive spectrum.

Let us now return to the central concern, discussed in section three, which Carroll (1990) raised about Pretend Theory long ago. Carroll argued that Pretend Theory is ill equipped to adequately account for the involuntary character of our responses to well-presented and well-executed fictions. There is an illuminating overlap in the way we irresistibly respond to a well-crafted horror film – with a mix of both fear and pleasure – and the ways in which women psychologically respond to their own, self-constructed rape fantasies. It seems that both cases involve having a complex and mixed array of emotional responses, all at once.

The mere fact that conflicting attitudes can co-exist and are both in play in response to these sexual fantasies is no reason, by itself, to prefer the idea that these cases involve only quasi or pretend emotions as opposed to real but modulated emotions.[15] Just as there is little doubt that in these cases the women are experiencing various degrees of sexual arousal, there is no reason to deny that they are also experiencing various degrees of fear. Here it is important to bear in mind that while such fantasising may need to be edgy enough to invoke a 'sense of danger, excitement, and passion', this needs to be carefully balanced so that the

14 For detailed examples of three main types of rape fantasies and the way they are generally presented (see Bivona & Critelli 2009: 40–42).

15 Indeed, it is standardly assumed that 'emotion comes into play at several points and at several levels within the context of a sexual situation. […] The sexual situation itself may evoke a positive or negative emotional response. Or, the specific acts/events of sexual arousal or sexual behaviour, because of their rewarding nature, may engender a strong emotional response. […] The role of emotion is likely to be quite different at distinct points in the process of sexual arousal' (McAnulty & Burnett 2006: 56).

imagined events of such fantasising do not begin to 'correspond *in toto* to actual rape' (Critelli & Bivona 2008: 67).

In making explicit the links with art-horror, it becomes less puzzling that women might fantasise about their own imagined rape. It is not much harder to understand the reasons for doing so than it is to understand why the wider populace engages with fictions that depict terrifying and unwelcome happenings. They do so because it titillates and excites. The discussion of art-horror in the previous section is a salient reminder that we very often engage with fictions and fantasies that portray events that we would never wish to occur in actuality. Still, within the safety of an imagined context, we can allow ourselves to engage with such fictions and we do so precisely because they can affect us so powerfully – viscerally and affectively.

Importantly, these embodied effects are achieved – irresistibly so – even when we know fully well, (or to quote Walton, when we are 'perfectly aware') that we are only dealing with the products of pure make-believe. In responding to fictions of this sort we can give our affective motors an effective workout in complete safety from external harms, protected from actual effects of the green slime or unwelcome sexual assaults. None of this lends any succor to Pretend Theory, for close inspection of how such fantasising yields such results raises doubts about whether Pretend Theory is in a position to provide the best explanation of such cases.

Pretend Theory places great weight on the fact that we cannot have emotions without also having other attitudes of the right sort, and it focuses on the fact that those who knowingly engage with fictions do not believe in the existence of the things with which they imaginatively engage. It is true that sometimes having a certain emotion does depend on having certain beliefs. For instance, if I am upset with you because I believe you insulted me, my emotions will shift should I discover you did not. While that is true, it hardly follows that *all* of our emotional responding depends on having contentful beliefs. For Gaut (2003) is surely right that the kind of case just cited 'merely shows that *if* an emotion is grounded in a belief, removal of the belief tends to remove the emotion grounded in it (p. 19, emphasis in the original).

In line with the earlier discussion of sexual arousal, there are good reasons to suppose that our most basic or primary forms of emotional responding are not content-involving at all. It is possible to 'just deny fear requires belief in danger' (Sainsbury 2010: 18). And, Sainsbury also correctly observes, 'Breaking the link between emotions and belief does not involve abandoning the view that emotions are in some sense cognitive' (Sainsbury 2010: 19). Usually, this observation is swiftly followed by the thought that 'Cognition is a broader category than belief' (Gaut 2003: 19). Thus it might be supposed that some contentful attitude other than belief might be in play and grounding our responses to fictions. Gaut (2003) suggests exactly this, holding that 'Charles does not believe that he is endangered but only *imagines* it, and given this, his desire not to be threatened does not motivate flight' (Gaut 2003: 21). But it is possible to take a further and more radical step. We might allow that 'cognition is a broader category than having contentful attitudes.' Radical enactivists propose exactly this: they argue that not all cognition, and certainly not its basic forms, need be content-involving (Hutto & Myin 2013).[16]

In a Radically Enactive conception of the imagination, while the content of a fiction certainly makes a difference, the true driving force in the way we consume fiction and what explains its effects on us is 'the *manner* in which that content is presented and processed' (Medina 2013: 329, emphasis in the original). Pressing the same basic line, Moran (1994) makes clear that it is not the content of a work of art that is crucial if we are to be emotionally moved it. Rather it is 'all the resources of figuration, allusion, rhythm, repetition, assonance, and dissonance […] that make what we are reading or hearing less like something we could make-believe is real' (p. 83).

The point is whether, and to what degree, we are moved by an imagining has less to do with '*what* is imagined' and more to do with '*how* it is imagined' (see Medina 2013: 328).[17] Gaut illustrates the point neatly:

> Disgust, for instance, is (certainly in the broad sense) an emotion. But it is odd to say one has to know whether something really occurred if one is to be disgusted by the thought of it. If I describe *in vivid and detailed fashion* the jam-and-live-mouse sandwich I breakfasted

16 For a clear and up-to-date statement on what a Radically Enactive account of the imagination looks like see Medina (2013). Defending an enactive approach to the imagination Medina draws important connections between the work of various philosophers, including Wittgenstein, Moran and myself.

17 Clarifying, Medina writes: 'The intensional and representational contents of our experiences of fiction do matter, but there is something even more basic and fundamental in emotionally engaged experiences of fiction: the directedness of those experiences, which is processed in an embodied, active, and interactive way. Both in fiction and in real life, our emotional responses are always directed at something. But it would be a mistake to think of this directedness as equivalent to intensionality, that is, to construe it always and necessarily in terms of internal representational contents, for our emotional responses do not always require such contents' (Medina 2013: 329).

on the other day, you might well be disgusted without supposing that I am telling the truth" (Gaut 2003: 17, my emphasis).[18]

The heavy lifting in our imaginative and emotional engagements with fictions – that which moves us emotionally – is *the way* a fantasy is presented, far more than its content.

Just as musicians play their instrument in specific ways to achieve particular effects, so fictions work on us in the reverse manner. It might be said that a film, text or imagining *plays us*. When well constructed, these artefacts operate on us such that we are played by them in certain, perhaps predictable, but irresistible ways. If this analysis holds water, it puts paid to Pretend Theory's idea that keeping track of the real/pretend divide is what does the major work in determining how we respond to fictions and in deciding whether we can genuinely emotionally engage with them at all.

The final analysis

Is there some way that Pretend Theory might accommodate these facts? It might be thought that it can deal with this challenge if, like genuine emotions, quasi-emotions also come in degrees. After all, Walton proposed that they do track the properties of real emotions in this way when first introducing the construct. Returning to the earlier example of Charles and the green slime, he writes:

> It is fictional not just that Charles is afraid, but that his fearful experience has a certain character and progresses in a certain fashion. These more specific fictional truths depend largely on the character and progress of his quasi-fear sensations. If *it is fictional that his fear is overwhelming*, or that it is only momentary, this is so because his quasi-fear sensations are overwhelming or momentary. Fictionally his fear *grows more or less intense* or *becomes almost unbearable or finally subsides*, as his quasi-fear feelings change in these ways (Walton 1990: 246, my emphases).

The trouble with this line of reply is that it reveals the explanatory emptiness of Pretend Theory. To be sure, our responses to our own fantasising are involuntary and can be overwhelming. It is difficult to square how this can be so with Pretend Theory – for, as Carroll (1990) pointed out, it is not as if we are merely

18 Such basic emotional responses are natural. The mere fact that they are contentless does not make them irrational. They are better understood as arational. It is not irrational, to borrow one of Gaut's (2003) examples, for 'a visitor to the CN Tower in Toronto, while knowing and believing himself to be perfectly safe [to be] irresistibly nervous and even terrified' (p. 19). It would be irrational for the person to endorse that natural response or to allow it to influence their practical reasoning about the safety of visiting the tower.

pretending that our psychological states have these properties. That surely is not under our imaginative control; it is not something that we decide. This, as Carroll averred, really is a major problem for Pretend Theory. In this light, we can give up pretending that Pretend Theory is the best way to understand how we emotionally engage with fictions, for a simpler and more attractive enactivist alternative has been articulated.

References

Bermúdez, J. (2011) 'The force-field puzzle and mindreading in non-human primates'. *Review of Philosophy and Psychology* 2(3): 397–410.

Bivona J, & Critelli, J. (2009) 'The nature of women's rape fantasies: an analysis of prevalence, frequency, and contents'. *Journal of Sex Research* 46(1): 33–45.

Bivona, J.M., Critelli, J.W. & Clark, M.J. (2012) 'Women's rape fantasies: an empirical evaluation of the major explanations'. *Archives of Sexual Behavior* 41(5): 1107–1119.

Carroll, N. (1990) *The Philosophy of Horror: or, Paradoxes of the Heart*. New York/London: Routledge.

Clark, J.A. (2010a) 'Hubristic and authentic pride as serial homologues: the same but different'. *Emotion Review* 2: 397–398.

Clark, J.A. (2010b) 'Relations of homology between higher cognitive emotions and basic emotions'. *Biology and Philosophy* 25: 75–94.

Critelli, J.W. & Bivona, J.M. (2008) 'Women's erotic rape fantasies: An evaluation of theory and research'. *Journal of Sex Research* 45(1): 57–70.

Cobley, P. (2014) *Narrative*. London: Routledge.

Currie, G. (2010) *Narratives and Narrators: A Philosophy of Stories*. Oxford: Oxford University Press.

DeLancey, C. (2001) *Passionate Engines: What Emotions Reveal about Mind and Artificial Intelligence*. New York: Oxford University Press.

Ekman, P. (1999) 'Basic emotions'. In T. Dalgleish & M.J. Power (eds) *Handbook of Cognition and Emotion*. Chichester, UK: John Wiley and Sons.

Fodor, J.A. & Pylyshyn, Z. (2015) *Minds without Meanings: An Essay on the Content of Concepts*. Cambridge, MA: MIT Press.

Friend, S. (2003) 'How I really feel about JFK'. In M. Kieran & D.M. Lopes, D.M. (eds) *Imagination, Philosophy and the Arts*. London: Routledge.

Gaut, B. (2003) 'Reasons, emotions and fictions'. In M. Kieran & D.M. Lopes (eds) *Imagination, Philosophy and the Arts*. London: Routledge.

Goldie, G. (2000) *The Emotions: A Philosophical Exploration*. Oxford: Oxford University Press.

Goldie, P. (2003) 'Narrative, emotion and perspective'. In M. Kieran & D.M. Lopes (eds) *Imagination, Philosophy and the Arts*. London: Routledge.

Goldie, P. (2012) *The Mess Inside: Narrative, Emotion, and the Mind*. Oxford: Oxford University Press.

Griffiths, P.E. (1997) *What Emotions Really Are: The Problem of Psychological Categories*. Chicago: University of Chicago Press.

Griffiths, P. (2013) 'Current emotion research in philosophy'. *Emotion Review* 5(2): 1–8.

Hutto, D.D. (2012) 'Truly enactive emotion'. *Emotion Review* 4(2): 176–181.

Hutto, D.D. (2013) 'Why believe in contentless beliefs?' In N. Nottelmann (ed) *New Essays on Belief: Structure, Constitution and Content*. New York: Palgrave Macmillan.

Hutto D.D. & Myin, E. (2013) *Radicalizing Enactivism: Basic Minds without Content*. Cambridge, MA: MIT Press.

Hutto, D.D. & Satne, G. (in press) 'The natural origins of content'. *Philosophia*.

Huxley, A. (2008[1932]) *Brave New World*. New York: Random House.

Leitenberg, H. & Henning, K. (1995) 'Sexual fantasy'. *Psychological Bulletin* 117: 469–496.

McAnulty, R.D. & Burnett, M.M. (eds, 2006) *Sex and Sexuality: Sexual Function and Dysfunction*. Westport, CT: Praeger.

Medina, J. (2013) 'An enactivist approach to the imagination: Embodied enactments and "fictional emotions"'. *American Philosophical Quarterly* 50(3): 317–335.

Moran, R. (1994) 'The Expression of Feeling in Imagination'. *Philosophical Review* 103(1): 75–106.

Person, E.S., et al. (1992) 'Associations between sexual experiences and fantasies in a nonpatient population: A preliminary study'. *Journal of the American Academy of Psychoanalysis* 20(1): 75–90.

Radford, C. (1975) 'How can we be moved by the fate of Anna Karenina?' *Proceedings of the Aristotelian Society*. Supplemental Vol. 49: 67–80.

Radford, C. (1977) 'Tears and Fiction'. *Philosophy* 52: 208–213.

Sainsbury, M. (2010) *Fiction and Fictionalism*. London: Routledge.

Stock, W.E. & Geer, J.H. (1982) 'A study of fantasy-based sexual arousal in women'. *Archives of Sexual Behavior*. 11(1): 33–47.

Sue, D. (1979) 'Erotic fantasies of college students during coitus'. *The Journal of Sex Research* 15(4): 299–305.

Thurston, C. (1987) *The Romance Revolution*. Urbana and Chicago: University of Illinois Press.

Walton, K.L. (1978) 'Fearing fictions'. *Journal of Philosophy* 75: 1: 5–27.

Walton, K.L. (1990) *Mimesis as Make-believe. On the Foundations of the Representational Arts*. Cambridge, MA: Harvard University Press.

Whipple, B., Ogden, G. & Komisaruk, B. (1992) 'Physiological correlates of imagery induced orgasm in women'. *Archives of Sexual Behavior* 21(2): 121–133.

Wollheim, R. (1984) *The Thread of Life*. Cambridge, MA: Harvard University Press.

Gunnel Brander

Sexual Fantasies in Sexological Psychotherapeutic Settings

Like sexual identity in a broad sense, and sexual practice, sexual fantasies are a part of sexuality on the individual level. Sexual fantasies are complex structures and can on one hand be seen as problematic in various ways and on the other hand be regarded as beneficial for our sexual well-being. In the present chapter, such fantasies will be considered from a sexological clinical perspective with a starting point in sexual script theory and its conflict levels: the cultural, interpersonal, and intrapsychic levels. In addition, contemporary psychodynamic developmental and mentalisation-based psychodynamic theory will be used to understand the handling of sexual fantasies within individual, relational, and cultural contexts.

In their review of research literature on sexual fantasies, Leitenberg and Henning (1995) define a sexual fantasy as a fantasy with the purpose to enhance sexual pleasure. They conclude from studies made from 1948 to 1992 that sexual fantasies are very common among both women and men. Men seem to use sexual fantasies more frequently in daily life and when masturbating than do women, but the use of fantasies during intercourse seems to be equally frequent among men and women. Sexual fantasies seem to decline linearly for both men and women with age. Some people have strong guilt feelings about their fantasies and in those cases they seem to be associated with having more sexual problems. Regarding the content of sexual fantasies, men are more likely to imagine more explicit sexual scenes and that they are actively doing something with their partner, whereas women have more emotional and romantic fantasies and passive imaginations of something being done to them by a partner. Submission fantasies are more common among women than among men, while men are more prone to fantasise about multiple partners than are women.

Very little is known about how small children fantasise but adult people, when asked to recall when they began to have sexual fantasies, remember them from eleven to thirteen years of age. Men tend to report slightly earlier occurrence of fantasies than women. Furthermore, there seems to be no clear connection between having deviant fantasies and acting them out in reality according to Leitenberg and Henning (1995). Furthermore, Leitenberg and Henning disagree with Sigmund Freud's idea of sexual fantasies in adults as signs of depravation and a dissatisfied sex life. So do others, like Friedman and Downey (2000). In their review of psychoanalytical thinking on sexuality they use findings from empirical sexological research in order to see what psychoanalytic ideas have been invalidated by sex research and what ideas in psychoanalysis might still be useful. They reflect on sexual fantasies and point out that since psychoanalytic theory is built upon psychoanalytic treatment of well educated, middle class and Western European individuals around the turn of the last century it is difficult to draw any conclusions outside this context.

What Freud has contributed is that he saw relationships and sexual relationships as inherently ambivalent with passion as well as antipathy constantly present. We experience desire side by side with fear-anxiety and rage-hostility. These ambivalent feelings are also present in our sexual fantasies. These fantasies have roots in bodily experiences descendant from the early mother-child relationship. Friedman and Downey (2000) also point out that newer research on sexual fantasies from a psychodynamic perspective is rare.

In sexual therapy, sexual fantasies can be a useful tool for the therapist. To better understand how sexual fantasies play a significant role in forming and exerting influence over us as sexual beings, a holistic perspective is essential. For the therapist, various theories and concepts can be helpful in recognising each individual client's sexuality and in what ways the client's sexual fantasies, and his or her relation to their sexual fantasies, might have functioned disruptively or may function supportively for that client.

Theories for the practice

Sexual script theory (Simon & Gagnon 2003) is presented in the introduction to this volume, but to reiterate briefly Simon and Gagnon saw sexual scripts as manuscripts for understanding human sexuality as socially constructed on three different levels. These are the cultural, interpersonal, and intrapsychic levels. Conflicts can appear both in and between the levels.

The dual control model assumes a balancing between excitation and inhibition (Bancroft & Janssen 2000; Bancroft, et al. 2009). Rather than seeing excitation and inhibition as a gliding scale, the dual control model conceptualises them as two different systems that interact. Every individual varies in their balance of these two interacting mechanisms. For instance, fear of pregnancy or performance anxiety may function as inhibitory, whereas certain situations, fantasies, or images may function excitatory. To understand sexual responses as well as sexual problems and dysfunctions, the dual control model is useful.

According to Bowlby's *attachment theory* from 1969 (Broberg, et al. 2008), every child needs a secure base to attach to. Otherwise it will not be able to develop into an independent grown-up individual. This secure base can be a caregiver of any kind. Attaching to a secure base is essential for the child, enabling it to investigate and also, in case of danger or threats, to return to what Bowlby called a 'haven of safety'. Early in childhood children start to build a conception of themselves and their relations to other people. Bowlby called these conceptions 'inner working models' and they are helpful in the interaction with the surrounding world. There are three major attachment styles, according to Ainsworth (1978): secure, anxious-ambivalent, and anxious-avoidant.

Secure attachment means having experiences of 'good-enough mothering' where the primal caregiver is able to be a secure base for the child to return to during its exploration of the world. This gives the child trust in the caregivers' availability. Anxious-avoidant attachment is based upon strategies to avoid distress concerning separation from the caregiver to survive as an independent person, and anxious-ambivalent is based upon strategies of dealing with the caregivers' emotional unreliability when it comes to separation as well as reunification. All three are to be seen as variants of normal development. Later on one more attachment style has been recognised, 'disorganized attachment' (Broberg, et al. 2008). That means absence of stability in relation to the attachment person and it creates fear and feelings of an unsolvable situation. It has been demonstrated that these attachment styles tend to be stable across life and thus hard to change. However, this does not mean that they are unchangeable if needed (Broberg, et al. 2008).

A psychological concept that has proved to be very interesting when working with sexological treatment in order to understand individual sexualities and sexual lives is our *mentalising ability*. The concept per se originated in French psychoanalysis and was an elaboration of Bowlby's attachment theory about the child's inner working models and early relationships. The theory of mentalisation was further developed by Allen, Fonagy, and Bateman (2008) as a theory of self-development, focusing on the early attachment relation to significant caretakers. They define mentalisation as the ability to 'hold mind in mind'; that is, the ability to think of inner mental states in ourselves as well as in others. Through mentalisation we become capable of subjectivity and self-reflection. To quote Rydén and Wallroth (2008), mentalisation ability 'enables us to look upon ourselves from the outside and others from the inside' (my translation).

According to Allen, et al. (2008), the mentalisation ability is genetically determined, but Karterud and Bateman (2011) make it clear that it must be developed through relationships with other individuals and that this mentalisation ability provides the self with a context. Early relationships give the child possibilities of attachment in which the little child can become reflected by someone meaningful and sympathetic to him or her, thereby transposing knowledge about the child back to him or her. Already before the age of one year, the child can separate the goals from the means that create the goals. At two years, the child has usually established an awareness of intentionality in others and after about an additional two years it can separate fantasy from reality, in so doing also realising that thoughts and feelings are representations of reality. A child of six has created a so-called autobiographical self, with the ability to transform knowledge to experiences of its own and to have manifold representations of its own self. By this age the child develops correspondent representations of others. This makes us capable of understanding both ourselves and others and at the same time to include elements in the situation as a whole, also those outside oneself and the relationship with the other. Our mentalisation ability is fragile and we can, for one reason or another, at times lose it. Depending on our individually different developmental experiences, we have different capacities to reestablish this ability (Karterud & Bateman 2011).

Our mentalisation ability helps us in obtaining emotional agency in our relationships – both sexual and non-sexual – with others. A well-functioning mentalisation ability is essential when it comes to handling sexual fantasies, identities, and activities in our relationships. In sexually oriented therapy settings this is pronounced, as will be demonstrated below in the case examples concerning sexual fantasies.

Recent research on sexual fantasies and psychodynamic therapy

As mentioned, research on sexual fantasies from a psychodynamic perspective has been rare. However, some research has been done in the past years. For instance, Birnbuam (2007) examined two studies on associations between attachment orientations and content of sexual fantasies. He notes that there is empirical evidence that sexual motives, attitudes, and behaviours are shaped by and dependent on our attachment processes. Sex-related themes in fantasies were more often seen in anxiously attached persons than in others. These were also more likely to sexualise their relationships and tended to romanticise their sexual interactions at the same time. Furthermore, they more often used sex as a way of showing care for their partners.

Anxiously oriented persons reported sexual fantasies with submission themes. Among them the women more often fantasised about unrestricted sex and the men reported more romantic-oriented fantasies. In addition, these men more often expressed a desire of irresistibility and presented themselves as affectionate and helpless. The women more often had fantasies about other people than their romantic partners than did the men, whereas the men more often than the women wanted to sexually satisfy the others in their fantasies. More anxiously attached individuals were likely to sexually fantasise more frequently than others, while highly avoidant attached persons fantasised on intimacy themes, which are more romantic than sexual themes. Birnbaum (2007) concludes that different attachment orientations reflected relational goals in the content of sexual fantasies rather than compensating for attachment-related concerns, that is, sexual fantasising mirroring attachment needs.

In a later article, Birnbaum, et al. (2012) presented a study of the effects of explicit and implicit insecurity on content of sexual fantasies. They found that sexual fantasies can be used as coping strategies in order to regulate reactions in situations being attachmentally stressful by enhancing interpersonal distance and even hostility. This seems to be done without apparent relation to the attachment style of the individual.

Newbury, et al. (2012) focus on how therapists deal with sexual fantasies in therapeutic settings working with couples. Through a qualitative study, they investigated how six psychosexual therapists approached sexual fantasies in treatment. In the analysis, five themes emerged. The first theme was the importance of fantasising. According to DSM-IV, lack of sexual fantasies is one factor in diagnosing hypoactive desire. All six respondents in the study saw the role of sexual fantasies as important or even essential in restoring sexual functioning. The second theme was help with fantasising. Here, they all agreed that the best help was to encourage clients' imaginative processes and to accept the outcome whatever it was, instead of working to get rid of so-called 'partner replacement fantasies', that is to help clients not to have sexual fantasies during sexual activities with a partner.

Acceptance of fantasies was the next theme. Respondents agreed that sexual fantasies can be either adaptive or maladaptive in clients and that it is necessary to note the difference. The fourth theme was disclosure of fantasies. Two of the respondents used a systematic disclosure strategy with their clients while the others said it was practiced when needed. The last theme concerned whether partner replacement fantasies are necessary. They all agreed that sexual fantasies are meaningful and have important functions. One participant said that in relations, it is necessary to be intimate and separate at the same time. Therefore partner replacement fantasies are useful to 'mediate tensions between self and other, autonomy and union' (Newbury, et al. 2012: 368).

Newbury, et al. (2012) challenged the widely spread assumption that sexual fantasies would be harmful for couple intimacy. They also highlighted the need of an 'informal attachment assessment', that is an investigation into the individuals' attachment styles, before letting the couples reveal their sexual fantasies in couple therapy.

Sexual fantasies are important for our well-being, self-confidence, and enjoyment. They may be creative and playful for the individual, but if they, as sometimes happens, become more of a controlling force, the situation may be anything but playful (Rosenqvist 2010). The multifaceted function of sexual fantasies in people's lives will be demonstrated below through a few sexually oriented therapy cases in which sexual fantasies were of importance.

Case vignettes

The cases are fictitious, constructed out of many different real-life cases, in order not to risk that individuals will be identifiable for the reader. They are examples of what kind of cases concerning sexual fantasies, or lack of them, one might encounter in a clinical setting for sexually oriented therapy. The purpose is not to go deeper into treatment but rather to reflect on sexual fantasies in relation to sexual script theory and psychological developmental models, and to discuss how fantasies can be present in therapeutic contexts.

Case 1

Carl, a man around forty years old, contacts the sexual therapy clinic due to sexual difficulties in relation with his female partner, Ella. As a matter of fact, she had recommended for him to call the clinic for help. He explains that he, since a year, is engaged in a relationship with a woman of approximately the same age as himself. This is his first long-lasting and serious relationship. For the past couple of months they have lived together and around that time he started to have erectile problems. Furthermore, Carl tells the therapist that the problems began when they decided to be 'honest about everything' with each other and he therefore told her about his sexual fantasies.

These sexual fantasies have their origin in an incident when he was a young boy, when he witnessed his mother arguing with another woman in the neighbourhood. This was a both exciting and frightening experience for him. Eventually, the memory of this experience became sexualised, and came to function as a sexual trigger during masturbation or while having sex with a woman. The image he now brings to mind shows his mother mud-wrestling naked with another woman. Never causing any problems for him until now, the fantasies have been an exciting and joyful part of his sexuality. Now, however, Ella is upset and disappointed, calling him sick and perverted. She does not want him near her until he has got rid of his nasty fantasies. Scared that Ella does not want him anymore, Carl has tried really hard to think of other things when they are having sex, which resulted in erectile difficulties. Now, he is worried that he is as perverted and sick as Ella says he is.

In therapy, two apparent themes recurred, one about his sexuality and the other about the relationship. Carl was quite unsure about his own sexuality. He had never had any reason to question it before, since his masturbation and even sexual encounters with others had worked out fine so far. He began to reflect upon his own fantasies from both his own and Ella's perspectives and could eventually see that their respective perspectives differed a lot and that this is unavoidable. After some time, he could understand how his fantasies affected Ella and that she understood them within a framework of her own experiences and feelings. The more he could appreciate her reaction, the more he could handle his fantasies in a, for him, more constructive way. In therapy his sexuality in general and his sexual fantasies in particular were validated and acknowledged as normal. This made him more confident with his sexuality and ultimately he could meet her sexual wishes and needs without abandoning his own while trying to adjust to hers. His erectile problems disappeared, probably because they were secondary to the other problems they had.

Carl's other concern was about relating to Ella in an honest and respectful way in order to maintain a long-lasting relationship between them. He reflected on how to be honest without revealing himself completely. By mentalising and reflecting about his own fantasies, he understood that he and Ella were and always would be two different individuals with different fantasies and sexualities, even though they shared an intimate relationship. From this he learned that respectful honesty is also about having and keeping secrets. Thus, Carl could find ways to guard his integrity concerning his fantasies by for example not readily admit and confess to the fantasies when she asked about them, and to select what to tell and what not to tell instead of disclosing everything coming into his mind without reflection.

Case 2

Oscar, thirty-two years old, was a single man who turned to the sexual therapy clinic to get help with his sexual fantasies. When he came to the clinic he was markedly depressed and had pronounced self-contempt. He had fantasies about young boys, about ten years of age. They were posing naked in different settings for him. Now and then he had had these fantasies ever since he was a boy himself. As an adult they were particularly frequent in periods when he did not have a sexual partner. His sexual preferences were and had always been sex activities with women of his own age. Now he had not been having sex with anyone for a long period of time as a consequence of being very engaged in and occupied with his work.

During this period he had been involved in masturbation and sexual fantasies as a substitute for a partner and, he said, it had been working well for him until he read in the newspaper about an illegal child pornographic network being discovered by the police. This made him worried about his sexual fantasies. He feared that he might be a paedophile and that he therefore would end up as a child molester. He found no way to get rid of these thoughts and worries, and increasingly felt more and more uncomfortable in social contexts outside his apartment. He had even begun to worry that people might see his thoughts. He was very scared to be revealed as a paedophile, not least since he had a child of his own, a four-year-old boy.

Oscar and his partner had separated about two years prior to our meeting in the clinic, after having conflicting views on his dedication to his work. The separation affected his self-image and self-esteem badly and he was convinced that he was not at all made for relationships or parenthood. He then started to work excessively and had no social life except having his son with him every other weekend. In therapy he, at first, reflected on how likely it was for him to develop into a child molester, and, later on, he focused on his sexual preferences. He became more and more emotionally reassured: it was not actually the case that he was interested in having sex with young boys but with adult women in real life practice. The fantasy pictures were a compromise for him in his present life situation and he realised that he had no wishes to set them into practice at all. He could see more and more clearly that his boundaries against acting upon his fantasies were still strong. This made him feel more confident and as his self-esteem grew he became increasingly interested in rebuilding his social life. He started to go out with some other single people from the company he worked at and could see that he was highly appreciated by them. This led him to discover the interest in him shown by a female colleague of his own age and he could respond to that. After a while they started dating and his masturbation fantasies about young boys became progressively more rare and eventually transformed into other fantasies.

Case 3

Katta was a young woman of twenty-five. She contacted the clinic because she was unable to have sex with her boyfriend, Jim. Katta expressed a clear wish to be helped so that she would be able to have pain-free sexual intercourse with Jim, since she was afraid that he would leave her if she did not become more sexually available for him.

Katta was diagnosed with an eating disorder at the age of seventeen. Before that she had taken care of her mother and two younger brothers after her parents' dreadful divorce when she was twelve years old. Her life had been filled with struggles to literally survive and to keep her family together after the divorce. Now, she was free from the eating problems and her life had begun to be more harmonious in many ways. In consequence, she wanted to be like all the other young women around her, having lives that seemed perfect, with friends, relationships, and working careers.

During the first session, her inability to talk about and define her own sexuality and sexual identity became apparent. Being disconnected to her own feelings, she tried to comply and adjust to Jim's desire to have sex with her. Intercourse was very difficult for her, she explained, because it was too painful. Consequently, their sexual life did not work at all and it made her both sad and anxious. Jim, in his turn, was becoming more and more insecure and he dared not even take initiative to physical closeness and intimacy due to the fear of hurting her. In therapy, she kept coming back to the first request of getting help to have sexual intercourse with Jim.

Focus in treatment was on helping her to define herself as a sexual being with her own feelings, needs, and desires. Initially, it was very hard for Katta to understand sexuality as something intrapsychic and not only interpersonal or cultural. She conceived sex as something one *does*, rather than something emotional on an individual level. Her experience had been to suppress her own feelings for the benefit of other people's needs. Gradually she identified herself sexually as being heterosexual, but came to the realisation that she could not think of herself in an intimate sexual relationship with Jim at all. Katta was painting pictures as a hobby, something she had done since she was ten years old, and when asked by the therapist what she felt about her own paintings she answered dismissively 'nothing really, it is a lot of hard work only'. She usually classified them as good or bad, and most of them were bad. All paintings were variations of her self-portrait, trying to make it perfect. This disclosure of aspirations to perfection led the therapist to focus on desire and passion as helpful feelings for sexual activities as well as in painting, and also in the long run to use sexual fantasies as facilitators of desire. She was surprised to discover that agency was possible even in her own sexuality. With the help of her own feelings she could act in ways she decided herself, either to spark or to inhibit desire.

Katta was encouraged to do mentalisation training in her daily life, such as trying to identify feelings of desire in herself as well as their appearance in other people by reflecting on what she experienced in different situations and in encounters with others. In the beginning, this was a frightening process, because she was convinced that other people could see what she felt. Nonetheless, persisting in the training, it eventually led to a situation on a trip abroad, in which she felt sexual desire towards a male associate and started to fantasise about having sex with him. Then, she understood that these feelings were missing in her relationship with Jim. She decided to leave him in order to free them both. Later on she met the male colleague again and had very satisfying sex with him a couple of times without feeling obliged to engage in a relationship with him.

Case 4

Tilde was around twenty years of age when she sought help at the clinic because she was afraid that she might be a homosexual. Just the idea that she might be would be a disaster for her. She was quite certain that her mother would disapprove, since every time Tilde visited her mother she wondered if Tilde had met any nice boy yet. She had recently moved away from her family, consisting of only herself and her mother. She had grown up on a farm in the countryside quite far from the city where she was going to study at the university. When growing up she was quite alone, since her sisters were twelve and fifteen years older than her and they left home when she was ten and twelve years old respectively. She and her sisters had not had much contact after their leaving home. Her only way to meet friends was when her mother could drive and fetch her, something she hardly ever had the possibility to do. So she was a bit isolated at home with her mother, who had a lot to do at the farm and also, eventually, was taking care of the father who had cancer.

Her father died from his cancer when Tilde was fourteen years old. At that point in time he had been more or less disabled by the illness for three years. She missed him, but could not remember them ever being very close. Her sexual experiences were scarce. Remembering trying to explore masturbation after the youngest older sister had left home, she conveyed that these incidents had resulted in a lot of shame and guilt: she had felt it was inappropriate to engage in such activities while her father was so ill.

During her high-school time she went out a few times, making friends with young boys as the other girls did, but she was uncertain about her feelings since she thought they were a bit scary. When she fantasised about having sex it was easier for her to think about being with another girl than a boy. She now lived in a student flat sharing a kitchen with about ten other unfamiliar students from all over the country and the world. It was a very nice place, she thought, but she was having a hard time trying to socialise and make friends with them. The last time she had attended a party, a very nice young man had shown her some interest and wanted to kiss her, and when he did, all she could think of was another girl. This really made her worried so she ran away from it all. After that she was really upset and afraid of going into the kitchen to meet some of the other students there. Also she did not attend her classes but stayed isolated in her room most of the time. At night she was dreaming about that boy being a girl and she woke up in the middle of the night feeling fearful and lonely.

In therapy she started to investigate her feelings about possibly being gay and she began to reflect more generally on her sexuality. At the clinic there were a lot of photos of homo- as well as heterosexual intimacy on the walls from HIV- and condom use campaigns. These photos inspired her to reflect over her own feelings, thoughts and dreams in comparison to reality. She then started to apply these thoughts in all kind of situations such as on the way home from therapy, at university lectures, and so on. Although she felt very insecure and nervous, she tried to stay in social situations at school and with the people she lived with. Sometimes it worked and other times she had to escape. On one occasion, on a visit at her mother's, she dared to start a conversation with her mother about being lonely during childhood and they talked about how her life situation had been then and how it was at present. Her mother was surprised at hearing about her life situation. In her eyes, Tilde seemed so strong and capable of taking care of herself. They talked about her mother's life after the death of Tilde's father and why she never met any new partner, despite having been young when her husband had passed away. This conversation made it clear to Tilde that she did not need to worry about her mother's life and that she herself was okay in her mother's eyes. There were not any unexpressed demands on her mother's part regarding Tilde's life. It was not, as Tilde had feared, that difficult to discuss herself or even to show her feelings in front of her mother.

After that she started to reflect on what other people might feel meeting her, and what she herself felt meeting other people. This was very important for her, since she gradually understood that other people's thoughts and feelings could be very different from her own without either one necessarily being right or wrong. She became increasingly tolerant toward her own sexual thoughts and let them inspire her sexual fantasies during masturbation. Reflecting on her thoughts, she recognised the girl in the fantasy as being more of a symbol for herself exploring her own desire and sexuality than a homosexual partner. Soon other sexual fantasy themes, like having sex with other people, were introduced and accepted by her. She left therapy after a year, when she and a fellow girl student were going to Australia as exchange students for a period. At termination of therapy she was more self-confident and secure about her sexuality. Her thoughts about her sexual identity were freer and therefore also bearable for her.

Why and how sexual fantasies matter in sexually oriented psychotherapy

Sexual fantasies cannot be separated from our sexualities, but play a significant role in forming and influencing us as sexual beings. They are commonly used to enhance and/or maintain sexual arousal and pleasure, both in masturbation and in sex with partners, but also simply as relaxing daydreams. As stated earlier, there is no evident connection between having deviant fantasies and acting them out (Leitenberg & Henning 1995). As seen in the cases described above, sexual fantasies may, however, function both in positive ways by reinforcing our sexual well-being, and in negative ways by provoking feelings of shame, by leading to insufficiencies in our psychological self, self-esteem, or self-image, or even by causing sexual dissatisfaction and dysfunction. They can cause problems by being inhibited or blocked off.

In the case of Carl, sexual dysfunction was caused by the shame he felt in relation to his sexual fantasies due to his partner's reaction to them. Interestingly, in this case the sexual dysfunction disappeared simply by addressing how to handle the sexual fantasies and how to balance honesty and integrity in a relationship. In Oscar's case, on the other hand, the shame experienced due to his sexual fantasies damaged his self-esteem and self-image.

A holistic perspective is essential to better understand sexualities. For the therapist, the sexual script theory (Simon & Gagnon 2003) is a useful tool for recognising each individual client's unique sexuality. For instance, a therapist might encounter a client like Carl, whose case can be seen, from a perspective that takes the sexual script into account, as consisting of conflicts on all levels: On the cultural level, because they contain elements that are 'forbidden' or taboo in society, i.e. fantasising about his mother mud-wrestling naked with another woman. In addition, sexual fantasies in general are sometimes discussed as problematic because they are deviant, frequent, or might be acted upon in real life, which seems to have affected the scripts of Carl's partner more than Carl himself. On the interpersonal level, the couple's very different scripts and pre-understandings gave rise to a conflict between them. Finally, on the intrapsychic level the conflicts Carl experienced with his fantasies on the other script levels resulted in his being unable to become aroused and get an erection.

The case of Oscar, who fantasised about young boys although he had no desire to actually have sex with others than women of his own age, illustrates conflicts between cultural and intrapsychic scripts of sexual fantasies, demonstrating the importance of identifying the different and contradicting levels of the scripts to help clients to restore sexual functioning and well-being. In the third case, Katta had repressed her sexuality to the benefit of other more urgent feelings and needs during childhood and adolescence. She seemed not to have any sexual scripts of her own and she could not get in touch with her sexual feelings. Trying desperately to be like others of her age, she imitated their behaviour, which was not a successful strategy. And in the last case, of Tilde, a somewhat different conflict of intrapsychic character can be identified. Tilde confused her sexual fantasies with a very demanding and controlling sexual identity based upon a cultural script, that is, she believed herself to be a lesbian in line with the social construction of homosexuality. Thinking and fantasising was for her the same thing as reality, in a way that became so demanding that she had difficulties in handling it. Notable is that her fantasies tended to affect the development of her own sexual identity.

The cases also demonstrate that some difficulties can be dealt with by psychoeducative interventions on sexuality and sexual fantasies. Bancroft and Janssen's (2000) dual control model can be useful for this purpose. For example, in Carl's and Oscar's therapies, the dual control model could help them understand how the sexual fantasies may affect sexual functioning, feelings, and behaviour. In order to reduce clients' feelings of shame associated with fantasising, it is also helpful to address the purpose and usefulness of sexual fantasies.

By assessing attachment styles in the above mentioned cases, all four very likely could be described as anxiously or even disorganised-attached, that is, they are unable to use some kind of organised strategy for attachment: relationships are chaotic and scary because the very person one loves is the person one is most afraid of. In the cases of Tilde, Carl, and Oscar, their sexual fantasies are sex-related (and not more romantically intimacy-related) and probably more frequent than average sexual fantasies overall. All three of them seem to be anxiously attached persons (Birnbaum 2007). Maybe the case of Katta is an example of a more disorganised attachment style and this can explain her lack of sexual fantasies and her disconnection to her own sexuality. Carl's erection difficulties could probably be interpreted as having emerged through sexually caring for his partner at the expense of himself.

Oscar's way of using his sexual fantasies, when his relationship is ended, can perhaps be understood as a coping strategy to enhance interpersonal distance (Birnbaum 2012). Also, it is interesting to note that Oscar tends to escalate the fantasies to assure himself of distance to relationships and presumptive partners in a restrictive and somewhat obsessive way. This defensive strategy emotionally hurt his self-respect, his self-esteem, and his self-image.

Working with sexual problems in individual therapies, it is also useful to make an 'informal attachment assessment' as Newbury, et al. (2012) have described it, trying to understand how sexual fantasies are used by the individual. In some cases identifying their sexual fantasies is helpful in interventions to facilitate for clients to make better contact with their own sexual feelings. It is also interesting to note clients' views of the concept of 'partner replacement fantasies', since these can be seen as a way for us to regulate closeness in our sexual relationships (Newbury, et al. 2012). Maybe that is what Carl, Oscar, and Tilde are trying to do in their respective ways with help of their sexual fantasies.

Sexually oriented therapy can also deal with developing mentalisation ability and sexual agency by reflecting on fantasies, feelings, and sexual needs during sessions. In this way, the therapy room is a place for playing with feelings, thoughts, and fantasies, in this case within sexualities. The sense of emotional agency in our sexualities and sexual fantasies is necessary for our sexual well-being, by helping us to feel secure enough to be free to handle our manifold individual possibilities without fear, pressure, or shame. Mentalisation helps us reach this emotional agency (Karterud & Bateman 2011), that is, to use our feelings as a guide to eventual fulfilment of the emotional needs when it is possible. By mentalisation, Carl, in the first case, learned how to differentiate himself and his sexuality from those of his partner. Oscar was brave enough to challenge his shame and could thereby focus on reflecting on himself and his sexuality, including his sexual fantasies. This led to emotional agency and ability to restore his self-image. In the third case, through encouraging mentalisation the therapist enabled Katta to identify her sexual feelings and enhance her sexual fantasies.

Finally, in the last case, probably from the beginning of adolescence sexual thoughts had been used as an inhibitor of arousal and sexual feelings. By urging reflections and mentalisation the therapist helps 'enhance' fantasies and emotions, which stimulates the client's ability to mentalise sexual themes and feelings. In this case Tilde was able to reach a better sense of agency of her sexual thoughts and feelings. In the long run, she will also be able to use them in sexual fantasies, enhancing desire and excitement.

Concerning the use of sexual fantasies as intervention in therapeutic treatment Newbury, et al. (2012) show us that the couple therapists in their study all agreed on the importance of addressing and using sexual fantasies as tools in their therapeutic work. It is worth mentioning that working with sexual fantasies is not restricted to couple therapy but has importance also in individual psychotherapeutic settings. In a sexological perspective, sexual fantasies can be useful in measuring sexual well-being throughout therapy (Rosenqvist 2010) and function as a tool used to enhance sexual feelings or arousal. Playfulness and creativity in relation to sexuality are essential in the therapy room.

The traditional psychoanalytical view of deviant sexual behaviour as immature expressions of sexuality (Rosenqvist 2010) is worth discussing, not least since the question arises of what then might constitute mature sexual behaviour. Sexualities, including fantasies, identities and practices, are manifold and built upon the individual's experiences and possibilities. Therefore, from a sexually oriented therapy perspective, it is not at all particularly useful to label or categorise clients as sexually mature or immature. Rather, out of respect for the client's right to sexual well-being, it is preferable and more useful to regard each individual's sexuality as unique.

Notably, the significance of mentalising ability and mental agency for the enhancement of our sexualities and in other parts of our lives, is often disregarded by clinicians and therapists seeing people in psychotherapeutic treatment. On the issue of sexualities, especially sexual fantasies, these are seen as much too complicated and therefore more difficult to handle than other themes and emotions coming up in the therapeutic situation. Few therapists, beside those who are specialised in sexology, see the sexuality perspective as a powerful and useful theme in psychotherapy. Further scholarly studies on human sexualities from a perspective of psychological development are needed, and those ought to include sexual fantasies, sexually oriented therapy, and therapeutic methodology – and no less so, extended discussions focusing on sexualities from a holistic perspective that takes sexual well-being into account.

References

Allen, J. G., Fonagy, P. & Bateman, A.W. (2008) *Mentalizing in Clinical Practice.* London: American Psychiatric Publishing, Inc.

Bancroft, J. & Janssen, E. (2000) 'The dual control model of male sexual response: a theoretical approach to centrally mediated erectile dysfunction'. *Neuroscience and Biobehavioral Reviews* 24: 571–579.

Bancroft, J., Graham, C.A., Janssen, E. & Sanders, S.A. (2009) 'The dual control model: current status and future directions'. *Journal of Sex Research* 46(2–3): 21–142.

Broberg A., Risholm Mothander, P., Granqvist, P. & Ivarsson, T. (2008) *Anknytning i praktiken. Tillämpningar av anknytningsteorin.* Stockholm: Natur & Kultur.

Birnbaum, G.E. (2007) 'Beyond the borders of reality: attachment orientations and sexual fantasies'. *Personal Relationships* 14: 321–342.

Birnbaum, G.E., Simpson, J.A., Weisberg, Y.J., Barnea, E. & Assulin-Simhon, Z. (2012) 'Is it my overactive imagination? The effects of contextually activated attachment insecurity on sexual fantasies'. *Journal of Social and Personal Relationships* 29(8): 1131–1152.

Friedman, R.C. & Downey, J.I. (2000)'Psychoanalysis and sexual fantasies'. *Archives of Sexual Behavior* (2)96: 567–586.

Karterud, S. & A. Bateman (2011) *Mentaliseringsbaserad terapi.* Stockholm: Liber.

Leitenberg, H. & Henning, K. (1995) 'Sexual fantasy'. *Psychological Bulletin* 117(3): 469–496.

Newbury, R., Hayter, M., Wylie, K.R. & Riddell, J. (2012) 'Sexual fantasy as a clinical intervention'. *Sexual and Relationship Therapy* 27(4): 358–371.

Rosenqvist, L. (2010) 'Sexuella fantasier'. In P-O Lundberg & L. Löfgren-Mårtenson (eds) *Sexologi*. Stockholm: Liber.

Rydén, G. & Wallroth, P. (2008) *Mentalisering: Att leka med verkligheten.* Stockholm: Natur & Kultur.

Simon, W. & Gagnon, J. H. (2003) 'Sexual scripts'. In Parker, R. & P. Aggleton (eds) *Culture, Society and Sexuality*. London: Routledge.

Contributors

Blizzard, Deborah is Associate Professor at the Department of Science, Technology, and Society at Rochester Institute for Technology. Her research interests are among other things the (re)creation of the human-machine relationship through erotic dolls, but she has also focused on sociocultural constructions of fetoscopy and contemporary close-up magic.

Brander, Gunnel is authorized psychologist, psychotherapist and specialist in Clinical Sexology. She has taught Sexology at Malmö University for many years.

Carlbom, Aje, Ph.D. in Social Anthropology, is Senior Lecturer at the Faculty of Health and Society Malmö University. He has specialized in cultural and religious aspects of integration, as well as ideological, cosmological, and representational issues.

Carlström, Charlotta, Ph.D. student, Department of Social Work, Malmö University, Social Worker, Master of Sexology. She specializes in alternative sexualities and her Ph.D. thesis is about BDSM practice.

Hutto, Daniel D. is Professor of Philosophical Psychology, holding this appointment jointly at both the Universities of Wollongong and Hertfordshire. His research is a sustained attempt to understand human nature in a way which respects natural science but which nevertheless rejects the impersonal metaphysics of contemporary naturalism.

Johnsdotter, Sara, Ph.D. in Social Anthropology at Lund University in 2002, is Professor in Medical Anthropology at the Faculty of Health and Society, Malmö University. Her research projects have included genital modifications and sexuality, and also the interface between sexuality and language.

Larsson, Mariah, Ph.D. in Film Studies at Lund University in 2006, is Associate Professor in Health and Society, Sexology, at Malmö University, and Research Fellow at Department of Media Studies, Stockholm University. Her research concerns sexuality and film, particularly pornographic film.

Månsson, Sven-Axel, Professor Emeritus of Social Work, received his Ph.D. in Sociology at Lund University in 1981. He is currently a member of the

Centre for Sexology and Sexuality Studies, Faculty of Health and Society, Malmö University. He has published extensively on issues such as prostitution and human trafficking, sexuality on the Internet, and the use of pornography by young people.

Ouis, Pernilla has a Ph.D. in Human Ecology and is Associate Professor in health and society, specialized in ethnic relations at Malmö University, where she teaches Sexology and Social Work. Her research interests include sex and Islam, the honour complex and sexual rights in traditional societies.

Ryberg, Ingrid, Ph.D. in Cinema Studies, is a researcher at Valand Academy, University of Gothenburg. Her dissertation, *Imagining Safe Space: The Politics of Queer, Feminist and Lesbian Pornography* (Stockholm: Acta 2012) investigates a recent transnational wave of interest in pornography as a form of queer, feminist and lesbian activism.

Vossen, Emma is a PhD candidate at the University of Waterloo and an editor at the game studies publication *First Person Scholar* where she frequently writes about gender and games. Her dissertation examines female desire and pornography consumption focusing on the comics medium. Her other publications include discussions of romance and sexuality in The Walking Dead comics, and the pornographic fetish art of Superman's co-creator Joe Shuster.

www.ingramcontent.com/pod-product-compliance
Ingram Content Group UK Ltd.
Pitfield, Milton Keynes, MK11 3LW, UK
UKHW021011120926
8556IPUK00039B/1002

9 783631 649404